Picture Grammar for Children 1

Contents

Title	Grammar	Page
Alphabet fun!	Alphabet skills	2
At school	I, you ... My, your ...	8
Birthday party	Present simple to be	14
Review 1		20
Continents and animals	This, That/These, Those	22
Dressing up	Possessives	28
Explore your town	There is/There are	34
Review 2		40
Family and home	Prepositions	42
Get up and go!	Imperatives	48
Have a sale!	have got/has got	54
Review 3		60
Grammar summary		62
Words and phrases		64

Alphabet fun!

Words you need

1 *Point to a letter and say it. Find the matching word.*

2 *Underline and say five words you know.*

Extra words you know

book ....

....

....

Word check

1 *Match and write.*

H	t	hat	H *is for hat.*
S	h	yo-yo	S ____________________.
T	k	glove	T ____________________.
Y	j	kite	Y ____________________.
J	s	table	J ____________________.
G	y	jigsaw	G ____________________.
K	g	spoon	K ____________________.

2 *Circle the nouns. List in A-B-C order.*

anappleacomputerabicycleapencilanorangeaviolinanewspaperanumbrellaandatable

a *pple*

b______________ p______________

c______________ t______________

n______________ u______________

o______________ v______________

3 *Complete. Add a noun to each list.*

I wear it.	*I play with it.*	*I eat it.*
_ _ t	_ _ _ o t	_ _ _ _ g e
__________	__________	__________

4 *Spell a word on a friend's back.*
Use your finger.

Show what you know

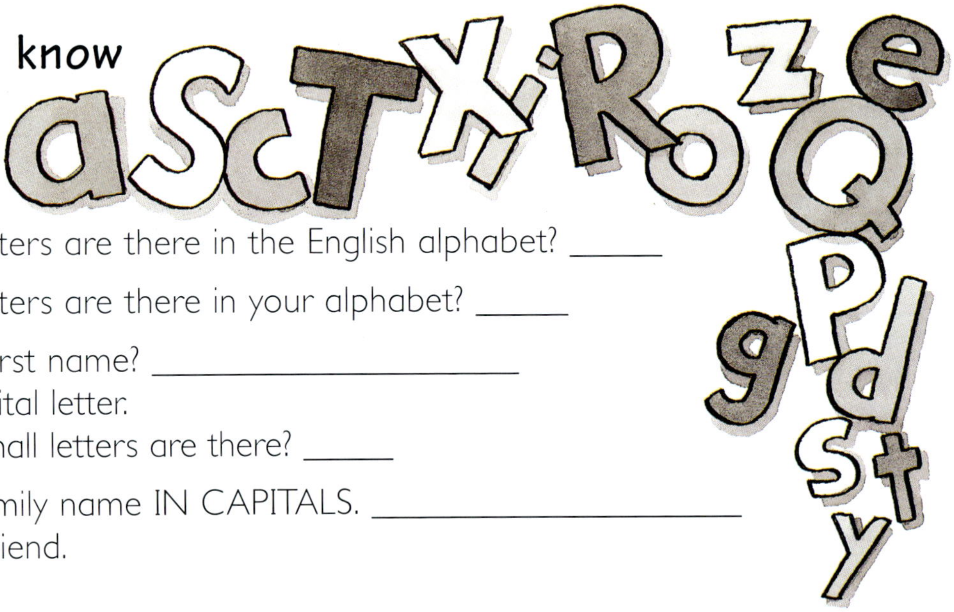

1 *Complete.*

1. How many letters are there in the English alphabet? _____
2. How many letters are there in your alphabet? _____
3. What's your first name? ____________________
   Circle the capital letter.
   How many small letters are there? _____
4. Write your family name IN CAPITALS. ____________________
   Spell it to a friend.

2 *Add the missing vowels (**a, e, i, o, u**).*

1. _ p p l _ 
2. _ r _ n g _ 
3. _ g g 
4. _ m b r _ l l _ 
5. _ c _ c r _ _ m 

3 *Sort the vowels and consonants.*

	Vowels	*Consonants*
computer	o _ _	c m _ _ _
umbrella	_ _ _	_ _ _ _ _
xylophone	_ _ _	_ _ _ _ _ _
jigsaw	_ _	_ _ _ _

4 *Look and complete.*

1. It's *an apple.*

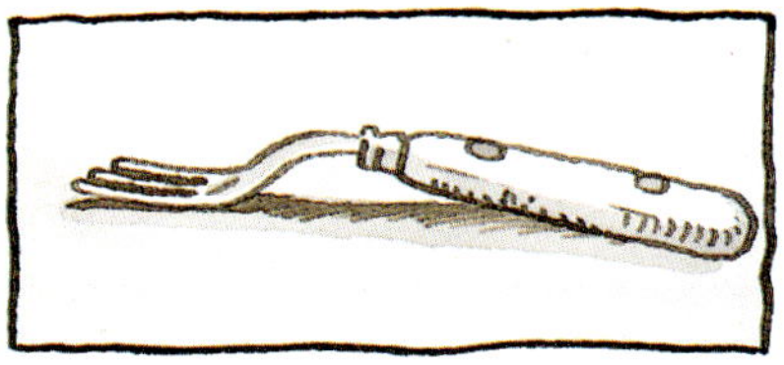

3. It's ___ __________

5. It's ___ __________

2. It's *a knife.*

4. It's ___ __________

6. It's ___ __________

Practice

1 *Make the shape of these letters with your hands or body.*

E n g l i s h

2 *Complete. Say the message.*

my name is

3 *Join the consonants in alphabetical order. Now colour the picture.*

What is it?

It's an ______________________

Practice

4 *Add the missing vowels.*

lmp *l a m p*

1. cmptr __________
2. mrrr _______
3. qn ______
4. wndw _______

5 *Add **a** or **an**. Draw quick pictures.*

Draw *an* apple on the table.

1. Draw ____ egg on the table.
2. Draw ____ glove on the table.
3. Draw ____ hat on the table.
4. Draw ____ orange on the table.
5. Draw ____ ice cream on the table.
6. Draw ____ yo-yo on the table.

Extra *Make an eye chart with alphabet letters. Test a friend.*

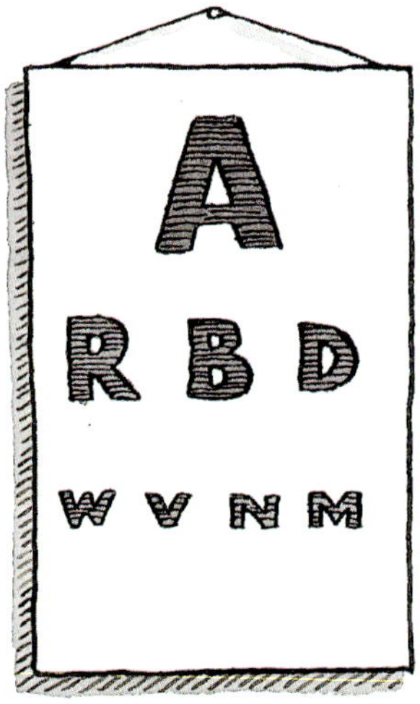

Now you know

1 *Find and circle. Make your own. USE CAPITAL LETTERS.*

c	p	e	n	c	i	l	b
b	e	l	l	i	m	d	i
i	n	m	i	r	r	o	r
c	s	o	p	e	r	l	y
y	e	m	l	u	r	l	k
c	q	u	e	e	n	t	i
l	a	m	p	t	y	e	t
e	w	i	n	d	o	w	e

2 *Find and sort.*

3 *Put a mirror on the line and read.*

an apple a doll an egg a hat an orange a mirror

Think with your teacher

1 *Find and say the blue letters. What are they?*

Aa Bb Cc Dd Ee Ff Gg Hh Ii Jj

Kk Ll Mm Nn Oo Pp Qq Rr Ss

Tt Uu Vv Ww Xx Yy Zz

2 *When do you use **a**? When do you use **an**?*

At school

Words you need

1 *Underline three words you know. Learn three new words.*

2 *Point to ten things in your classroom. Say what they are.*

Word check

1 *Read and colour.*

The *floor* is brown, the *door* is red,
The *table* is orange and so is our pet.
The *ceiling* is yellow, the *walls* are, too.
Two *bags* are pink, three *bags* are blue.
Look at the boy on the green *chair*,
His *pencil* is black and so is his hair.

2 *Complete.*

Singular	*Plural*
1 pen	**2 p *e n s***
1 pencil	4 penc _ _ _
1 crayon	5 c _ _ _ _ _ _
1 ruler	3 r _ _ _ _ _

3 *Find and circle.*

b	b	b	l	a	c	k
r	g	r	e	y	o	y
o	a	p	s	r	f	e
w	h	i	t	e	e	l
b	l	n	a	d	d	l
l	e	k	a	b	l	o
u	b	r	o	w	n	w
e	g	r	e	e	n	y

Extra words you know

shelf

Show what you know

1 Find and circle **My, Your, His, Her, Our, Their.**

2 Match.

I am Linda.	His name is Michael.
You are Jack.	Their names are Michael and Sue.
He is Michael.	Our names are Linda and Jack.
We are Linda and Jack.	My name is Linda.
They are Michael and Sue.	Your name is Jack.

3 Complete with **I, You, He, She, We, They.**

1. _I_ am Linda. My hair is brown.
2. _____ are Jack. Your hair is black.
3. ___ is Michael. His eyes are brown.
4. _____ is Sue. Her eyes are blue.
5. ___ are Linda and Jack.
   Our names are Linda and Jack.
6. _______ are Michael and Sue.
   Their names are Michael and Sue.

Practice

1 Who are they? Complete and answer.

1 What's her name? _____ name is *Linda*.

2 What's his name? _____ name is ________________ .

3 What's her name? _____ name is ________________ .

3 4 What are their names? _____ names are ________________ and Jack.

2 Complete the chart for you and your friends.

Things in my class

Names	*Blue things*	*Sentences*
(me) *Jack*	*pen*	My *pen is blue*.
1. (me) ________________		My ________________________ .
2. (girl) ________________		Her ________________________ .
3. (boy) ________________		His ________________________ .
4. (boy) ____________ and (girl) ________________		Their ________________________ ________________________ .

Practice

3 *Use the colour key. Colour and complete.*

KEY
b = blue
br = brown
g = green
o = orange
r = red
y = yellow

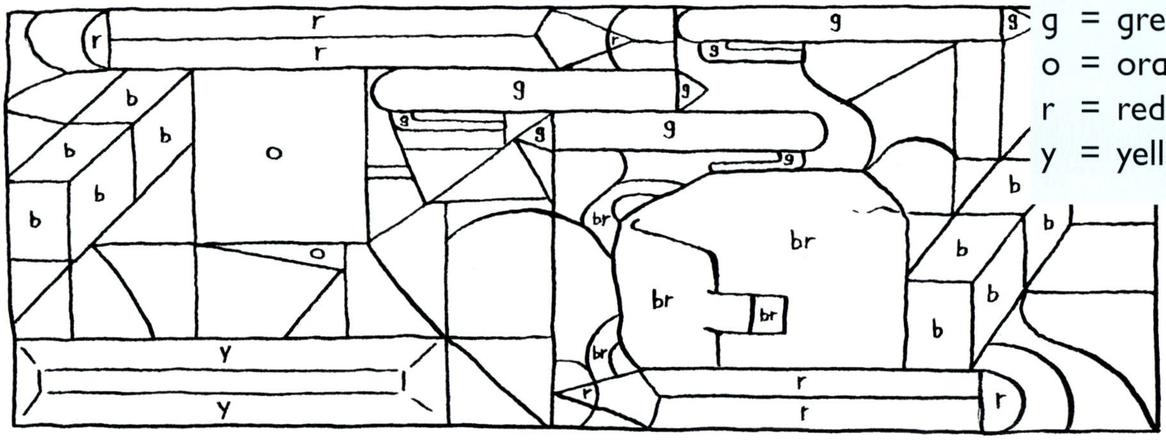

1. **The pencils** *are red*.
2. The pens ____ ______ .
3. The rubbers ___ ______ .
4. The book ___ _______ .
5. The ruler ___ ______ .
6. The bag ___ ______ .

4 *Complete to make your own class quiz. Test a friend.*

His hair is *black*. **His eyes are** *brown*. **Who is** *he*?

Answer: *He* **is** *Jack*.

1. Her hair is __________ . Her eyes are _______ . Who is ____ ?

   Answer: ______ is ______________ .

2. His hair ______ _______ . _______ eyes are _______ . Who is ____ ?

   Answer: ______ is ______________ .

3. Their hair is _______ . _______ eyes _______ _______ . Who are _______ ?

   Answer: ______ are ______________ and ______________ .

Extra *Play a guessing game. Make questions about your classroom.*

Now you know

1 *Ask and answer about your class. Complete the chart.*

Names form your class	Eyes				Hair			
	brown	grey	green	blue	black	brown	blonde	red
Linda			✔					

2 *Use the chart above. Complete sentences.*

She is *Linda.* *Her* eyes are *green.* *Her* hair is *brown.*

1. *I* am ________ . *My* eyes are ________ . ___ hair is ________ .
2. You are ________ . _____ eyes are ________ . _____ hair is ________ .
3. ___ is ________ . _____ eyes are ________ . *Her* hair is ________ .
4. ___ is ________ . *His* eyes are ________ . ___ hair is ________ .
5. *We* are ________ and ________ . *Our* eyes are ________________ .
   (your name) (your friend) ___ hair is ________________ .
6. *They* are ________ and ________ . _____ eyes are ________________ .
   (boy) (girl) *Their* hair is ________________ .

Think with your teacher

Underline the nouns. Some of the nouns end in 's'. Why?

1. The table is red.
2. My eyes are green.
3. The chairs are red.
4. His pencil is yellow.
5. My hair is brown.
6. Her pencils are orange.

Birthday party

Words you need

1 Label Linda's presents.

2 Point to the balloons. Say what the children are.

Extra words you know

video

Word check

1 Complete.

	Name	Age	What are they?
	Luke	*7*	*foot*ball *play*er
1.	Barbara	___	_ _ _ cer
2.	Jane	___	_ _ _ _ _ figh _ _ _
3.	Sue and Jack	___	_ _ _ _ _ st _ _
4.	Carlos	___	_ _ _ _ _ _ _ aut
5.	Michael	___	_ _ _ _ _ oy
6.	Linda	___	_ _ _ wn

2 Match.

1 5 × + – 8

five plus one minus eight times

3 Complete and write. Make sums for a friend.

5 + 5 = *10* **Five plus five equals ten.**

1. 6 + 1 = ___ _____ plus _____ equals ________ .
2. 5 - 2 = ___ Five ______ two ________ ____________.
3. 3 x 3 = ___ ________________________________.
4. 7 + 4 = 11 ________________________________.
5. 10 - 10 = ___ ________________________________.

4 Sort the presents.

For my birthday

I want *I don't want*

Show what you know

1 Match.

	Verb to be	*Short forms*
I	is	I'm
you	are	you're
he	are	he's
she	are	she's
it	is	it's
we	is	we're
they	am	they're

2 Circle the apostrophe. Write the missing letter.

I'm not = I *a*m not
1. You're = You _re
2. She's = She _s
3. He isn't = He is n_t
4. We're = We _re
5. They aren't = They are n_t

3 Look at page 14 and answer.

Is Carlos an astronaut? *Yes, he is.*
1. What is Jack? He's _ ____ ____ .
2. How old is Luke? He's _ _____ ____ .
3. Who is the cowboy? Michael ___ ____ ________ .
4. Is Sue eight? No, she ____ . She's ____ .
5. How old are Jack and Sue? They ___ ____ .
6. Is Barbara a dancer? Yes, ___ ___ .

Practice

1 *Complete. Use* **am, is, are.**

My name *is* Linda.

1. Today ________ my birthday.
2. I ________ eight years old.
3. I ________ a clown.
4. My best friends ________ Jack and Sue.
5. They ________ rock stars.

2 *Draw and complete for you and two friends.*

1. My name ___ ______________________ .
2. I ___ ______________ years old.
3. My best friends _______ _________________ and ______________________ .
4. They are ___________________________ years old.

3 *Complete. What are these birthday presents?*

Question		*Answer*
What is it?		*It's a computer.*
What are they?		*They're videos.*
1. What is it?		It'__ a ________________ .
2. What is it?		_______ a _____________ .
3. What are they?		They'___ _____________s.
4. What are they?		_______'___ _____________s.

Practice

4 Play this game.

5 Draw and write about your friend.

My friend

His/Her name ___ ____________ .

He/She ___ ____________ years old.

His/Her favourite colour is ____________

His/Her favourite toys are

a/an ____________________ and

a/an ____________________ .

6 You are a reporter. Complete and ask a friend.

Your questions	*Your friend's answers*
1. Wh___ is your name?	My name ___ ____________ .
2. H____ old _____ you?	I'_ ______ years old.
3. What'_ the name of your school?	Its name ___ ____________ .
4. Who _______ your friends?	They ___ __________ and ________ .

Extra *Do an age survey in your class for brothers and sisters.*

Now you know

1 *Write a similar chant for your age. Read it to a friend.*

How old are you?
3 x 3 is 9.
8 is 6 + 2.
I am 12 – 4 years old.
Tell me: How old are you?

2 *Draw and write about your favourite star.*

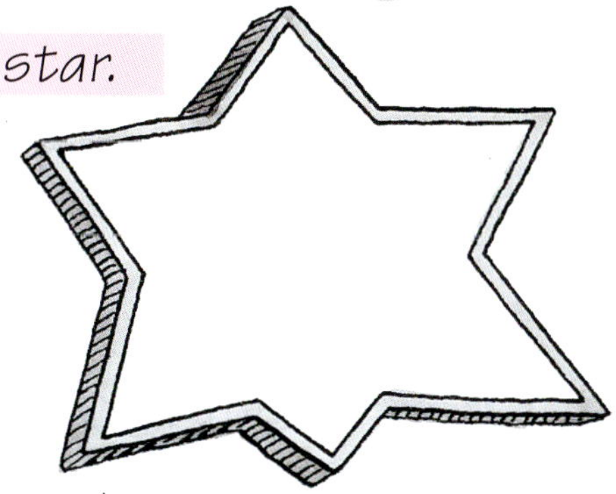

His name is Jordan Jones. | _______ name is ___________ _________ .
He's a basketball player. | _____'__ ___ ___________________________ .
He's 32 years old. | _____'__ __________________ years old.
He's fantastic! | _____'__ fantastic!

3 *Play 'Who am I?' Mime your favourite star.*

Think with your teacher

1 *Look at page 14 and complete.*

Carlos ___ 6 years old.
Sue and Jack ______ 9 years old.
Barbara ___ 7 years old.
Jane ___ 5 years old.
Linda ___n't 6 years old. She's ___ .

Is Sue 3 years old?
No, she ___n't. She's ___ .

Are Sue and Luke 5 years old?
No, they _____'__ . Sue ___ 9, Luke ___ 7.

2 *Tell your teacher how to say your age in your language.*

Review 1

A The alphabet

IamsixyearsoldMynameisCarlosMyeyesarebrown

1 Circle the words. (1 point)

2 Say the three sentences. (3 points)

3 Sort the letters. (3 points)

vowels	consonants	CAPITAL LETTERS
a, i, ______	m, s, ______	I, ______

B a/an

1 Complete with a **or** an. (3 points)

1. Draw ___ orange table.
2. Draw ___ red apple.
3. Draw ___ yellow hat.

2 Draw and colour the pictures. (3 points)

C Vocabulary

Play 'I Spy'. (5 points)

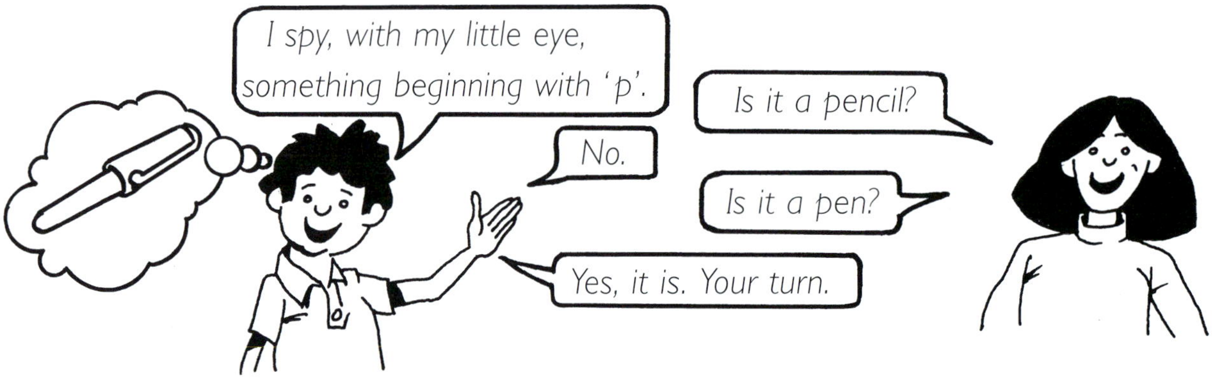

D Pronouns and possessives

Complete. (10 points)

A boy in my class	*A girl in my class*	*Two friends*
His name is ________ .	___ name is ______ .	______ names are ________ and ________ .
___ is __ years old.	___ is __ years old.	______ are __ and __ years old.
_____ eyes are ______ .	_____ eyes are ______.	______ eyes are ________ and ___________ .

E Verb *to be*

1 You are a reporter.

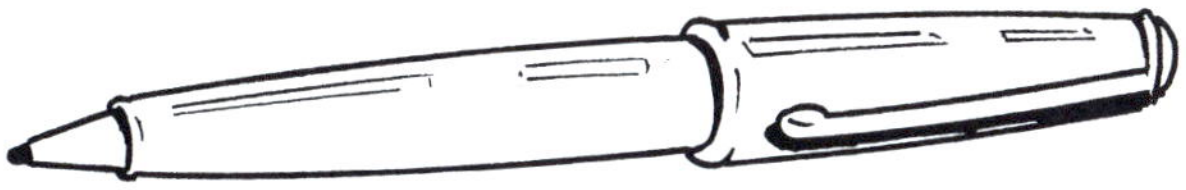

Complete and ask a friend about his/her favourite teacher. (10 points)

Your questions	*Your friend's answers.*
1. Who ___ your favourite teacher?	_____ name ___ ____________ .
2. Where'__ _____ from?	___'__ from ________________ .
3. What's _____ favourite colour?	_____ ________ ________ ___ ________ .
4. What colour ___ ______ hair?	It'__ ______________ .
5. What colour _____ ______ eyes?	They'___ ___________ .

2 Complete with am not, isn't **or** aren't. **Answer.** (12 points)

1. It isn't a clown. It *isn't* a robot. What is it?
   It's a ________ .

2. I ___ _____ 7. I ___ _____ 9.
   How old am I?
   You're ______.

3. They ______ cowboys.
   They ________ clowns.
   What are they?
   They're ________________ .

4. This ____________ an apple.
   This ____________ an orange.
   What is it?
   It's an _____ .

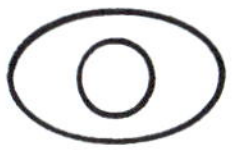

40-50 very good | 25-39 OK | 0-24 have another try

Score /50

Continents and animals

Words you need

1 Underline the words you know. Learn the new words.

2 Find one animal for each continent.

Word check

1 Complete.

One lion. Two lions.

1. One ______________ Two seals.
2. One ______________ Three snakes.
3. One ______________ Four rhinoceroses.
4. One ______________ Five ostriches.
5. One ______________ Six foxes.
6. One ______________ Seven wolves.
7. One ______________ Eight butterflies.
8. One mou__________ Nine mice.

2 Correct these words.

Aafcir A f r i c a

1. tarcanticA _ _ _ _ _ _ _ _ _ _
2. meriAca _ _ _ _ _ _ _
3. opeurE _ _ _ _ _ _
4. aiAs _ _ _ _
5. trailAusa _ _ _ _ _ _ _ _ _

3 Match.

big strong fast short

weak long slow small

Extra words you know

camel ____________________

____

____

____

Show what you know

1 Add **This** or **These**.

1. __________ are foxes. 2. __________ is an ostrich. 3. __________ are mice.

2 Add **This** or **That**.

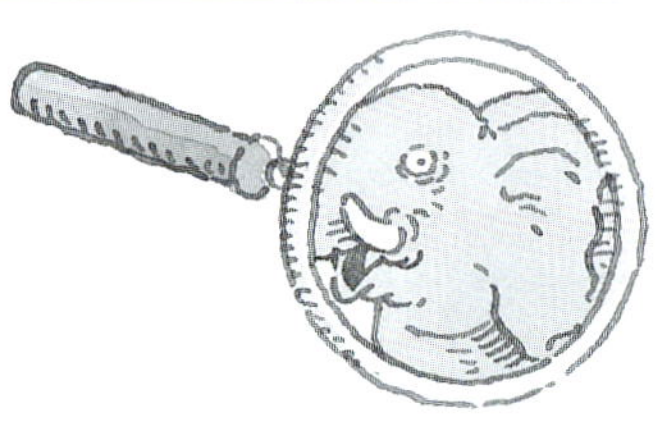
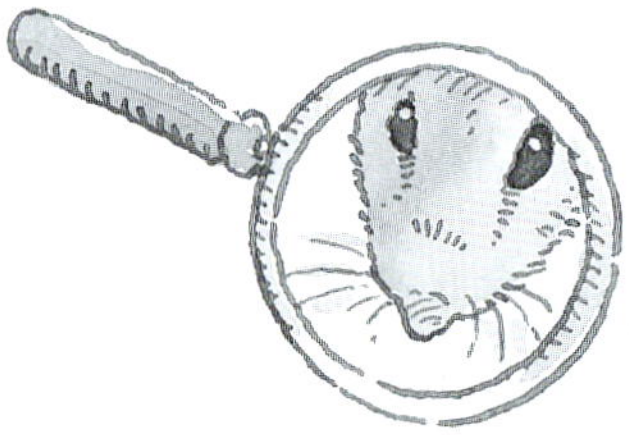

1. __________ is an elephant. 2. __________ is a mouse. 3. __________ is an antelope.

3 Add **These** or **Those**.

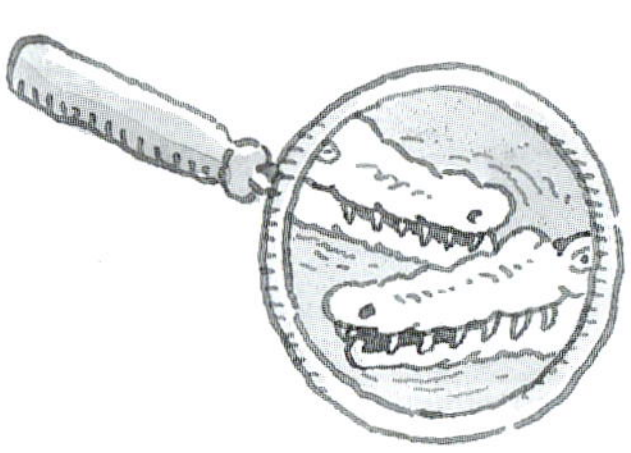

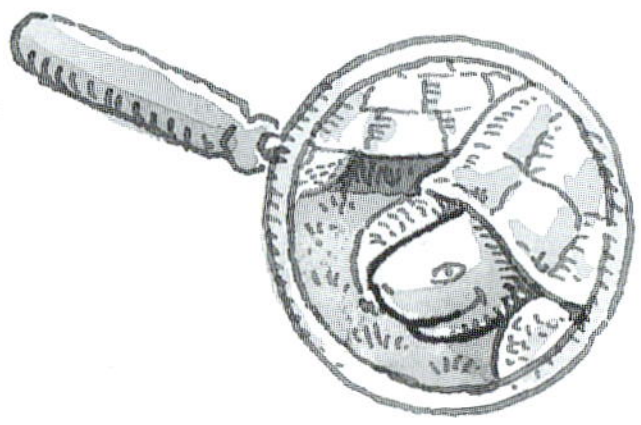

1. __________ are crocodiles. 2. __________ are lions. 3. __________ are tortoises.

Practice

1 Add **This, That, These,** or **Those.**

1. __________ is a jaguar.
2. __________ is an elephant.
3. __________ are crocodiles.
4. __________ are antelopes.
5. __________ is a fox.
6. __________ are mice.
7. __________ is a rhinoceros.
8. __________ are butterflies.

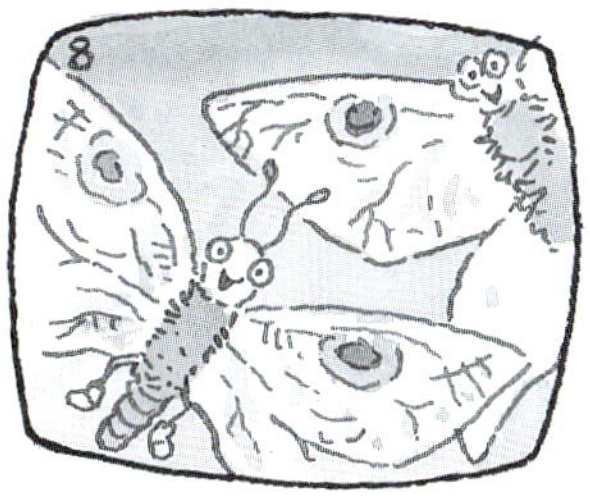

2 Read and colour the snakes.

Practice

3 Complete using **this** or **these**.

What's the name of *this* animal? *snake*

1. What's the name of ________ animal?  ____________

2. What are the names of ________ animals?

____

3. What are the names of ________ animals?

____

4. What's the name of ________ animal?  ____________

4 Use the key. Complete using **that** or **those**.

Where's *that* tiger from? It's from *Asia*.

Where are *those* lions from? They're from *Africa*.

1. Where'__ ______ gorilla from? It's from ________________.
2. Where ___ ______ kangaroos from? They're from __________.
3. Where'__ ______ wolf from? It's from ________________.
4. Where'__ ______ mouse from? It's from ________________.
5. Where ___ ______ seals from? They're from ____________.
6. Where'__ ______ elephant from? It's from ____________.

Key AF = Africa AN = Antarctica EU = Europe
AS = Asia AU = Australia NA = North America

Now you know

1 *Colour the picture. Write where the animals are from.*

That elephant is from A f r i c a.

1. That tiger is from _ _ _ _ .
2. Tho_ _ wol_ _ _ _ _ _ from Eur_ _ _ .
3. _ _ _se rhinoceroses _ _ _ from _ _ _ _ _ _ a.
4. Th_ _ gorilla _ _ from Africa.

2 *Complete the spellings.*

One clever crocodile.	Two clever crocodil e s .
One big butterfly.	Three big butterfl i e s .
1. One tall tiger.	Two tall tiger_
2. One small snake.	Three sm_ _ _ sn_ _ _ _ .
3. One red rhinoceros.	Four re_ r_ _ _ _ _ _ _ _ _ _ _ _ _ .
4. One orange ostrich.	Five o_ _ _ _ _ o_ _ _ _ _ _ _ _ _ .
5. One fast fox.	Six f_ _ _ f_ _ _ _ .
6. One white wolf.	Seven w_ _ _ _ w_ _ _ _ _ _ .

Think with your teacher

1 *Match and explain.*

1. This is a tiger.
2. That is a tiger.
3. These are tigers.
4. Those are tigers.

a. b. c. d.

2 *What animals have the same names in your language?*

______________________ ______________________ ______________________

Extra *Make an animal alphabet.*
A is for antelope.
B is for ...

Dressing up

Words you need

Look at the key and complete the labels.

Word check

1 *Write in A-B-C order.*

skirt socks shorts shirt shoes

s h i r t   s h o _ _   s h o _ _ _   s _ _ _ _   s _ _ _ _

Key

Extra words you know

tracksuit ______________________

____

____

____

2 Complete and match. Colour three pairs you have.

a pair of *gloves*

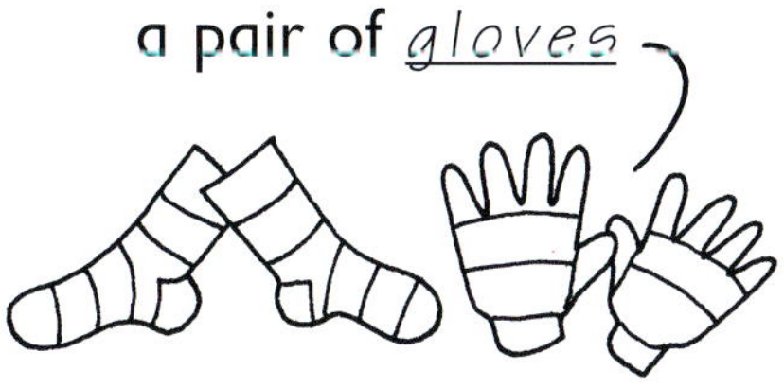

1. a pair of _ _ _ n s
2. a pair of _ _ c k s
3. a pair of _ _ _ r t s
4. a pair of _ _ o t s

Show what you know

1 Can you remember? Complete using ***Jane's*** or ***Peter's.***

This is *Jane's* skirt.

1. These are __________ shoes.

2. This is __________ T-shirt.

3. This is __________ watch.

4. This is __________ hat.

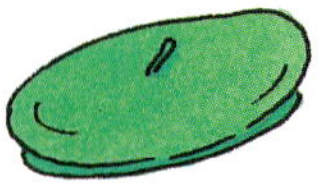

5. These are __________ jeans.

6. These are __________ boots.

2 Find and answer.

Whose shirt is it?

It's *Michael's shirt*.

1. Whose skirt is it?
   It's __________ __________ .
2. Whose boots are they?
   They're __________ __________ .
3. Whose blouse is it?
   It's __________ __________ .
4. Whose necklace is it?
   It's __________ __________ .
5. Whose gloves are they?
   They're __________ __________ .

3 Match and colour.

1. The robot's shirt is blue.
2. The robot's shirts are blue.
3. The robot's hat is red.
4. The robot's hats are red.

Practice

1 Complete using **Linda's** or **Jack's**.

This orange T-shirt isn't *Jack's*. His T-shirt is red.

1. This blue hat isn't ____________ . Her hat is pink.
2. These pink shorts aren't ____________ . His shorts are blue.
3. These blue sandals aren't ____________ . Her sandals are orange.
4. This yellow watch isn't ____________ . Her watch is green.
5. These black sunglasses aren't ____________ . His sunglasses are green.

2 Whose clothes is the robot wearing?

1. This pink hat isn't *Jack's*.
   His hat is *blue*.
2. This green watch isn't ____________ .
   His watch is ____________ .
3. These orange sandals aren't ____________ .
   His sandals are ____________ .
4. These green sunglasses aren't ____________ . Her sunglasses are _____ .

3 Complete, colour and answer.

Whose is **this pink hat?**  **It's *Linda's*.**

Whose are **these blue shorts?**  **They're *Jack's*.**

1. ________ ___ this orange T-shirt?  It's ______________ .
2. ________ ___ this green watch?  It's ______________ .
3. ________ ______ these blue sandals?  They're ______________ .
4. ________ ______ these green sunglasses?  They're ______________ .

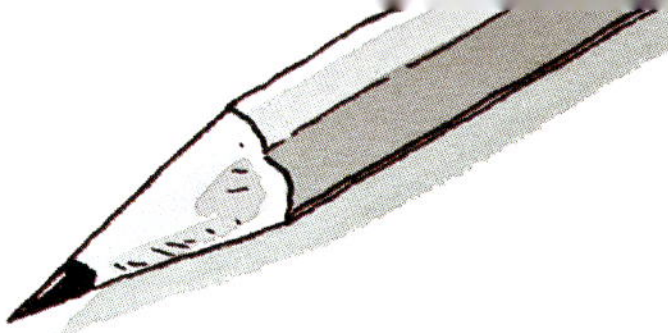

Practice

4 Draw and describe your friends' clothes.

This is *Rosa's* skirt.

1. This is ________ shirt.

2. These are ________ jeans.

3. This is ________ jacket.

4. These are ________ boots.

5. This is ________ skirt.

5 Circle the correct words.

Is this (your)/you necklace?

1. Whose/Who's are these boots?
2. They're her/she shoes.
3. Are these they/their coats?
4. They're our/we gloves.
5. Is this me/my scarf?

Extra *Make a class Lost Property box.*

Now you know

1 *Complete the chart for you and your friends.*

	Name	white	blue	black	red
	Linda	blouse	sweater	shoes	shirt
(boy)					
(girl)					
(you)					

2 *Look at your chart. Complete and answer.*

Whose is that white blouse? It's Linda's.

Whose are those black shoes? They're Linda's.

1. Whose is this ________ ________ ? It's ________'__ .
2. Whose are those ________ ________ ? They're ______'__ .
3. Whose ______ ________ ________ ________? They're ______'s.
4. Whose _____ ________ ________ ________? It's _____'__ .

Think with your teacher

Circle the apostrophes. What do they tell us?

Who's this? It's Linda.
Whose is this white blouse? It's Linda's.

Explore your town

Words you need

1 *Underline and say five buildings in your town.*

2 *Play 'Where's the building?'*

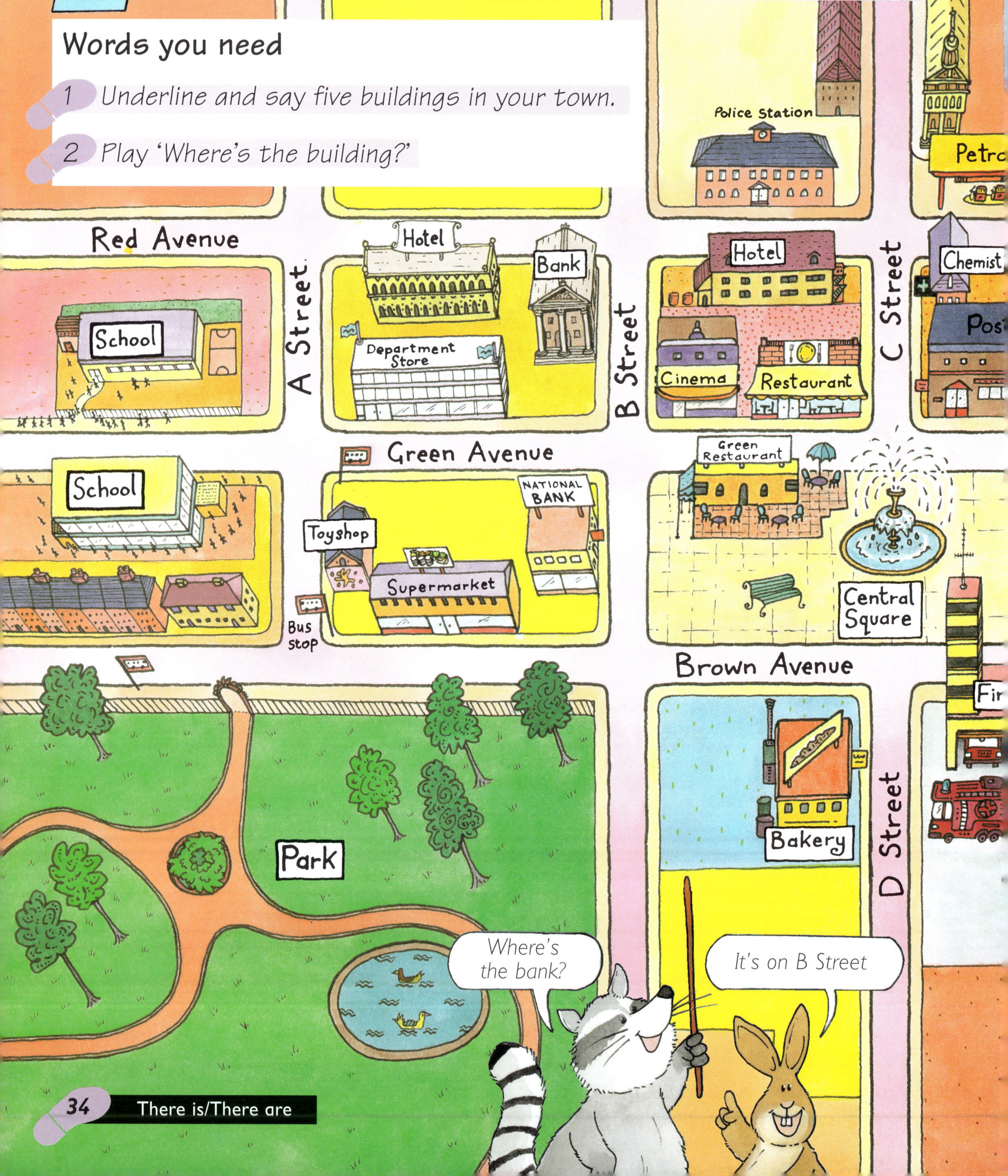

Map of Summerville

Word check

1 Complete.

N *o r t h*

W _ _ _

E _ _ _

S _ _ _ _

2 Add to these lists.

Sells things	Doesn't sell things
department store	*police station*

3 Complete and match.

bus s *t o p*

post o _ _ _ _ _

fire st _ _ _ _ _

ba _ _

hos _ _ _ _ _

po _ _ _ _ station

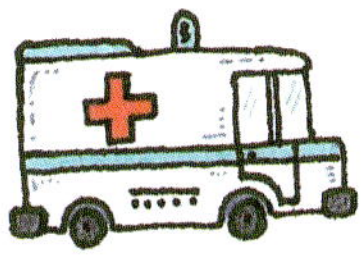

Extra words you know

airport

Show what you know

1 *Look at the map section. Add the Street or Avenue names.*

There's a department store in this Avenue. *Green* **Avenue.**
1. There's a bank and a cinema in this Street. ________ Street.
2. There are two hotels in this Avenue. ________ Avenue.
3. There's a school in this Avenue. ________ Avenue.

2 *Look at the map on pages 34–35. Complete.*

Is there **a toyshop in A Street?** *Yes, there is.*
Are there **two banks in C Street?** *No, there aren't.*
1. ___ ________ a police station in Red Avenue? ____, ________ ___ .
2. ___ ________ a restaurant in A Street? ____, ________ ________ .
3. ______ ________ two bus stops in B Street? ____, ________ ________ .
4. ______ ________ two restaurants in Green Avenue? ____, ________ ______ .

3 *Look at the map again. Read and answer.*

How many schools are there in Summerville? *There are two.*
How many toyshops are there in A Street? *There's one.*
How many airports are there in Summerville? *There are none.*
1. How many hotels are there in Red Avenue? ________ _____ _____ .
2. How many supermarkets are there in C Street? ________ _____ _______ .
3. How many cinemas are there in B Street? __________ ______ .
4. How many parks are there in Summerville? ________ _____ _____ .

Practice

1 *Work in pairs. Hide these buildings in your grid.*

Building	***Colour of squares***
school	6 red squares
supermarket	5 blue squares
hotel	4 green squares
restaurant	3 yellow squares
police station	2 black squares
bakery	2 orange squares

My grid

a	b	c	d	e	f	g	
							1
							2
							3
							4
							5
							6
							7

My partner's grid

a	b	c	d	e	f	g	
							1
							2
							3
							4
							5
							6
							7

2 *Now ask your partner questions and fill in the colours on your partner's grid.*

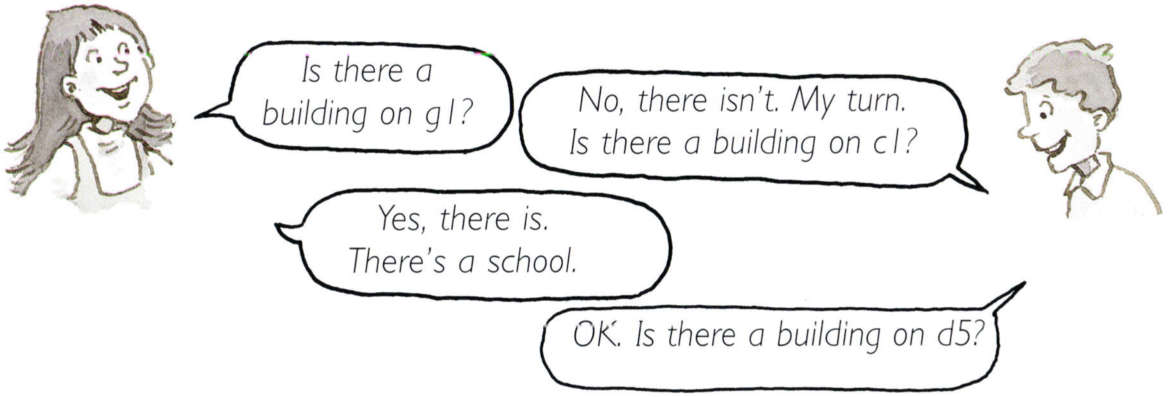

Practice

3 Read, complete and colour.

Dear Paul,

This is a postcard of S________.
There's a big ________ pool.
There are two big ________.

Please write about your town.
Best wishes,
Jack

4 Draw a postcard for your town. Write about it to a new penpal.

____
____
____
____
____
____
____
____

Extra Make a big tourist poster or leaflet for your town. Display it.

Now you know

1 *Read and 'walk' on the grid with your fingers. Draw a line.*

Start at ‼

You are on the corner of Red Avenue and A Street. Walk north two blocks. Stop.
Turn east. Walk east three blocks. Stop.
Turn south. Walk south three blocks. Stop.
Turn west. Walk west two blocks. Stop.
Where are you? Say the Avenue name and Street letter.

Give similar instructions to a friend.

2 *Complete for your town.*

There is a big swimming pool in my town.

1. There's a ____________ in my town. It is near __________________ .
2. There__ a ____________ in my town. It is near __________________ .
3. There ______ two __________________s in my town.

Think with your teacher

1 *Complete and answer the questions about your town.*

1. How many _______________s are there? There ______ one.
2. How many _______________s are there? There _______ two or three.
3. How many _______________s are there? There _______ none.

2 *When do we use* ***there is ...*** *? When do we use* ***there are ....****?*

Review 2

A *Vocabulary*

Match. (4 points)

bread	teacher	yo-yo	car	money
toy shop	bank	bakery	school	petrol station

B *This, that, these, those*

1 Read and colour. (8 points)

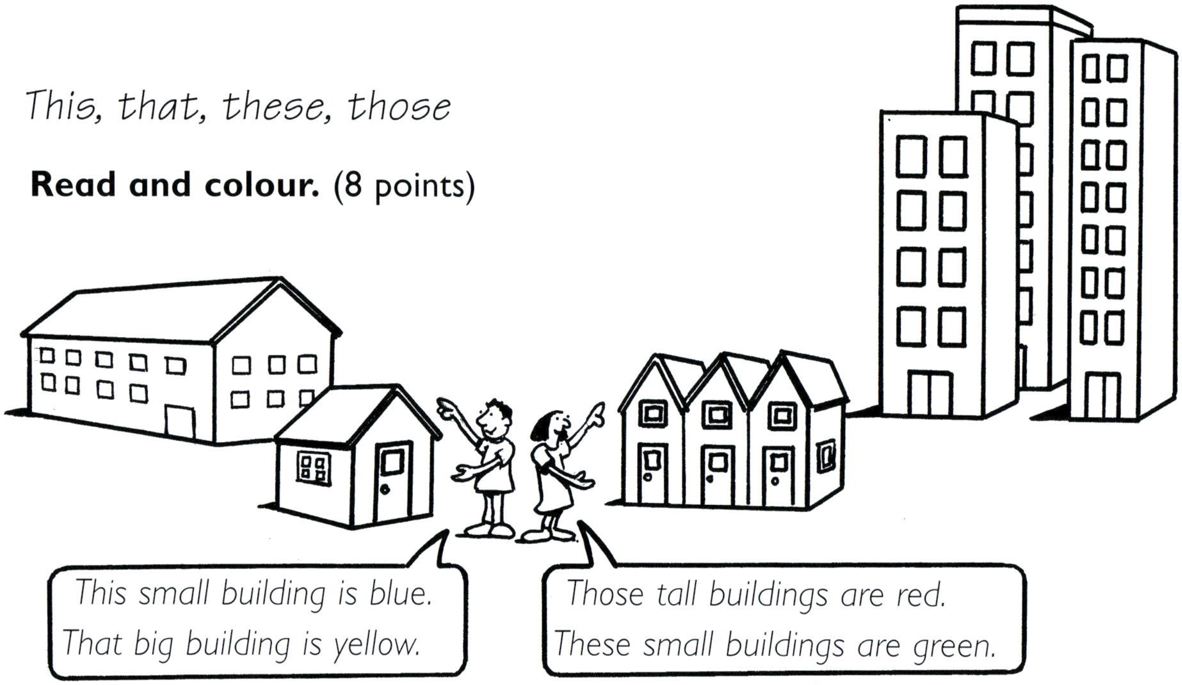

2 Complete with this, that, these, those. **Answer.** (10 points)

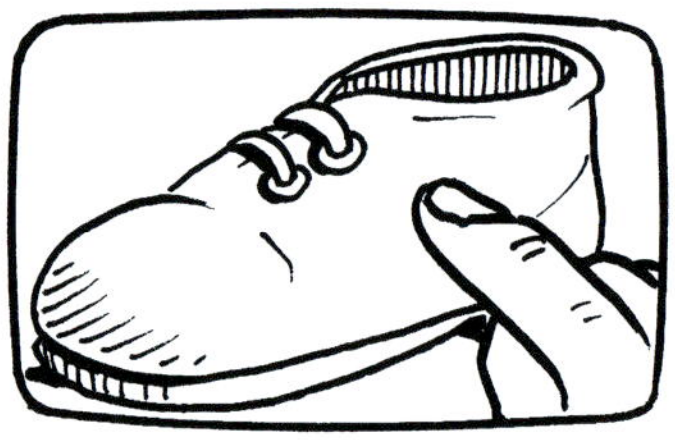

1. What's __________ ?
It's __ __________________ .

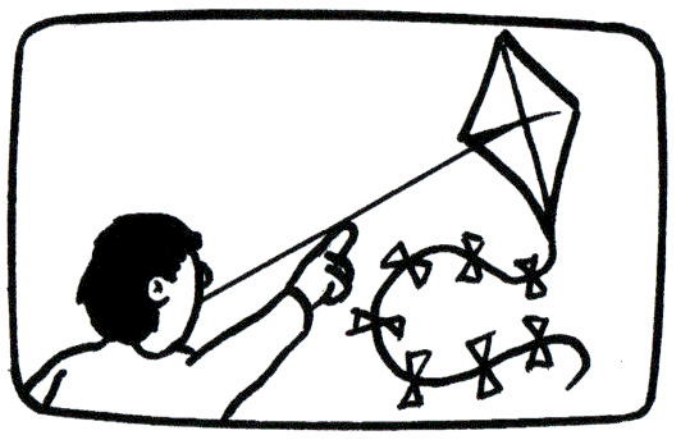

3. What's __________ ?
It's __ __________________ .

2. What are __________ ?
They're __________________s.

4. What are __________ ?
They're __________________s.

C *Whose and possessives*

1 **Complete and answer.** (14 points)

Whose *are* these boots? 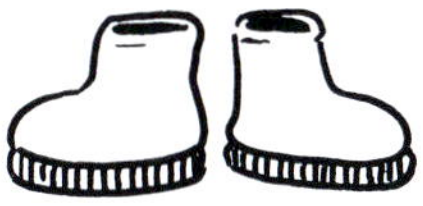 They're the *astronaut's*.

1. Whose _____ these shoes?  They're the _______________ .
2. Whose _____ this hat?  It's the _______________ .
3. Whose _____ this hat?  It's the _______________ .
4. Whose _____ these boots?  ______ ______ ____________ .
5. Whose _____ this watch?  ______ ______ ____________ .

2 **Complete with** your, his, her. (5 points)

1. Is this ______ hat?  No. It isn't my hat. It's the clown's.
2. Are these ______ shoes?  Yes. They're her shoes. They're the dancer's.
3. Are these ______ gloves?  Yes. They're his gloves. They're the astronaut's.
4. Is this ______ jacket?  No. It isn't her jacket. It's the firefighter's.
5. Are these ________ shoes?  Yes, they're my shoes.

D *There is/are*

Complete. (9 points)

Is there a bank in B Street?	Yes, there is.
1. ___ ______ a supermarket in Red Avenue?	No, there isn't.
2. _____ ________ two restaurants in E Street?	No, there aren't.
3. Are there three bus stops in Green Avenue?	No, ________ ________ .
4. Is ________ an airport in Summerville?	No, ________ ________ .

40-50 very good
25-39 OK
0-24 have another try

Score /50

Family and home

Words you need

1 *Point to and say five things in the picture.*

2 *Choose a room. Ask your friend to name three things in it.*

Extra words you know

uncle ....

....

....

....

Word check

1 Circle the odd words out.

Kitchen	Living room	Bedroom	Bathroom
cooker	armchair	bed	bath
saucepan	carpet	clock	shower
fridge	cooker	drawer	tap
bed	television	fridge	sink
fork	picture	desk	television

2 Match to make new words.

arm down sauce book bed

room shelf chair stairs pan

3 Complete.

4 Sort the family words.

mum dad brother sister grandma grandad

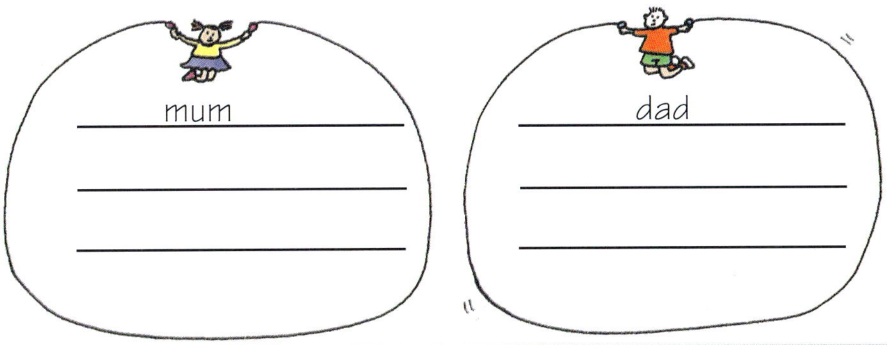

Show what you know

1 *Match. Write the number.*

1. The cat is in the basket.
2. The cat is on the chair.
3. The cat is under the chair.
4. The cat is behind the chair.
5. The cat is in front of the basket.
6. The cat is next to the chair.
7. The cat is near the chair.
8. The cat is between the chair and the basket.

2 *Complete with* **in, on, under, next to, between, behind.**

There's a picture *on* the wall.

1. There's a chair ____________ the bed.
2. The chair is ______________ the bed and the desk.
3. There are two yellow socks ______ the drawer.
4. There's a red book ____________ the chair.
5. There's a cat _____ the bed.
6. The lamp is ______________ the computer.

3 *Cover the picture and ask a friend.*

Practice

1 Read and label the family.

Grandma is on the sofa between my brother and my sister.
Mum is in the armchair next to the lamp.
Dad is in the armchair next to the television.
There's a picture behind Mum's armchair.

2 Look at the picture. Complete the sentences.

1. The book is __________ the floor.
2. There's a basket __________ the armchairs.
3. There are two newspapers __________ the armchair.
4. There's a sock __________ the sofa.
5. There's a picture __________ thc wall.

3 Write two more sentences about the Mouse House.

1. *There is* ____

____.

2. *There are* ____

____.

Practice

4 Draw the cat's tail.

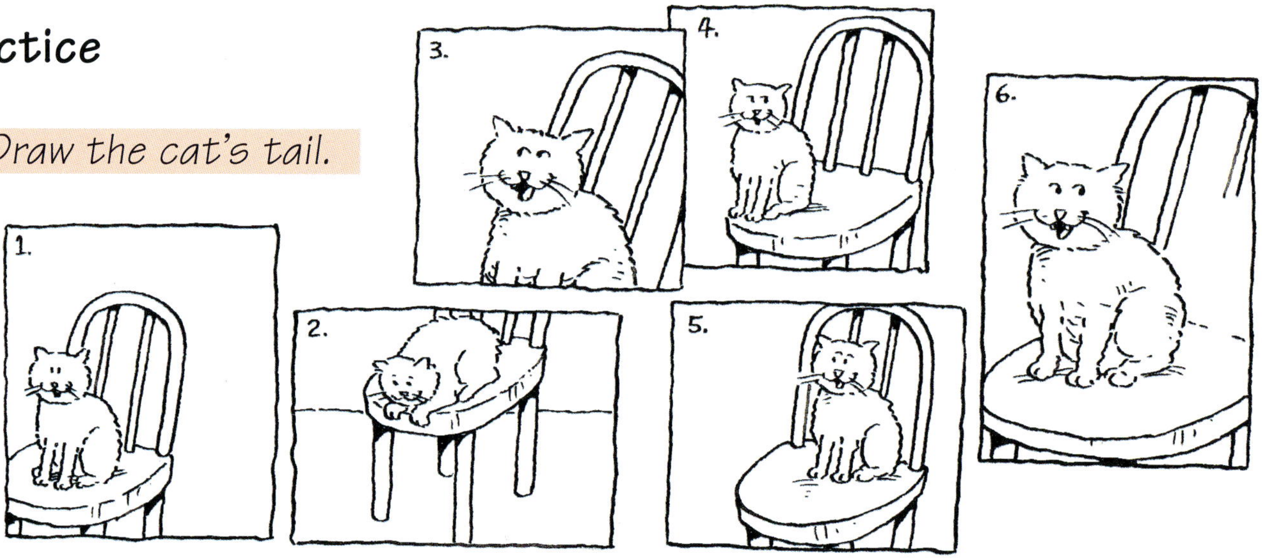

1. behind the chair
2. under the chair
3. between the cat's ears
4. next to the cat, on the chair
5. in front of the cat's feet
6. in the right place

5 Choose and draw four things. Ask and answer.

6 Look at the table. Tell your friend where things are.

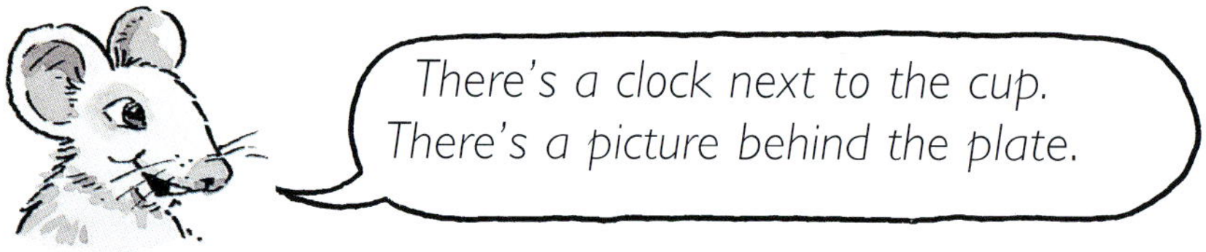

Extra Draw and label your family and home.
Describe your picture to a friend.

Now you know

1 *Look for 60 seconds. Cover the picture and answer.*

Where's the table? It's *in front of* **the window.**

1. Where's the clock? It's ____________ the television.
2. Where's the armchair? It's ________________________ .
3. Where's the lamp? ____________________ the window and the picture.

2 *Look at the picture. Play 'true or false' with a friend.*

The clock is under the sofa.

False!

The picture is ___________________________ .

True!

Think with your teacher

1 *Write about your classroom.*

Our Classroom

There are ________ desks. There ___ one ________________ .
The ________ is next to the ______ . The ____________ is under the ____________ . The __________________ is behind the __________________ .
On my desk there is a _______________ . In my bag there are ________ ___________ .

Get up and go!

Words you need

1. Circle three instructions your teacher uses in class.
2. Underline three instructions your parents use at home.
3. Mime an instruction for a friend to guess.

Extra phrases you know

Put your pencil down.

Word check

1 Number in the best order.

Clean your teeth. __
Eat your breakfast. __
Go to school. __
Get up. _1_
Wash your hands. __
Brush your hair. __

2 Add the missing words.

Stand up.

1. _____ to school.
2. Sit ________ .
3. ________ your hair.
4. ________ shout!
5. ________ off the light.
6. Go ________ bed.

3 Circle the correct words.

(Open)/Turn on your book.

1. Close/Turn off the light.
2. Open/Turn on the light.
3. Close/Turn off the door.

4 Write three instructions for a friend to do.

Open your book.

1. ______________________________ .
2. ______________________________ .
3. ______________________________ .

Show what you know

1 *Write in the best order. Tell your friend.*

open your book sit down come in

Come in, sit down and open your book.

1. eat your breakfast wash your hands clean your teeth

   ____________ , ____________ and ____________ .

2. go to school eat your breakfast get up

   ____________ , ____________ and ____________ .

3. do your homework put your pencil down pick up your pencil

   ____________ , ____________ and ____________ .

2 *Complete.*

Open the door.	*Don't open* **the door.**
1. Stand up.	____'t ______ up.
2. Come in.	Do_ '_ come in.
3. Turn on the light.	______ ______ on the light.
4. Sit down.	______ ______ down.
5. Turn off the light.	______ ______ off the light.

3 *Complete.*

Pick up your book.	**=**	**Pick your book up.**
1. Turn off the light.	=	Turn the light ______ .
2. Pick up your pencil.	=	______ your pencil ______ .
3. Put down your book.	=	______ your book ______ .
4. Put up your hand.	=	________________________ .
5. Turn on the light.	=	________________________ .

Practice

1 Play 'Simon says'.

Rule: You are OUT of the game if you follow an instruction that DOESN'T begin with *Simon says...* .

2 Complete. Match the signs to rules.

Don't chew bubble gum in class. c

1. ______ eat in class. ☐
2. ______ sleep in class. ☐
3. ______ read comics in class. ☐
4. ______ shout in class. ☐

d

c

a

b

e

3 Complete with **up, in, off, down, here, on.**

Come in.

1. Stand ______ .
2. Sit ______ .
3. Pick it ______ .
4. Turn it ______ .
5. Turn it ______ .
6. Come ______ .

Practice

4 *Read this road safety code.*

Look right. Look left. Look right again. Is the road clear? Cross quickly.

Complete for your country.

Look ______ . ______ ______ . Look ______ again. Is the road clear? ______ quickly.

5 *Complete with* ***wash, clean, eat, give, do, go, watch, don't.***

Dear Linda,
We are at a party tonight.
Please ________ your dinner. (________ your hands before you eat.)
________ the cat her dinner. ________ your homework.
________ your teeth. ________ to bed at 10 o'clock!
Sleep well.

Love,
Mum and Dad

P.S. Don't ________ television and ________'__ telephone all your friends!

6 *Say and do.*

Point to yellow, point to white.
Turn to the left. Turn to the right.
Point to green. Point to red.
Left foot first. Walk straight ahead.

Extra *Make a road safety poster. Display it.*

Now you know

1 *Unscramble. Write under the signs.*

teeth/your/clean

____________________.

your/wash/hands

____________________.

a/wear/hat

____________________.

2 *Think and complete. Pick up the pencils in the correct order.*

Pick *up* **the** *red* **pencil.**

1. Pick _____ the __________ pencil.
2. Pick _____ the __________ pencil.
3. Pick _____ the __________ pencil.
4. Pick _____ the __________ pencil.

Think with your teacher

1 *Complete with* **be, come, don't, open, sit, write, shout.**

1. _______ in and _______ down.
2. _______ your books and _______.
3. _____ quiet.
4. Please don't _______ and _______ eat in class.

Thank you! Back in 2 minutes!

Miss Smith (your teacher)

2 *Mime these instructions. Now tell your teacher in your language.*

1. Sit down. 2. Be quiet. 3. Open your book.

Have a sale!

Words you need

1 *Underline three words you don't know. Learn them with a friend.*

2 *Write things you can bring to the sale.*

Word check

1 Complete.

	Singular	Plural
1.	________	teddies
2.	____________	skipping ropes
3.	watch	____________
4.	________	kites
5.	rollerskate	____________
6.	computer game	computer ________

2 Write in A-B-C order.

shoes	*remote control car*
robot	1. ____________
skipping rope	2. ____________
remote control car	3. ____________
skateboard	4. ____________
rollerskates	5. *skipping rope*

3 Choose and write.

Things I want to buy

clothes

Extra words you know

tennis racket

Show what you know

1 Match.

I	has got	I've got
You	has not got	You've got
He	have got	He's got
She	have got	She hasn't got
We	have not got	We've got
They	have got	They haven't got

2 Write two toys or games for each.

I have got ______________________________

My friend has got ______________________________

We haven't got ______________________________

3 Complete and answer.

Have **you got a teddy?** *Yes, I have./No, I haven't.*

1. ________ you got a remote control car? ____, ___ ______________.
2. Has your friend got a bike? ____, ___ ______________.
3. _____ your friend got a computer game? ____, she __________.
4. _____ Sue and Linda got robots? No, they __________.
5. _____ you and your friend ____ ______? Yes, we have.

4 Complete these sentences.

My friend has got a *doll* **but she hasn't got a** *robot***.**

1. I have got a _______ but I haven't got a _______.
2. My friend has got a _______ but he hasn't got a _______.
3. My friend ____ ____ a _______ but she hasn't ____ a _______.
4. We have ____ _______ but we haven't ____ _______.
5. Michael and Jack _____ ____ robots but they _______ ____ skateboards.

Practice

1 *Look again at page 54–55 and complete.*

Michael has got a <u>bike</u>. He <u>has</u>n't got a <u>skateboard</u>.

1. Linda has got a ______________ . She _____n't got a ______________ .
2. Sue _____ got a watch. She ___________ _____ a baseball bat.
3. Jack _____ _____ a robot. He ___________ _____ a bike.
4. ___________ _____ _____ a jigsaw. _______ ________ ______ a computer game.
5. I _________ _____ a _____________ . I haven't _____ a ______________ .

2 *Colour the robot and doll. Write questions for a friend to answer.*

Has your robot got green eyes? No, it hasn't. It has got black eyes.

Have your robot and your doll got brown hair? Yes, they have.

Your questions	*Your friend's answers*
1. Has _____ _____ _____ _________ eyes?	Yes, _____ _________.
2. Has _____ _____ _____ a _________ dress?	_____, _____ _________.
3. _____ _____ _____ got _________ shoes?	_____, _____ _________.
4. _____ your _____ and your _____ got _____ hair?	_____, _____ _________.
5. Have your _____ and your _____ _____ _____ socks?	_____, _____ _________.

Practice

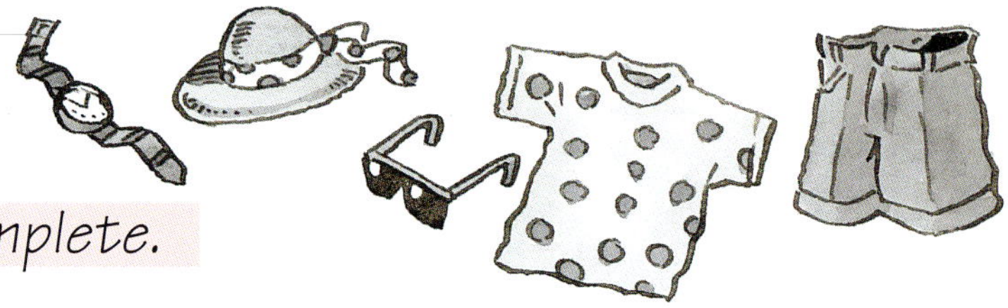

3 *Guess or find out how many. Complete.*

1. How many pairs of jeans *have* you got? — I ______ ______ ______ pairs of jeans.
2. How many T-shirts ______ you got? — I ______ ______ ______ T-shirts.
3. How many sweaters ______ your friend got? — He/She ______ ______ ______ sweaters.
4. How many pairs of shoes has your mum(dad) ______? — ______ ______ ______ ______ pairs of shoes.
5. How many jackets ______ you and your friend got? — We ______ ______ ______ jackets.
6. How many hats ______ your friends got? — They ______ ______ ______ hats.

4 *Complete the chart for you and your friend.*

	We have got these clothes for parties	We have got these clothes for sport	We have got these clothes for the beach
Linda	*red dress, white shoes*		

5 *Use your chart. Complete.*

I *have got* a *white sweater* and *blue jeans* for parties.
My friend *has* got a *red dress* and *white shoes* for parties.

1. I ______ ______ a ______ ______ and ______ ______ for parties.
2. I ______ ______ a ______ ______ and ______ ______ for sport.
3. My friend ______ got a ______ ______ and ______ for the beach.
4. My friend ______ got a ______ ______ and ______ ______ for parties.

Extra *Make a poster for a sale. Have a sale!*

Now you know

1 *Add two friends' names. Find out. Complete.*

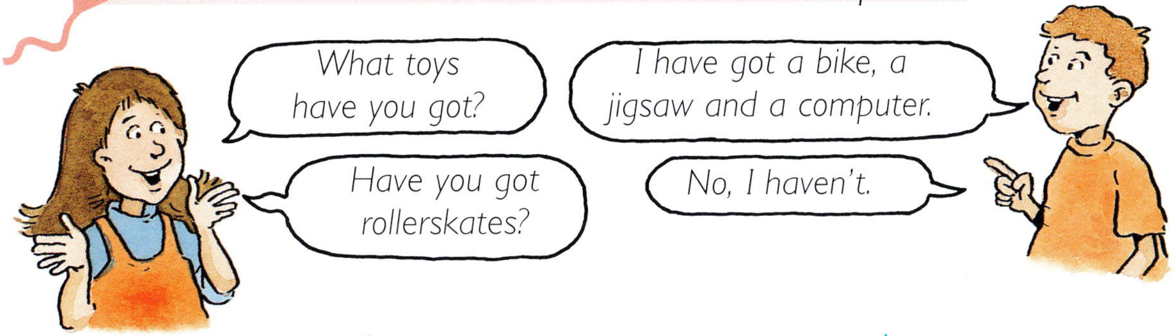

	has got these toys	*hasn't got these toys*
Michael	bike, jigsaw, computer	rollerskates

2 *Use your chart above to make sentences.*

Michael has got a bike.
Linda has got rollerskates but I haven't.
Michael has got a bike but my friend hasn't.

1. ____________ has got a ____________ .
2. ____________ has got a ____________ but I ____________ .
3. ____________ has got a ____________ but my friend __________ .
4. I ___________ got a ____________ but my friend ________ .
5. My friend ___ _____ a __________ and I have got a _________ too.

Think with your teacher

Complete. Explain to your teacher.

Statement	*Negative*	*Question*
I have got	I haven't got	Have I got ?
You have got	*You haven't got*	______ you _____?
She _____ _____	She __________ ___	_____ she _____?
He _____ _____	He __________ ___	*Has he got?*
It has got	*It hasn't got*	_____ it _____?

Review 3

A Prepositions

1 Write the names on the T-shirts. (4 points)

I'm Sue. The cat is in front of me
and Sara is behind me.
My brother Ben is between my sister Maria
and my sister Sara.
My brother Tom is next to me. My mum is behind Tom.
My dad is next to Tom. My grandma is in front of Maria.

2 Look and complete using behind, in front of, next to, between, in, under. (6 points)

1. The picture is ________________ the kite.
2. There are two pens ________________ the cup.
3. The hat is ________________ the doll.
4. The comics are ________________ the jigsaw.
5. The watch is ________________ the skipping rope.
6. The clock is ________________ the picture and the cups.

B Imperatives

Write the instructions under the signs. (5 points)

______________ ______________ ______________ ______________ ______________

______________ ______________ ______________ ______________ ______________

C *have/has got*

1 Colour the animals. Complete the chart. (13 points)

	eyes	ears	hair	legs	tail
The mouse has got ...	2				
The cats have got ...		4			
I have got ...					

2 Look at your chart and pictures.

Complete. Use have/haven't got **or** has/hasn't got **and a colour.** (18 points)

The mouse _has_ _got_ a _brown_ tail.

1. The mouse _____ _____ 2 _______ eyes.
2. The cats _______ _____ _______ eyes.
3. The cats _______ _____ _______ hair.
4. The mouse _______ _____ 4 _______ legs.
5. I _______ _____ _______ hair.
6. I _______ _____ a _______ tail.

3 You are doing a 'home survey'. Complete the questionnaire. (4 points)

Have you got a brother? _Has_ your mum got a car?

1. _________ you got brothers and sisters?
2. _________ your mum and dad got a car?
3. _________ your house got a big kitchen?
4. _________ you got a big bedroom?

40-50 very good | 25-39 OK | 0-24 have another try | Score /50

The English alphabet

There are 26 letters.
There are 5 vowels: a, e, i, o, u
There are 21 consonants:
b, c, d, f, g, h, j, k, l, m, n, p, q, r, s, t, v, w, x, y, z
A,B,C,D,E,F,G,H,I,J,K,L,M,N,O,P,Q,R,S,T,U,V,W,X,Y,Z

a/an

an apple, an egg, an ice cream, an orange, an umbrella
BUT: a bicycle, a computer, a doll, a fork, etc.

Possessive adjectives my, your, his, her, its, our, their

Our class
My name is Linda. Your name is Jack.
My hair is brown. Your hair is black.
Their names are Michael and Sue.
His eyes are brown. Her eyes are blue.

Plurals

One big lion	Two big lions
One long snake	Two long snakes
One big butterfly	Three big butterflies
One fast fox	Five fast foxes
One orange ostrich	Six orange ostriches
One white wolf	Seven white wolves
One small mouse	Two small mice

This, that, these, those

What's this? This is a mouse.

What are these? These are mice.

What's that? That is a lion.

What are those? Those are lions.

The verb *to be*

Affirmative	Negative	Questions	Negative answers
I am = I'm	I am not = I'm not	Am I a clown?	No, you are not.
You are = You're	You are not = You aren't	Are you a cowboy?	No, I am not.
She is = She's	She is not = She isn't	Is he a clown?	No, he is not.
He is = He's	He is not = He isn't	Is she an astronaut?	No, she is not.
It is = It's	It is not = It isn't	Is it a robot?	No, it is not.
We are = We're	We are not = We aren't	Are we clowns?	No, you are not.
They are = They're	They are not = They aren't		No, we are not.
		Are they firefighters?	No, they are not.

Possessives and Whose...?

Whose is that red hat?	It's Linda's (hat).
Whose is this white shirt?	It's Michael's (shirt).
Whose are those black boots?	They're Jack's (boots).
Whose are these blue jeans?	They're Sue's (jeans).

There is/There are

Describing	Questions	Answers
There is a bank in this street.	Is there a park in this street?	Yes, there is./No, there isn't.
There are five shops in this street.	Are there two banks in this street?	Yes, there are./No, there aren't.

How many...?

How many oranges are there on the table? There are three./There is one.

Prepositions

The cat is near the chair.
The mouse is under the chair.

The mouse is behind the box.
The cat is in front of the box.

The cat is next to the cups.
The mouse is between the cups.

The cat is in the box.
The mouse is on the box.

Imperatives

Sit down, please.
Be quiet.
Don't shout!

have/has got

Questions	Affirmative	Negative
Have you got a car?	Yes, I have.	No, I haven't. I have got a bicycle.
	Yes, we have.	No, we haven't. We have got bicycles.
Have they got cars?	Yes, they have.	No, they haven't. They have got bicycles.
Has he/she got a brother?	Yes, he/she has.	No, he/she hasn't. He/She has got a sister.

WORDS AND PHRASES

This wordlist contains all the vocabulary items illustrated in the Words you need pages of each unit.

Unit Alphabet Fun

apple
bicycle
computer
doll
egg
fork
glove
hat
ice cream
jigsaw
kite
lamp
mirror
newspaper
orange
pencil
queen
robot
spoon
table
umbrella
violin
window
xylophone
yo-yo
zebra

Unit A

black
blue
board
book
brown
ceiling
chair
class
classroom
crayon
desk
door
eye
floor
green
hair
orange
pen
pencil
pencil case
pet
pink
playground
purple
red
rubber
ruler
school bag
scissors
table
teacher
wall
white
window
yellow

Unit B

astronaut
clown
computer game
cowboy
dancer
eight
eleven
equals
firefighter
five
football player
four
minus
nine
one
plus
rock star
seven
six
ten
three
times
twelve
two
zero

Unit C

Africa
Antarctica
antelope
Asia
Australia
big
butterfly
crocodile
elephant
Europe
fast
fox
giraffe
iguana
jaguar
kangaroo
lion
long
mouse
North America
ostrich
penguin
rhinoceros
seal
short
slow
small
snake
South America
strong
tall
tiger
tortoise
weak
wolf

Unit D

blouse
boots
coat
dress
gloves
hat
jacket
jeans
necklace
sandals
scarf
shirt
shoes
shorts
skirt
socks
sunglasses
sweater
swimsuit
T-shirt
watch

Unit E

avenue
bakery
bank
bus stop
central square
chemist
cinema
department store
East
fire station
hospital
hotel
North
park
petrol station

How to get Published in South Africa

How to get Published in South Africa

A Guide for Authors

Second Edition

BASIL VAN ROOYEN

SOUTHERN
BOOK PUBLISHERS

ISBN 1 86812 661 7

First edition, first impression 1994
Second edition, first impression 1996

Published by
Southern Book Publishers (Pty) Ltd
PO Box 3103, Halfway House, 1685

Cover design by Tracey Mackenzie
Set in 10 on 12 point Stone Serif
Typesetting and reproduction by PG&A, Ottery, Cape
Printed and bound by Colorgraphic, Durban

To Mariétta, for her understanding and support

Table of Contents

Preface ix

Contributors xi

Part 1: The book publishing industry in South Africa

1. A short overview of the book trade 3
2. General non-fiction 10
3. Literary publishing *Peter Anderson* 19
4. Children's book publishing in South Africa *Alida Potgieter* 29
5. The Afrikaans market *Kerneels Breytenbach* 38
6. Publishing in African languages *Dumisani Krushchev Ntshangase* 47
7. Educational publishing *Kate McCallum* 55
8. Tertiary-level publishing 64
9. Book club publishing *Mike Jacklin* 77
10. Publishing overseas 80
11. Self-publishing *Monica Cromhout* 84

Part 2: How to find the right publisher

12. How to choose and approach a publisher 95
13. How a publisher decides what to publish 99
14. The people you deal with 105

Part 3: How publishing works

15. The publishing contract and royalties 113
16. The publishing process 126
17. How a book is costed 138
18. Paperback versus hardback 143

Part 4: How to prepare a manuscript

19. How to prepare text 149

20. How to prepare illustrations 155
21. How to structure a book 159
22. Good writing 168
23. House style 173
24. How to read proofs 182
25. How to prepare an index 187

Part 5: A directory of South African publishers 191

Miscellaneous information 233

Further reading 238

Index 245

Preface

I was pleasantly surprised by the fact that the first edition of this book sold out within about 18 months. I was less pleased when faced with the necessity to update it, but was inspired to do so by the excellent feedback I received from so many people after publication of the first edition.

The two parts of the book that had to be extensively revised were *Part 1: The book publishing industry in South Africa,* and *Part 5: A directory of South African publishers.*

It was clear to me from comments in both the media and in letters addressed to me by readers that greater detail was needed in some areas of publishing. I accordingly approached some more experts in the publishing field for contributions.

The biggest single complaint about the first edition was that the first part seemed to concentrate so heavily on non-fiction and educational books, and said very little about areas such as literature and children's books. The reason for the emphasis was that the former are the books that are most commonly published in South Africa. However, that was clearly not good enough for users, many of whom are interested in writing creative work.

Peter Anderson of David Philip Publishers and Alida Potgieter of Human & Rousseau stepped into the gap to give expert views on how to get published in the fields of literature and children's books respectively.

Another point on which the first edition was criticised was that it devoted a separate chapter to Afrikaans publishing but ignored publishing in African languages. I had to admit that the emphasis on languages other than English needed to be balanced, and was fortunate enough to get Dumisani Ntshangase to do a chapter on African language publishing.

Finally, I came in for some criticism for being so negative about self-publishing by authors. I reconsidered the matter and decided that I have no reason to change my mind on the subject: I firmly believe that self-publishing is the quickest way I know of losing money. However, I also have to acknowledge a certain amount of bias in the matter by virtue of the fact that I am a publisher myself. So, while I still hold that it is better to get published through a publisher than to attempt to publish yourself, I asked Monica Cromhout to write on this subject. She has more experience in this area than anyone else I know of, and if you have to go that way, it is better to follow her advice than to try and re-invent the wheel all on your own.

The Directory section had to be extensively updated, as is to be expected, and a number of publishers have been added. It is still anything but exhaustive, but covers the most likely publishers an author is likely to want to approach.

For the rest I corrected an embarrassingly large number of errors, made the odd improvement, and brought the text up to date to reflect the ever-changing but ever-fascinating world of publishing in South Africa.

Readers can write to me to point out shortcomings in the text at the following address:

Southern Book Publishers
P.O. Box 3103
HALFWAY HOUSE 1685

THE AUTHOR

Contributors

The following people contributed chapters to this book:

Peter Anderson lives in Cape town, where he works as an editor for David Philip Publishers. He was educated at UCT and the University of Oxford, serves as the poetry editor of an established South African literary journal, and is himself a poet.

Alida Potgieter grew up in the Eastern Cape, has a B.A. in languages and a Higher Diploma in Librarianship from the University of Stellenbosch, and a B.A. Hons. in English from Unisa. She has worked as librarian in Natal, Grahamstown and Cape Town. From 1975 to 1982 she was the book selector at the Cape Provincial Library Service. She joined Human & Rousseau in 1982 and was involved in children's book publishing for 14 years. She recently moved to the adult fiction section at the same publishing house.

Kerneels Breytenbach was born in Johannesburg and matriculated in Alberton in 1975. He started working in the arts section of *Beeld* and later *Die Burger,* eventually becoming arts editor of *Die Burger* from 1982 to 1989. In 1989 he joined Human & Rousseau, where he was appointed general manager in 1995. In 1992 he won the CNA prize for the best debut with the short story collection *Morsdood van die Honger,* and in 1993 he published his first novel, *Glimlag.*

Dumisani Krushchev Ntshangase is a publisher of African languages at Juta and Co. based in Johannesburg. He was a lecturer in African languages at the University of the Witwatersrand and the Johannesburg College of Education. He had also been a commissioning editor at Macmillan Boleswa. His current fields of interest are the sociolinguistics of South Africa, African literature, African languages publishing, broadcasting policies and language management, planning and policy. He is currently working on the biography of B.W. Vilakazi, a Zulu novelist and poet, for his Ph.D.

Kate McCallum is the Managing Director of Oxford University Press Southern Africa, and has worked in South African publishing since 1980. She is presently the chairperson of the Education Publishers' Group within the Publishers' Association of South Africa, as well as chairperson of its Research and Statistics Committee. Her writing includes a book, *Words for Africa,* the South African editorship of *The Just Seventeen Advice book,* and papers and chapters in both published and unpublished collections.

Mike Jacklin runs a joint venture with Time Warner in South Africa, which includes Time Life Books, Time and Fortune magazines, The Disney Book Clubs and the old Daan Retief Book Clubs, now called Read and Learn Programmes where local publishing opportunities occur in English, Afrikaans, Zulu, Xhosa and Tswana.

Monica Cromhout is editor of *Writers' World* Magazine and publisher of Options Publishing. She is co-chairperson of the Book Development Council (Western Cape Committee), Executive Committee member, Book Development Council of South Africa and co-chairperson of the Home Based Business Association. Her work involves promoting the interests of writers in South Africa, and finding and developing as many opportunities as possible for their success. One of these opportunities is self-publishing.

Part 1

The book publishing industry in South Africa

1

A short overview of the South African book trade

Nothing much happened in publishing terms in South Africa until the early part of the twentieth century. Prior to that, we imported all our books from the "mother countries", that is the United Kingdom and The Netherlands. The pioneers of publishing in this country were exceptional individuals, immigrants from the "mother countries" who started small family businesses. Some of the businesses grew and prospered and their names are still with us. Van Schaik, Juta, Shuter and Shooter, Maskew Miller are still household names, even though the founding families may no longer be involved in the companies.

Major international publishing houses also established themselves over the years in this country. In a number of cases the South African subsidiaries became important publishing houses in their own right. Some of them merged with local publishing houses to become a kind of hybrid, half locally owned and half internationally owned. And indeed, the importation of books continues to make up a large part of the activities of these companies. The British educational publishers, in particular, have made a real impression in this country: names such as Longman, Heinemann, Macmillan and Butterworth spring to mind.

As the international publishers were developing, the major Afrikaans houses also came into existence, mostly as a side-line of the emerging media conglomerates which included newspaper and magazine publishing. Nasionale Pers and Perskor are examples of this type of publishing house. Other companies have had their origin in the anti-apartheid struggle, building up a reputation as "liberation publishers". The names of Ravan, David Philip Publishers and the SACHED Trust can be mentioned in this context.

There are also numerous institutional publishers in South Africa. Many government departments, municipalities, religious organisations, professional associations, private companies and educational institutions publish their own books. However, this book deals principally with organisations whose main business it is to publish and market books.

Finally, an important segment of the publishing industry is run by individuals or very small enterprises. Often the publisher is also the author. Although this segment of publishing is an important source of books published in this country, it again falls outside the scope of this discussion.

It is estimated that the annual turnover of the South African publishing industry is in the region of R2 billion.

Among the more useful statistics I was able to obtain, were those from the CNA, which are probably reasonably representative of the total general trade market in the country.

The percentage of local to overseas books sold by the CNA over the past few years has varied as follows:

Year ending	Local	Overseas
March 1989	77%	23%
March 1990	82%	18%
March 1991	77%	23%
March 1992	75%	25%
March 1993	78%	22%
March 1994	77%	23%
March 1995	79%	21%

The high proportion of local books in the mix will come as a surprise to most readers—clearly far more copies of the average local title is sold than of the average overseas one.

Within the area of local books, the CNA estimates that the split between fiction and non-fiction is:

6% fiction
94% non-fiction.

The profile of books sold by other booksellers might be significantly different, but the CNA on its own probably represents a good 30–40% of total general book sales in South Africa.

It is important to understand that the books which make up this turnover are not similar products. Most publishers, except the very biggest, all specialise to a greater or lesser extent. The complexities of publishing in South Africa are easier to grasp if you bear in mind the following broad segmentation:

Educational publishers

School publishing makes up the bulk of publishing activity taking place in South Africa. The reason for this can be found in a simple examination of our demographics. With such a high percentage of the population at school, and the general level of education in this country up to now having been so low, it is inevitable that school publishing will lead the field.

Some of the main school publishers in the country are as follows (not necessarily in sequence of size): Educum, Nasou, Via Africa, Kagiso, Juta, Maskew Miller Longman, Shuter & Shooter, Heinemann, Hodder and Stoughton Educational, J.L. van Schaik, Oxford University Press.

Tertiary publishers

This category includes those organisations publishing for the tertiary market: universities, technikons, teachers' training colleges, private colleges, etc. It is probably the smallest segment of the publishing industry in South Africa, since most books falling in this category are imported from the United States and Britain. Some of the major publishers in this area are Butterworth, Juta, J.L. van Schaik, Kagiso, Heinemann, Oxford University Press, International Thomson Publishing.

General book publishers

General book publishing or "trade" publishing is aimed at entertaining or instructing the person in the street. It includes both fiction and non-fiction. Important publishers of non-fiction are Struik, Tafelberg, Human & Rousseau, Southern Book Publishers, Jonathan Ball Publishers, Vlaeberg, David Philip, Penguin, Perskor. When it comes to fiction, the list is much shorter. Afrikaans fiction publishing is well served by major houses such as Tafelberg and Human & Rousseau as well as "book club" publishers such as J.P. van der Walt, but most publishing of popular fiction by South African authors in English actually takes place in Britain.

General publishing also includes the publication of poetry, short stories, plays—art forms which may be commercially unimportant but which are of great importance in cultural terms.

These different areas of publishing are discussed in greater detail in the rest of Part 1. For a more complete breakdown of who publishes what, see the directory in Part 5 of this book.

Booksellers

A survey of the publishing scene in South Africa would not be complete without a look at the distribution channels available. The retail distribution of general books is dominated to a startling degree by the CNA-Gallo group, which operates not only the hundreds of CNA outlets but also the more up-market Exclusive outlets. Some strong independent booksellers still remain, such as Adams in Durban, but they are few and far between. Another major distributor of general books is Leserskring/Leisure Books, part of the Nasionale Pers Group.

A welcome development was the creation of a new chain of upmarket bookshops to compete with the Exclusive Group. The new chain, Facts and Fiction, was in fact formed by breakaway managers of the Exclusive Group, with financial backing from construction company Stocks and Stocks. In 1995 they set up branches at Menlyn in Pretoria and in Woodmead, Sandton City, Rosebank and Balfour Park in Johannesburg. New outlets were being planned for other major centres in South Africa.

Another interesting development over the last few years has been the development of the PNA chain of bookshops in the Gauteng area. Based on a concept similar to CNA, it is run as a franchise operation. By the end of 1995 it already had 18 branches. In 1996 it took over the Paperbacks chain of bookshops in Cape Town. With major shareholding in PNA held by the powerful Pick 'n Pay Group, it looks as if the CNA might finally have to face competition on a country-wide scale.

Tertiary books are mostly distributed by campus bookshops. These are dominated by major chains, such as Van Schaik and Juta. Once again there are a few strong independents such as Armstrongs in Johannesburg.

In 1995 MAST sold its Johannesburg and Cape Town based shops to Van Schaik Boekhandel, which now dominates academic book sales in South Africa in much the same way that the CNA-Gallo Group dominates general trade sales.

In the school publishing area the dividing line between publishers and booksellers is often blurred. Most of the major school publishers, such as Nasou and Juta, also operate bookshops. Many school bookshops tend to be depots rather than bookshops and most of the selling is done by representatives calling on schools. Few of the sales actually take place over the counter. In some cases education departments purchase direct from the publisher.

In summary, it can be said that South Africa has a strong and vibrant infrastructure when it comes to the publishing and distribution of books when compared to the rest of Africa. Compared to Europe and North America, however, the number of bookshops and publishers is tiny. This is so because the industry (with the exception of school books) mainly serves the small minority of affluent and educated people in major metropolitan areas. There can be no doubt that the great challenge facing the South African publishing industry is for it to expand its activities to the majority of South Africans who at the moment are not part of the book-buying public.

Major forces in the book trade

Much has been said about monopolistic tendencies in the South African book trade. It is true that the trade is dominated by two major groups, CNA-Gallo and Nasionale Pers. CNA-Gallo, as previously discussed, dominates the general retail trade through its control of the CNA and Exclusive Books. In addition, it has a 50 per cent stake in Struik Publishers and a major stake in educational publisher Heinemann. The other book trade giant, Nasionale Pers, owns no less than eight publishing houses: Nasou, Via Afrika, Human & Rousseau, Tafelberg, Jonathan Ball-HarperCollins, Kwela, Lexis and J.L. van Schaik. In addition they own the biggest academic book retail chain, Van Schaik, and the country's largest book club, Leserskring/Leisure Books.

These combined holdings give both groups immense clout in the book trade. To describe them as monopolies is, however, an exaggeration. Clearly there are many other important players in the field, not to mention hundreds of smaller ones. The dominance of these two groups may just be due to economy of scale and efficiency. There is certainly no queue of companies forming up to enter the book trade, which is notorious for being a high-risk industry with low returns.

South African National Bibliography

Few statistics exist regarding the South African book trade. A major source is the *South African National Bibliography*, published annually by the State Library and readily available in the reference section of most libraries. The *Bibliography* covers material published within the current and preceding two years which is sent to the State Library by publishers under the terms of the Legal Deposit of Publications Act, 1982. It includes monographs, pamphlets, government publications, microfilms, maps, technical reports, SABS specifications, periodicals, and so on, in addition to regular books.

The *Bibliography* is arranged in classified sequence of main entries (mostly following the Dewey System), and an alphabetical index which provides access to these full entries via title, names of authors, translators, editors, compilers and illustrators. It also provides a complete list of publishers—about 1 200 active ones—with address, phone and fax numbers. However, most are not publishers of the type discussed in this book.

Also published by the State Library, is the *Directory of South African Publishers*, which contains the complete list from the *Bibliography* as a booklet on its own.

The latest edition of the *Bibliography* provides some statistics of value, but the problem with the publication is that it is primarily organised as a tool for librarians. Its very inclusiveness limits its use as a source of book trade statistics. From the point of view of the publisher or the would-be author, it is of limited use, except for looking up details of specific topics.

Publishers' Association of South Africa

Most publishers in South Africa belong to the Publishers' Association of South Africa (PASA). An analysis of the membership of this association provides some useful insights into the composition of the South African publishing industry.

At the time of writing PASA had 107 full members. Not all publishers were members, but all major publishers were. A breakdown by size reveals the following spread:

Turnover band	Number of members in this band
R0–R99 999	36
R100 000–R499 999	18
R500 000–R999 999	10
R1 000 000–R2 999 999	6
R3 000 000–R4 999 999	7
R5 000 000–R7 499 999	6
R7 500 000–R9 999 999	4
R10 000 000–R19 999 999	6
R20 000 000–R34 999 999	8
R35 000 000–R49 999 999	2
R50 000 000 plus	4

It needs to be stressed that the membership included importers/distributors and not only publishers as such.

One of the frustrating problems for any one trying to analyse book trade statistics in South Africa, is that statistics are simply not available in any sensible form. PASA has made several efforts to conduct surveys of the South African book trade, but so far with little success. Survey results were so incomplete that no full picture could emerge. The government does not keep track of book trade statistics either. It is therefore impossible for any publisher to know what share of the market it controls.

In August 1996 massive changes were underway in the ownership of educational book publishers. Perskor and Kagiso had announced a merger, which could be viewed within the context of Black empowerment in the publishing industry, and Nasionale Pers was merging their two educational publishing houses, Nasou and Via Afrika, and had announced their intention of offering 50% of the shareholding to a Black consortium.

2

General non-fiction

Most of the general books (also known as "trade" books) published in South Africa could be classified as non-fiction. Up to about 30 years ago most books on South Africa were published in London; a fair number, especially those on politics, still are. South Africa was regarded as a passive consumer of books from elsewhere, despite the efforts of valiant pioneers such as Van Schaik. Immigrants have been responsible for much of the improvement in the quality of South African books over the last few decades. One such person was A.A. Balkema, who immigrated to South Africa from Amsterdam shortly after the Second World War, and set new standards of quality in the publication of Africana.

Two companies did a great deal of pioneering work in establishing a general book publishing industry in this country. They are Nasionale Pers and Struik, both now dominant in this market. Two publishing houses within the Nasionale Pers group, Human & Rousseau and Tafelberg, have been instrumental not only in putting Afrikaans general book publishing on the map, but in improving design standards by importing top designers such as Jurgen Fromm from Germany.

Struik, however, is beyond doubt the company that did more than any other to put South African general books on the map. They brought true professionalism to the production of large-format, full-colour, coffee-table books, of a type previously unknown in this country. Struik as we know it today was founded by the Struik family, who immigrated to South Africa from Indonesia. Father Struik was an Africana bookseller and publisher; after his death his three sons took over. Only one son, Gerry Struik, is still associated with the Struik company although he emigrated to Australia in 1996.

Southern Book Publishers started life as the South African offshoot of Macmillan UK, which had been bought out by management. It publishes a wide range of non-fiction books, especially natural history.

Non-fiction publishing in South Africa has grown to the point where it now accounts for the bulk of book sales of the CNA group.

There is no doubt that the quality of a great deal of the general publishing in South Africa is as good as anything elsewhere in the world, although exports are still limited. In comparable world terms, South Africa is about at the stage reached by Australia 10 years ago, but in advance of Canada and New Zealand.

Subjects for non-fiction publishing

There are as many subjects to write non-fiction books on as there are ideas in the world. Many non-fiction books are successes exactly because they address new issues and topics that no one had thought of before. However, there are certain main categories that form the staple stock of most bookshops.

Functional books. Most popular of all non-fiction books are probably the broad category of "functional" books; these include titles on gardening, cookery, do-it-yourself, hobbies and crafts, and so on. These are universal categories, not peculiar to South Africa. Non-fiction publishing in this country has developed to the point where many such categories are beginning to be over-published for the size of the market. Certainly, a cookery or gardening book needs a local author and local content to be really successful.

Wildlife and travel books. South Africa is a country where natural history as a publishing category is of exceptional importance. This importance can be explained by our situation in Africa and by the unique richness and variety of our wildlife. In addition, many tourists visiting this country come for the wildlife in the first place, and they constitute an important part of the buying market. Both field guides and coffee-table books are plentiful and of world quality. The travel category is, in the case of South Africa, closely related to wildlife because of the symbiotic relationship between the two. Certainly, the number of travel guides available at the moment from both local and overseas sources on the sub-continent is mind-boggling.

Books about politics. The other topic, next to wildlife, that has been uniquely important in this country over the years is politics. Apartheid made us the pariah of the world, but it was good for publishing. Books featuring South African political personalities, future scenarios, and so on used to be a mainstay of the local publishing scene and also did well overseas. When it became clear from 1990 onwards that the demise of apartheid was imminent, interest in the topic waned, even as the number of words devoted to it on television, radio and newspaper articles increased. Perhaps people just got fed up with hearing too much about politics. Whatever the reason, since the 1994 elections there has been a collapse of publishing for this category.

A notable exception to this trend has been *A Long Walk to Freedom* by Nelson Mandela, distributed in South Africa by McDonald Purnell, which turned out to be a runaway bestseller. By the end of 1995 this title (published in hardback in December 1994) had already sold 160 000 copies in hardback and 130 000 copies in paperback.

Choosing what to write about

Most authors of non-fiction books do not sit around trying to think up topics to write books on. They tend to be experts in some field or another—indigenous gardening, rock fishing, Malay cooking, crochet work, or whatever—and they want to share this knowledge with the world, either for gain or for pleasure. There are a few professional non-fiction authors who can write on any given topic, provided they have time to do the research, but they are few and far between.

For the most part then, the question of choosing a topic is not normally much of an issue; the issue is what to write a specific book about. If you are a gardening expert and want to write a book on South African gardening in general, you would have to think very hard about what you do and how you do it. In the first place, there are already half a dozen similar local books available in addition to dozens of imported ones. Secondly, you need to be a high-profile gardening writer, already perhaps with a magazine column, otherwise no publisher is going to be interested. Thirdly, you would have to find a publisher with both the capacity to handle a book like this and the cash flow to finance it. Since the major publishers in this field already have existing books or are committed to publishing new ones, you are going to find it a hard job.

If you still want to write a gardening book, you might therefore have to decide to produce a book on one particular aspect; perhaps bonsai, if that is a field of speciality for you. Before you set out to find a publisher, you will need to research what is available in the market-place. In fact there are numerous bonsai books on the market, several of which are South African. You will need to think up a new angle on the subject, or be able to persuade a publisher that you have better photographs, more successful growing methods, or whatever may be the case, to give your book an advantage above the others on the market. Only if you have either a unique topic, or a unique angle to a topic that is saleable in the market-place, should you approach a publisher. After all, quite apart from convincing the publisher, you need to be sure yourself that it is worth spending months of your time and a great deal of effort on developing the idea.

Having said that, general non-fiction writing is more accessible to the person in the street than other types of writing which require high literary skills. Generally speaking, as long as you know your topic well and are reasonably competent in your writing, the publisher's copy-editor will be able to lick your book into shape.

Books needed for this market

In general book publishing there are probably far more authors looking for publishers than there are publishers interested in and capable of producing and marketing books. It is therefore a very competitive market-place for the author, as opposed to other segments of the book market where the main competition is among the publishers for a limited number of authors.

This does not mean that publishers do not place a high premium on leading authors—clearly they do. However, once you are away from the really well-known authors whose books fill up 80 per cent of shelf space in bookshops, new authors and less well-established ones may find it hard to get published.

That is the negative side. To be positive, there is absolutely no limit to the number of topics that one can write books on. As discussed above, it is really a question of finding the right topic and the right angle. If you get both right, you should be able to find a publisher.

Other role players

In general publishing, illustrators and photographers can be as important as authors. We only have to think of the impact made by photographers such as Anthony Bannister and Herman Potgieter, and illustrators such as Barbara Jeppe and Ken Newman, to realise how true this is. Many non-fiction books have a high illustration factor, and many sell on the basis of their beautiful pictures and designs.

The role of commissioning

Because of the very nature of non-fiction publishing, commissioning by the publisher plays an important role. A publisher can sit down and plan a programme, irrespective of whether he or she knows any authors to write the specific books desired. Once the programme is complete, the publisher can send out editors to commission specific people to write specific books or parts of books.

The Reader's Digest specialises in this kind of commissioning. Everyone is familiar with The Reader's Digest's very distinctive packaged format. They publish large-format books with a great number of colour pictures, authoritative but simply written and aimed at a mass market. The driving force in putting together these books is clearly The Reader's Digest itself and not any specific author. In fact, the authors of such books tend to be very much in the background. In a real sense, the author is The Reader's Digest and not any particular individual.

The opposite approach to that of The Reader's Digest can be seen when a publisher does little to the author's manuscript, except to cast it into the form of a book and put it onto the market. This does happen, although it is not very common, for publishers who publish in this way are not likely to stay in business long. For non-fiction publishing to work well, there needs to be a close partnership between the publisher, the author and the illustrator or photographer. The designer, who may or may not be part of the publisher's staff, is another person who plays a major role. If the chemistry between these people is good, the likely result will be a good book. If the chemistry is not good, something is bound to go wrong.

Unfortunately in general publishing many things can and do go wrong. The book may have a good topic and be well written, but still not do well in the market for any number of reasons: the wrong title, the wrong cover, the wrong price, too many words or too few words, a paperback cover used instead of a hard cover plus a dust-jacket, and so on. The number of minor mistakes that can be made with such a book is endless. Unfortunately, even though they may be minor, they can kill off a book in the market.

The non-fiction general market is sensitive to the consumer's perceptions. It is also exposed to the perceptions of booksellers, who act as go-betweens for the publisher and the final customer. Booksellers, like anybody else, have set ideas on what they like in books and what they think is saleable. Sometimes they are reluctant to stock a book on a new theme because they have no precedent for it and no history of such a book doing well. If the bookseller concerned is an important one such as the CNA, then the prophecy of doom for a book of this kind becomes self-fulfilling: if it is not stocked in the bookshops, it naturally does not sell, which may be taken to prove that such a book will not sell. Let me hasten to add that I have not experienced this to be the case with the CNA—this is merely an example.

Now and then, fortunately not too often, booksellers act as an unofficial censorship board. As a group of people they may feel that a certain book is too right-wing, too erotic, or whatever, and thus effectively rob the consumer of the opportunity of choosing for him- or herself.

What to expect from a general publisher

If you follow the guidelines for approaching a publisher laid down in Chapter 12, you will not go too far wrong. Just remember that it is more of a buyer's than a seller's market. You as author are going to be keener to get hold of a publisher than a publisher is to get hold of you. This unfortunate fact means that you will have to put more effort into your presentation and be more patient with the publisher than you would have to be if you were, for example, an author of tertiary textbooks.

General non-fiction books are not usually written by multi-author panels, so the publishing contracts tend to be fairly simple ones from that point of view. What often complicates matters, however, is that the photographic or illustration dimension of the book may be very important. It is common for the author and illustrator, or the author and photographer, to share royalties; alternatively, the photographer or illustrator may be paid a one-off fee. In many cases the publisher will regard the illustrations and photographs as part of the manuscript to be delivered by the author; in other words, the responsibility for obtaining photographs or illustrations rests in the first place with the author.

General book publishers are more inclined to pay advances on royalties than other types of publishers. In the United Kingdom and the United States leading authors sometimes earn millions in advances. Nothing so extravagant is paid locally. Advances here might be paid to help the author defray travel, development or photographic costs.

Printing overseas

A fair proportion of the general books printed in full colour for the South African market are printed overseas, especially in Singapore and Hong Kong. In this South Africa is not unique: publishers the world over tend to print a large part of their high-quality full-colour illustrated books in the Far East. (Singapore especially has focused in on this segment of the printing market.) Their price levels and quality standards are such that few printers elsewhere in the world can compete with them, even when shipping charges are added to the printing costs.

The future

Many debates have been held around the question of the channels of distribution for books in this country. It is obvious to even the most casual observer that general bookshops are situated in the most affluent areas—Sandton, Rondebosch, and so on—and that most book-buyers are affluent English-speaking whites. The only book chain with branches in virtually every small town is the CNA, and most of their smaller branches sell little in the way of books except a few paperback best-sellers, Bibles and dictionaries. In a newly democratic South Africa, such a state of affairs is not acceptable. The question is, how do we change it? And if we do manage to change it, will other South Africans start buying books?

In this regard, the history of Leserskring/Leisure Books may be instructive. This book club was formed just over 12 years ago as part of the Nasionale Pers group's effort to reach a wider audience—particularly an Afrikaans-speaking one on the platteland—than could be reached by conventional bookshops. With the help of the giant German publisher Bertelsman, they created a book club that sells a wide range of books (which are also available in bookshops) via a quarterly catalogue that goes out to some 350 000 members. The project proved to be a success, and certainly had a major impact on the way books were sold in this country. It did not seem to take any sales away from booksellers, but rather to reach an audience interested in the more popular varieties of books but unlikely ever to make the long trek to a bookshop in another suburb or town.

What is certain is that the present bookselling structure in South Africa simply cannot deliver books to the black masses. The bookshops are not located in the right places and they do not carry the right stock at the right prices. A different way of retailing books will have to be found. It is hard to know what this will be and which kind of book is likely to sell, but the general book market in South Africa does not have a great future unless those people who do not form a traditional part of the book-buying population can be persuaded to start buying books.

Many people will put the blame for the state of affairs squarely on the shoulders of the CNA retail chain, accusing them of monopolistic practices and of extreme Eurocentricity. I believe these charges are unfair. It is after all not the fault of the CNA if there is such a great lack of small, vigorous and independent booksellers in various parts of the country. There is nothing to stop anybody from opening a bookshop. The fact is that very few do get opened, and many well-established ones have disappeared over the last two decades, simply because it is hard to make money out of selling books.

One reason why the CNA is successful is that the branches do not attempt to sell books only; they also sell birthday cards, stationary, CDs and cassettes, toys and a host of other merchandise, all of which helps to bring customers into their shops. The policy of keeping a limited number of well-proven lines works well for them. Apart from their larger shops in the major centres, CNA branches do not pretend to be well-stocked bookshops. It is therefore unfair to judge them by such standards.

3

Literary publishing

Peter Anderson

South African literature—whatever that is—is not the best guide to literary publishing in South Africa (though it is a useful indication of what might be considered literary). A good deal of South African literature is written by South Africans living overseas and published either there or locally, and our top authors, though they may live here, are soon signed up by foreign houses that are better placed to secure them the exposure, reputation and income they deserve. On the other hand, a good many (highly successful) novels have come out of South Africa that one would not, strictly speaking, call literature. To confuse matters further, there exist works of undoubted literary worth in fields not ordinarily considered literary—the historical writing of Jeff Peires or Charles van Onselen, for example. And what of Eugène Marais's studies of nature, or Louis Leipoldt's notes on cookery? And Xhosa literature has among *its* origins the work of several nineteenth century journalists.

Literature, then, is an imprecise business. This imprecision causes publishers no small amount of anxiety. Unlike educational publishing, where the express need for a geography textbook may be identified and met (with a syllabus to guide the way), literary publishing involves the most subjective of decisions about merit, a good deal of wishful thinking about the market reception of a work, and a blind faith in the project of literature itself, which has been, and continues to be, very much a minority interest.

Fortunately, the advantages of a literate society are manifold, and where people are taught to read the desire for books is sown. With that desire, to some extent, and after a variety of fashions, some literary aesthetic arises among an addict few. This is the market of the literary publisher.

There is one other strange truth about literature worth noting in this introduction, and it is this—there is, among those who delight in reading literature, a very high incidence of the desire to write it also. Somehow, the literary public has been bamboozled by old-fashioned notions of Genius, or of the edifying mission of literature, or of the neurotic origin of writing, into believing that everyone goes around "with a novel inside them". Sadly, this is not true. There should be no shame in not writing great literature. Many successful authors will promise you that they wish every day that they had not chosen writing—or that it had not chosen them—and that they long for the contemplative calm of fixing bicycles. They are quite right, but probably lying nonetheless. "After all"—you will say—"*they* have had a book published . . ."

There are four broad areas of literary writing, each with its own characteristic *genres*, forms and publishing considerations. Some publishers specialise in one or other of these classes, some publish them all, and others, of course, do not even consider literature. The four classes dealt with below are poetry, fiction, drama and *belles-lettres*.

Poetry

Some people confuse the brevity of much poetry (brief, that is, by comparison with most prose) with a kind of creative seizure, a dashing-off or a razzling-up. It is as if prose required lengthy cooking (indeed it does), whereas poetry provided literature of a pot-noodle kind—just add hot water. In reality, successful poetry is always the product of long labour and much drudgery. All the going-on about inspiration, honey-dew, the milk of paradise, the muse, angst, inky fingers, garrets and whatnot is a terrible illusion conjured up to frighten the public away from asking awkward questions about what you actually do that's useful and takes more than a moonstruck evening's effort.

Be warned: poetry is not chopped-up prose. Sadly, there is among aspirant poets very little knowledge of conventional prosody or the rudiments of form. And whilst these are by no means recommended in all cases, the absence of any formal know-how has the general effect of throwing poetry back upon the content of the poem, itself often egotistical, plaintive, agonised and agonisingly boring.

Nor is publishing your poetry going to be very easy. There exist only a handful of South African publishers interested in poetry, and the number of titles they publish each year is very small. Human and Rousseau, for example, published just six volumes of Afrikaans poetry in 1995. The independent Snailpress now carries the main load of English poetry publishing, and they produced just nine volumes in 1995, and six in 1994—and they feel that half a dozen per annum is about what they and their share of the market can cope with. David Philip Publishers published the handsome Mantis series in the 1970s, but have now reduced their output considerably. Fortunately, small presses have come and gone and kept the candle burning.

However, you should not be thinking of sending your poems to a publisher unless you have enjoyed reasonable exposure in one of the so-called "little magazines".

Without some track record in these journals, it is extremely unlikely that any publisher will pay much attention to your poems, and for several good reasons. The first of these is that the market for poetry is very small indeed, and publishers reason that the appearance of your work in the little magazines is something of a promotional exercise; your presence in the magazines has established your name among the discerning few who are likely to be the core market for a proposed book, and the publisher feels that the product (your poetry) is at least a known quantity where it counts.

In addition to this all-important commercial consideration, the publisher is likely to look to the little magazines for a general guarantee of the literary worth of your poetry. After all, it is the editors of these journals who view the country's poetry on a daily basis, and who monthly separate the good from the bad (though not infallibly). The little magazines are the nursery of talent and the schoolroom of hard poetic labour.

The advantages of these magazines are many, but they should not be taken for granted. Just as you should not approach a publisher for a critical appraisal of your poems (it is simply not their business to dish out free advice), so you should leave the (unpaid and hardworking) magazine editors to respond as they see fit. Persevere, but do not pester. If your poems are any good, then a quiet correspondence will one day open up.

Always send a stamped, self-addressed envelope with your poems, even if you don't need them back. Make sure that the postage is adequate. Be patient. Read a lot, and if you really care about literature in South Africa, then subscribe to the little magazines and buy those books which do appear under local imprints (how else will you discover what publishers are likely to approve of?). Here are some addresses of magazines or more learned journals that publish poetry:

ATIO: P.O. Box 32112, Braamfontein 2017
Barefoot Press: P.O. Box 1914, Midrand 1685
Blek-Sem: P.O. Box 621, Honeydew 2040
Carapace: P.O. Box 375, Cape Town 8000
Dye Hard Press: P.O. Box 32112, Braamfontein 2017
English Academy Review: P.O. Box 124, Wits 2050
Imprint: P.O. Box 5091, Rivonia 2128
New Coin: c/o ISEA, P.O. Box 94, Grahamstown 6140
New Contrast: P.O. Box 3841, Cape Town 8000
Scrutiny 2: Department of English, UNISA, P.O. Box 392, Pretoria 0001
Something Quarterly: P.O. Box 66384, Broadway 2020
Sunbelly Press: P.O. Box 2082, Bedfordview 2008

Fiction

Fiction undoubtedly comprises the largest category of literary endeavour. More people read it than poetry or drama, a broader spectrum of society writes it, and a good deal more of it is published than the more classical literary forms.

We are *not* talking here about popular fiction (the bodice-rippers, romances, westerns, whodunits and so on, which are the way to go if it's hard cash you're after). This type of fiction is published only very rarely by the English-language publishers in this country (see Chapter 10, *Publishing Overseas*), though the Afrikaans- and African-language houses do have popular lists. We are talking about works of fiction with sufficient gravity to rescue them from the airport bookstalls.

Short Stories and novellas. Publishers don't see collections of short stories nearly as often as they see novels, but generally the standard of the former is better than that of the latter. The short story certainly provides some relief in terms of scale, and it may be that this encourages the sort of concentration and polish which is so often lacking in the novels which land on publishers' desks.

The novella, especially in publishing terms, is something of a bastard form, falling as it does between the novel and the short story. It is increasingly the norm to find a novella published in association with a few short stories, for although the book itself may be substantial, short stories or a novella appear not to offer the consumer quite the sustained involvement that a novel does. This will caution a publisher's enthusiasm for your work, and it is probably true to say that short stories have a better chance of achieving publication if their author is already known as a novelist.

What is true for the poet in South Africa is fairly true for the short story writer also, so read the section on publishing poetry (above). Short stories lend themselves very well to magazine publication, and their success in magazines will enhance the prospects of a collection being accepted. Do not limit yourself to the sorts of literary journals listed above, for some of the large circulation magazines publish short fiction regularly—but do not assume that they all accept unsolicited submissions; phone first, or you will waste everybody's time and your own postage. You will, of course, have sent a stamped, self-addressed envelope with your story. Be on the lookout for competitions, which pop up occasionally under the auspices of arts festivals, literary journals, newspapers and so on.

Novels. A good number of people who buy this book will have done so either because they have a novel in mind or are ready for submission.

Oh for the key to the great South African novel!

Until very recently, South African novels—and there have been some fine ones—have been dominated, directly or indirectly, by the extremity of our social and individual experience. Our authors' imaginations, and their complex engagements with literary "truth", have drawn landscapes full of strangeness and conflict, and characters divided within and against themselves. This is not to say that our novels have all been politically engaged—far from it—but that they have been steeped in our politics, and not surprisingly.

Things have changed, or are changing, and our novels will change too. Yet it doesn't follow that novels about reconciliation are the coming thing: in truth, there is no formula for a successful novel's content.

One might as well know, though, that publishers do not share in the idea that art is largely about suffering. Misery, urban bleakness and angst are not what the book-buying public are going to take on holiday. Gratuitous violence and dollops of Tarantinoesque language do not place your novel in the *avant garde*.

It is often said that first novels are largely autobiographical, and this is probably more true of novels written than those published. There is a trap here which you should be careful to avoid: in general you will produce a better novel by writing about that which you know, but never take this advice too literally—you cannot expect the great interest which you have in your own life to be shared by countless strangers.

What publishers do look for are the following:

- a good plot (i.e. the way things happen should be interesting—but note that the events of a well-plotted tea party may well be more entertaining than a tale of gun-running interlarded with sexual conquests and shootouts);
- good style (your novel should be written well, in a style appropriate to the story, with dialogue that sounds right, and passages of descriptive prose that are pleasing rather than embarrassing);
- originality (don't reinvent the alphabet unless you have to, but do come up with something new);
- good characterisation (your novel should be populated by plausible characters, of the sort that will engage a reader's emotions; they must have depth; don't use stereotypes);
- good structure (chopping your story into chapters is not enough; structure is achieved by countless decisions about the order of events in your narrative, the point(s) of view you adopt, the way time passes in the book, the moments at which you disclose things, etc.—many authors have employed external "structures" to help them, like a correspondence by letter, regular conversations, seasons or times of day);
- a clean manuscript (good grammar, spelling, punctuation and presentation won't ensure publication, but it will persuade a publisher that your manuscript has been frequently re-worked and polished, and this should attract attention to the substance of your book);
- and something indefinable—"it" (a good novel, story or poem should have the effect of locating some seeming gap in

our knowledge of the world and simultaneously filling it; your work should find a new nerve and let the readers feel it touched within themselves).

Before sending your novel to a publisher it is a good idea to let a trusted friend or acquaintance read it. In writing (and of course rewriting) your book you will have become hugely involved, so much so that your confidence in the book is likely to be either overblown or undermined. You need a kind, but less partisan, opinion. Choose your reader carefully, though, for there is little point in learning only what you want to learn.

You will need to send your manuscript to an appropriate publisher. Use the directory of publishers at the back of this book to identify those who do consider fiction. Go to your bookshelf and your local bookshop and look at the kinds of novel these publishers are publishing. Does yours seem to fit the style or concerns of any of these houses? If so, then these are the publishers to try first. Read Chapter 12 of this book and then send off your manuscript—to one publisher at a time—and wait patiently.

On receipt of your manuscript (and your stamped, self-addressed envelope), the publisher will make some quick decisions about your work. It may be that the unsuitability of your book can be told at a glance (you may have chosen an inappropriate publisher, for example, or perhaps your book is simply not ready for publication). If the publisher reads and likes what you've written, then the manuscript will probably be sent to a reader—a kind of literary consultant whose taste, wisdom and knowledge of the field the publisher trusts and admires. You may never discover the identity of this important person (or people, for there may be more than one), even if your book is accepted, but they will have a great influence on the publisher's decision.

In due course you will receive a letter of acceptance, rejection, or interest (the publisher may feel, for instance, that your book shows promise, but needs rewriting). But do not expect a detailed evaluation of your work; this is not the publisher's role. Remember that the publisher receives manuscripts daily. Remember that only a very small percentage of first attempts get published. Remember also that several rejected novels have gone on to achieve great success later.

Juvenile literature. One field of literary publishing has grown substantially in the past few years, and this is fiction for older children and young adults, call them what you will. Publishers in this area tend to have substantial educational lists, and it is true that juvenile literature is—in publishing terms—very largely a concern of educational publishing. But whatever its provenance, there now exists another field of literary endeavour in this country, and one whose best representatives are a far cry from the inventions of *Sweet Valley High*.

These books have an enormous role to play in the creation of a reading culture in South Africa, and they exist specifically to encourage reading. If they can achieve this across the spectrum of South African languages, then so much the better. It is not hard to see why they are beloved of librarians and language teachers—and publishers.

You shouldn't try your hand at juvenile fiction, however, without having some familiarity with your market and with the *genre*. They are not simply short novels—specific lengths are preferred for specific age groups, an appropriate language level is essential, plot complexity must obviously vary and so on. Read several before you embark on your own. There has long been a tendency to write juvenile fiction with either girls or boys in mind, and whilst—or indeed *because*—young readers are hugely susceptible to this kind of direction, you should proceed very cautiously in order to avoid the crass stereotyping which has long dominated books for the younger reader.

Children are everywhere and always equally mature or immature, but today's children are a good deal more sophisticated than those of a generation ago. Television, popular music, the Internet—the whole information caboodle—have exposed the young to an enormous wealth of cultural diversity, technological know-how and general knowledge. It is important to recognise this sophistication (don't patronise) and, at the same time, not to lose sight of the essential child. Being too coy about the facts of life or of South African society is as likely to signal your own anxieties as it is to accommodate the (perceived) curiosities and anxieties of today's young South Africans. Note, also, that the great divide in South African experience today is between the urban and the rural; too much of juvenile fiction advantages the former.

Send your chosen publisher a sample chapter, and a synopsis of your story. This will give the publisher enough information to assess the suitability of your work. If you have particular experience of working with children of the age group for which you have written your book, then include a *curriculum vitae*, or ensure that you mention it in your covering letter.

Drama

If you're a playwright, then publishing your play will be a secondary consideration. Your first objective will be to get it produced. Success on the stage may induce a publisher to consider the play for publication, but, in this country, the play's suitability for prescription as a literary or dramatic setwork for schools or universities will be of great importance to a publisher. Once again, there is no reason why an excerpt from your play should not find its way into the little magazines as a purely literary exercise. If you want to write plays for use in schools, then you should read Chapter 7 on educational publishing.

Belles-lettres

This is a broad area of literary publishing, encompassing, for our purposes, such things as essays, diaries, biographies and autobiographies. In many instances these *genres* might well not deliver what we would consider literature (a biography of François Pienaar or Winnie Mandela, for example), and these books would fall under the broad category of general non-fiction. There are cases, however, when these sorts of books are published more for their literary merit than for their subject matter (and, at times, for both). Think, for example, of Sindiwe Magona's or Guy Butler's autobiographies, or Sol Plaatjes's Boer War diaries of the siege of Mafeking. These are exceptional cases, however, and if you are thinking of penning your reminiscences, or writing up your year in Ethiopia, then you would do best to approach a general publisher. Once again, don't make the mistake of assuming that the rest of the world will find your life as absorbing as you do.

The market for true *belles-lettres* is very small in this country, and you would be extremely lucky to have, say, a volume of your essays published unless you were reasonably well-known as a literary figure already. Things like diaries, commonplace books and so on would need to be of exceptional interest to find a publisher—though there is always an outside chance that your great-grandmother's letters home are indeed going to be the literary find of the next century.

4

Children's book publishing in South Africa

Alida Potgieter

There are factors unique to children's book publishing that any aspiring author needs to keep in mind. Although fiction and non-fiction overlap to some extent with books for the educational market, this section will deal only with children's books published for the general market. The general market in this case consists of the library market and the mass market.

Market constraints

The South African publisher of children's books for the general market faces one major problem: the economics of publishing small print runs. The size of the print run is a crucial factor, because it determines to a large extent the retail price of a book and the quality of the book one can publish. The larger the print run, the lower the unit cost.

Unless a publisher can convince a book club like Leserskring/Leisure Books or a major bookshop chain like CNA-Gallo to commit themselves to a large advance order of a book, or to an exclusive deal, he or she is largely dependent on orders from libraries, and is forced to limit the print run to a maximum of 2 500 copies.

Added to this there is a near-universal perception that children's books should be cheaper than books for adults, so publishers often have to keep the prices of their children's books lower than they should be. This is an unrealistic and unhealthy situation that often leads to compromises on quality. It also means that children's books that do retail at more "realistic" prices (in terms of costing) are seen as far too expensive by the bookshops and their customers, and are consequently either not ordered by the bookshops or taken in very small quantities.

Printing several languages together, thereby increasing the print run, is of course one way of making full-colour printing possible, but translation costs and market realities have to be borne in mind. Another route is the selling of rights abroad and copublishing with an overseas publisher, as Songololo Books, a David Philip imprint, have done with considerable success.

Language

The development of children's book publishing in South Africa reflects to a high degree the economic and cultural power of the different language groups in various stages of our history. For many years nearly all English children's books were imported, mainly from Britain, and the competition from these books was too daunting and severe for any publisher to invest money in the development of local English children's books. And for very different but well-known reasons, there was an absolute dearth of children's story books in African languages, the only books published in those languages being school textbooks.

Obviously, Afrikaans had a major advantage for many years, since Afrikaans children's books never had to compete with imported books. The official status of Afrikaans since 1925 and the growing economic and political power of the Afrikaner community led to a remarkable output of Afrikaans children's books (albeit of varying quality) since the 1930s. But the Afrikaans children's book really flourished in the late 1950s and the 1960s when the provincial library services came into being and started placing large orders for these books.

Although many overseas books are still being translated into Afrikaans and African languages in order to make the printing of full-colour books (picture books, collections of fairy tales, non-fiction) affordable, there are more locally written books for older children and teenagers being published in Afrikaans today than ten years or so ago.

In the last decade children's books have proved to be one of the few branches of general publishing where books are produced in most of the major indigenous languages. However, the number of titles published in African languages still lags far behind.

Awards and rewards

Afrikaans authors had another advantage in that a larger number of literary awards were created for them, and at an earlier stage, by institutions like the S.A. Akademie vir Wetenskap en Kuns (their Scheepers Award, for example, was established as long ago as 1955), and the South African Institute for Library and Information Science (SAILIS). Such awards encouraged writing in Afrikaans. The only award for English children's books was, for a very long time, the Percy Fitzpatrick Award (SAILIS), which was only established in 1969 and which, significantly, existed for many years before it was first awarded. The growth and development of local English children's books really only started in the mid seventies.

In recent years a number of new awards have been introduced, and many of them are linked to specific publishers, like the Nasionale Pers annual children's book award, the MER Award, for publishers in the group; the Old Mutual Award (every five years for a Human & Rousseau book); the Sanlam Award organised by Tafelberg Publishers; and the Young Africa Award organised by Maskew Miller Longman. These awards sometimes carry substantial monetary rewards, as well as publicity opportunities and exposure on television and in newspapers and magazines.

A cash prize, together with the attendant publicity as a bonus, probably acts as a much stronger incentive and motivation for authors than any purely literary award. Such awards and competitions have done much to nurture the development of children's literature locally, especially in Afrikaans and English. Proof of this is that English novels for children and teenagers have actually won awards like the prestigious M-Net Award against stiff competition from books for adults.

Many of these awards are now no longer limited to English and Afrikaans, but have been thrown open to authors from all language groups. In time this should provide the same impetus for writing in African languages as it did for the two former official languages.

Which manuscripts do which publishers want?

Some publishers specialise in publishing books for certain age groups or in certain categories, or perhaps publish mainly in

English or mainly in Afrikaans. Authors should know which publishers are likely to be interested in their work.

There are a few publishers who publish mainly picture books, e.g. Garamond, Songololo Books and Anansi, and some who target older readers, like Maskew Miller Longman, whose Young Africa series focuses on teenage novels.

Human & Rousseau and Tafelberg are the publishers with the largest children's book sections in the country and they both publish for the whole age range, from picture books to teenage novels. Human & Rousseau is well known for its full-colour illustrated children's books, many of which are coproduced with overseas publishers, and its list of local illustrated books, especially for the eight to ten year age group, as well as books for younger children and teenage novels. Tafelberg's children's list, with the impetus provided by the Sanlam competition, tends to include more teenage novels.

Beginner authors need to do some market research. By looking at new and recently published children's books in well-stocked bookshops or libraries they should get an idea of the standard of books currently being published.

It may also be helpful for new authors to realise from the outset that the production costs of even a modest print run of a children's book for the general market could be anything between R12 000 and R20 000. The publisher therefore takes a major financial risk when accepting a manuscript since—in spite of his or her knowledge of the market—there is no guarantee that the book will indeed sell well.

Non-fiction. For a non-fiction manuscript, an outline and first chapter, plus the author's credentials for writing on the particular subject, are usually enough for a first submission.

However, a non-fiction title in English stands little chance of being published locally unless it is strongly South African in content. A book in Afrikaans might stand a slightly better chance, but there are still the cost constraints of colour printing and a limited market to contend with. The beautiful, large format full-colour non-fiction books published by many overseas publishers created a standard of publishing that we just cannot match with our small print runs. Apart from Struik, who has managed to publish several attractive local books, and one or two other publishers, there has been little local publishing activity in this area.

The only children's non-fiction titles with which general publishers have reasonable success are those that also work for the mass market and are therefore bought in reasonably large quantities by mass-market buyers like CNA-Gallo and Lesers-kring/Leisure Books. These are books that are not so much aimed at imparting information but at stimulating children's leisure time activities and hobbies, like gardening, cooking and crafts.

Certainly, there is an enormous need for more information books, especially in the indigenous languages, but the general market for such books is currently almost non-existent. The market is therefore limited to school and public libraries, neither of which buy in large enough quantities to justify the risk a publisher runs in taking on projects which—as a rule—have very high origination costs. The information in many non-fiction books also dates very quickly so that such a book has to be updated regularly or replaced by another one on the subject, thus adding to the cost.

Fiction. Publishers have different policies regarding the submission of manuscripts, but for fiction they definitely expect to see a complete manuscript before risking an evaluation. It is practically impossible to assess the suitability and quality of a story from a summary and only one chapter.

Stories for smaller children need illustrations, and authors for this age group should realise that royalties will as a rule be shared by the author and the illustrator. However, it is better not to submit illustrations with a manuscript, even if the text requires it. If an author submits artwork it might not be suitable for various reasons. It might not be good enough, or there might be a technical problem (more expensive to reproduce). It is best to leave decisions concerning artwork to the publisher who knows the market.

The publisher will usually commission the illustrator in consultation with the author. If the author himself or herself is an artist and wants to do the illustrations, the correct procedure would be to submit not just a manuscript with the text, but a rough artist's dummy plus one piece of final artwork in the style and medium in which he or she wants to do the book. There are many famous author/artists (Maurice Sendak, Shirley Hughes, Niki Daly) who submit a new manuscript to their publishers or agents as a "total concept". But the combination of these two talents is rare indeed.

Although the general market for children's fiction is small, the unit cost of a softcover book printed in black only is usually not too high if the print run is between 1 500 and 2 500 copies. Such books are therefore more commercially viable than full-colour ones.

In writing a story it could be that an author might sometimes not be sure who his intended audience would be and to whom his story would appeal. This is something that the publisher, who knows the market, might more easily establish and decide. However, if one knows the target audience, one may have fewer problems in finding the right tone and approach for a story, as well as the right length and level of complexity.

This section cannot provide detailed guidelines on creative writing but there are several books on the subject that new authors should find very useful. One of them is Joan Aiken's *The Way to Write for Children*, published by Elm Tree Books, London. (Aiken is one of the best and most successful British writers of children's books.) Local publications include Frances Bond and Eileen Molver's *Guide to Creative Writing*, which contains a chapter on children's books; and certain sections in the two books containing the proceedings of the first national symposiums on children's literature held in South Africa: *Towards Understanding* (Maskew Miller Longman) and *Towards More Understanding* (Juta).

The basic guidelines for writing fiction successfully for children (whether it is a picture book text of 400 words or a children's novel of 40 000 words) can be summarised in two main points:

- The story should be written from a child's point of view, portraying emotions, characters and events as a child of that age would feel, see and experience them, and using dialogue that is completely natural.
- It should have a strong story line, whether it is a realistic story or a fantasy, an adventure or a story about family relationships.

There are other finer points to consider, especially in the different categories, but if a story complies with these two main criteria, it would most probably appeal to the majority of young readers. Of course, some subjects or themes are more popular than others, but many stories on widely different themes have proven popular with young readers through the ages. Serious publishers who have the well-being of children at heart, of whom there are fortunately several in this country, do not limit the range of their publishing programme to the popular categories only.

What is decidedly unacceptable? Things like stereotyping and didacticism. Children's books do not need to be simplistic in order to be accessible. They should not be written to convey "useful lessons" about life. Sermonising is out. If you want to write fiction for children and you don't have a story to tell, you should try your hand at something else altogether.

Assessing new manuscripts

It is virtually impossible for a publisher to spend a great deal of time guiding all beginner authors.

Once a publisher has received a manuscript with good potential and has decided to publish it, the editor will be prepared to spend as much time on that book and with that author as it takes to realise that specific book's potential. But the starting point for such guidance is usually a manuscript that already shows promise.

In evaluating manuscripts and coming to a publishing decision, the main factors the publisher has to keep in mind are quality and cost. This is why publishers are forced to be so selective. It is expensive to produce a book, and unfortunately 95% of manuscripts that land up on a publisher's desk are just not good enough to justify the high risk and cost of publication.

After years as an editor of children's books, I am convinced that there are few other areas of publishing in which editors have to wade through so much inferior writing in order to select the few manuscripts with potential from those that have none whatsoever. Of course, many beginner authors might be attracted to writing for young children because the text could be relatively short. But the main reason seems to be that most people have no idea what good children's writing is and entertain the mistaken idea that any little story about a humanised toy or animal would be acceptable for publication. This naive view is apparent in so many telephone calls and letters to publishers.

What does impress an editor and would cause her or him to look at a manuscript with objective interest, is just a short business-like covering letter and a story that speaks for itself. Many years of experience have shown me that the best stories arrive on one's desk without any lengthy author's explanation or justification.

In general, I would say that the one characteristic of all successful and good authors of children's fiction (no matter what age group the book is intended for) is that they have a good *story* to tell and they tell it as well as they can—usually with a fresh or original approach, even if the theme or subject is not new.

In a market as small as ours, with such modest returns for author, illustrator and publisher on a first print run, it would be unrealistic of any author to be motivated in the first place by the idea of making money or earning a livelihood from the writing of children's books. It is just not possible, unless you have written a children's novel that is—often many years after publication—prescribed for use in secondary schools. These books (but there are only a few of them) are ordered in such large quantities that the publisher has to reprint them regularly.

New authors should also keep in mind that most editors work under great pressure, and time is costly and valuable. So, although authors find this extremely frustrating, it is in fact usual practice for a publisher to return without comment and with just a short standard letter those manuscripts which have arrived unsolicited and which, in the publisher's opinion, have little or no potential, or which are not suitable for her or his publishing programme. To obtain a reader's report or a critical evaluation by an expert in the field is expensive. In most cases it will only be asked for if the publisher sees merit in the manuscript and wants to suggest to the author to work on it again for resubmission, or if the publisher feels that the works shows promise and wants to encourage the author in general, so that any future manuscripts would be submitted to the same publisher.

Future developments and possibilities

A larger, stable middle class might stimulate the development of a book culture, which in turn should stimulate the growth of the body of children's literature in indigenous languages. Literacy is extremely important, so the emphasis for many communities in

South Africa at the present time is obviously still more on being able to read—the technical aspect of it—rather than on a love for reading as an entertaining or enriching experience.

If a reading culture is considered a crucial aspect of non-formal education by the powers that be, and more money is allocated to school and public libraries, the publishing of children's books for the general market can certainly continue to grow.

5

The Afrikaans market

Kerneels Breytenbach

In most respects the Afrikaans market closely mirrors the English market in South Africa. A clear distinction can be made between publishing in Afrikaans for the educational, tertiary and general markets.

Educational and tertiary publishing are closely linked to the evolution of the South African educational system. The establishment of Afrikaans universities and schools early in the twentieth century necessitated the publishing of textbooks in Afrikaans; economical and scientific progress and the urge to keep abreast of the latest international developments in various fields made possible the publication of a growing body of academic research in Afrikaans.

The victory of the National Party in the election of 1948 and the consequences of the policy of apartheid had a marked effect on publishing in Afrikaans. The formalisation of a policy of bilingualism led to an avalanche of Afrikaans general books, but it also carried with it the germ of a problem for Afrikaans general publishers: Afrikaans readers had access to English publications, so English books did not need to be automatically translated into Afrikaans. On the other hand, few Afrikaans books have been translated into English, with only authors such as André P. Brink, Dalene Matthee, Marita van der Vyver, Karel Schoeman and Breyten Breytenbach having broken through to the international English market.

General publishing in Afrikaans

General publishing encompasses various fields, such as fiction, non-fiction, religious and inspirational books. Important publishers are Human & Rousseau, Tafelberg, Struik, J.P. van der

Walt, and Lux Verbi, but many companies do some general publishing in Afrikaans (see the Directory of Publishers in Part 5). The Afrikaans market is small compared to publishing in English. Some interest in Afrikaans publications is shown in the Netherlands, mainly as a result of the link between Afrikaans and Dutch, as well as the fact that various Afrikaans literary figures have become known in Dutch literary circles. One Afrikaans poet, Elisabeth Eybers, has also won the highly prestigious P.C. Hooft Dutch literary prize.

Literary publications in Afrikaans are taken very seriously indeed. Great importance and prestige are attached to literary prizes such as the CNA, Hertzog and M-Net prizes. These prizes uphold and reward literary values. It may be that too much importance has been attached to them. It has long been the ideal of various Afrikaans publishers to produce works of a more popular nature. Only a few authors such as Dalene Matthee have really produced books that could claim to be of literary value and genuinely popular at the same time. Afrikaans general publishers have in the early nineties expressed a certain desperation in their search for new popular fiction. With the launch of the CNA and Leserskring's Kolskoot campaign in 1996 publishers at last succeeded in gaining the support of the reading public for popular fiction similar to that already available to the English reading public.

Afrikaans fiction

Afrikaans fiction can be divided into several categories: adult, popular, juvenile and children's fiction, with the latter two classes again subdivided into local publications and co-productions with British, French, Dutch and other publishers.

In the main Afrikaans fiction has been sustained by various forms of prescription at secondary and tertiary level, but Afrikaans general publishers also tend to "subsidise" their fiction through the huge sales of non-fiction books, especially books on cookery, gardening and natural history. Mass-market children's titles have also proved to be very popular.

Some fiction titles have achieved huge popularity, but Afrikaans publishers are aware of certain fields in which growth must be stimulated. Thanks to the huge advance orders of Leserskring/Leisure Books and the marketing acumen of the CNA, but especially the requirements of the various provincial library services, Afrikaans general publishers can produce a large number of illustrated children's fiction (local and co-productions) and books for teenagers every year. The emphasis has shifted from books with a Eurocentric slant towards ones that mirror the diversity, problems and ideals of South Africa. Various books that were originated in Afrikaans have been translated into Xhosa, Zulu and Sotho at the request of provincial librarians. This segment of the market has some built-in difficulties, however: if Leserskring and the CNA do not purchase certain titles, and if the libraries were to stop their support for children's and juvenile fiction it will be extremely difficult to continue publishing books of this kind in Afrikaans as sales through the rest of the trade are minimal.

In adult fiction there is a definite dividing line between titles of a literary nature and those with a more popular appeal. The latter had a brief period of ascendancy in the fifties, but since the sixties greater emphasis has been placed on works of literary quality, to the point where a dearth of popular work existed in the eighties. General publishers have recognised the need for a more balanced approach to fiction in order to rejuvenate the Afrikaans market. Whereas there is a small but appreciative market for Afrikaans poetry, it is generally recognised that popular fiction, published in the form of trade and mass market paperbacks, should be promoted with more vigour. Aspiring authors should heed this need. The successes of *Griet Skryf 'n Sprokie* (Marita van der Vyver) and *Triomf* (Marlene van Niekerk) can be held up as examples.

Afrikaans non-fiction

A relatively small market has not stopped Afrikaans general publishers from exploring its potential to the full. If one looks at what has been published, certain trends can be discerned that are of importance to budding authors. As is the case with English books, fortune smiles on those who tackle fresh topics and issues. A keen sense of fads, fashions and relevancy can amount to an intuitive kind of market research. Certainly, whether you write about overcoming depression or how to practise container gardening, it would be foolish to start without taking stock of what is available, not only in Afrikaans, but also in English. Remember: most Afrikaans readers can read English as well, and therefore have a larger choice than English readers have.

There are a few main categories into which non-fiction publications can be divided.

Leisure books. Although there is a tendency to look on cookery and gardening books as coffee-table books, various authors have succeeded in capturing the Afrikaans market with a highly practical approach to their subjects. Mrs S.J.A. de Villiers' *Kook en Geniet* has instructed generations of Afrikaans readers, and the *Huisgenoot Wenresepte* series, written first by Annette Human and later by Carmen Niehaus, started a whole new tradition of a popular, practical style of cooking. Keith Kirsten has done much the same with his gardening books, which were published in English and Afrikaans simultaneously.

General publishers realise that a well-known Afrikaans or local author will ensure the success of the publication, but they are always on the lookout for novel but practical approaches to the field.

Afrikaans publishers have attempted do-it-yourself books and books on hobbies and crafts, but with little or unspectacular success.

Natural history. Natural history is a lucrative field of publishing, but most books in this field are published in English. Even Afrikaans publishing houses will tend to publish in English, and only translate if they are convinced of the viability of an Afrikaans translation. It is not really a question of having no promising manuscripts; it is rather a problem of the market being too small for a print run that will allow an affordable price. Thus many Afrikaans authors make proposals to local publishers, but are then forced to write the manuscript in English. Consequently a large number of Afrikaans readers interested in wildlife and other aspects of our wonderful country have had to read about them in English in both field guides and coffee-table books. There is however one exception: illustrated children's non-fiction, where the large school and library market is in great need of such books.

If you have an idea for a book in this field, it is advisable to enter into discussions with local publishers before you start writing the manuscript.

Inspirational and devotional books. Given the religious character of Afrikaans society, it is understandable that inspirational and devotional publications form a sizeable portion of the Afrikaans market. Inspirational books (religion with a popular approach) and devotional books (a more formal, dogmatic approach to the subject) as well as various forms of diaries and collections of meditations have proven to be popular. One of the most prominent authors in this field is Solly Ozrovec.

Politics and local history. Afrikaans has been closely linked to the political struggle and empowerment of the Afrikaner from the beginning of this century, so it follows that Afrikaans general publishers have frequently entered this field of publishing, especially during the first three decades of National Party rule. There have been signs of dissent, however; to a certain degree with Tafelberg's series of books by Dr A.D. Wassenaar, but especially from Human & Rousseau. Their publication of fiction by André P. Brink and others have set them apart from the mainstream of Afrikaans politics, and they have followed this up with the ground-breaking study on local political and social history, *Nuwe Geskiedenis van Suid-Afrika,* under the editorship of Trewhella Cameron, and books such as Carl Niehaus's *Om te Veg vir Hoop* and Beyers Naudé's autobiographical *My Land van Hoop.*

Afrikaans general publishers have tended to distance themselves clearly from sectarian politics. They still welcome manuscripts of a political nature, albeit with the knowledge that interest in the topic has waned since the 1994 elections, with only some of the really important studies on future scenarios doing well in the market. As far as Afrikaans books on Afrikaner politics pre-1994 are concerned, the axiom holds true that a growing share in a declining market spells death.

Life skills. This area has developed into a huge market in the United States and Europe. The same pattern has evolved in the Afrikaans market. Afrikaans translations of American bestsellers as well as locally written books on topics such as depression, alcoholism, self-improvement, co-dependency, managerial skills, new business approaches in South Africa, raising healthy children, communication and so on have scored spectacular successes. If you want to write a book in any of these fields, it is wise to remember, as has been pointed out before, that a knowledge of what has been published in the field (in both English and Afrikaans) is essential.

Gaps in the market

Most of the pitfalls and problems relevant to English publishing in South Africa (as discussed in the sections "Books needed for this market" and "Choosing what to write about" in Chapter 2) also apply to Afrikaans general publishing. There are however certain other factors to take into account.

First, if you specifically want to write an Afrikaans book on any topic, you should be absolutely certain that it will draw the attention of the Afrikaans reading public. Know your audience. Do some market research of your own, or have it done for you, about gaps in the market, and about how many potential readers there are. Publishers can help in this respect, as can booksellers, librarians and the purchasing staff of Leserskring and CNA. Not only should you know about the books that have been published on certain subjects, it is also imperative that you find out whether they have sold at all. Know your market, know the readers.

Second, consult a publisher if you are considering having your manuscript translated into English for simultaneous publication. General publishers are aware of the deluge of imported books they have to compete with in the local book stores, and will only agree to such simultaneous publication if they are convinced there is a need for such a book, and that they will be able to sell both editions. If you are a new author on the scene, be doubly cautious about deciding on a translation.

Once you have identified a suitable topic, persevere. You will have to compete with many established authors—but they too were once in the exact position you find yourself in now. And publishers thrive through the building up of a stable of well-known authors.

Commissioning

Because of the nature of their work publishers frequently identify gaps in the market and plan books—for which they must then find authors. This is where the commissioned author enters the scene. Frequently he or she is an experienced author or journalist. Among them are some of the most sought-after people in the field of publishing. They may also be called upon to assist inexperienced authors when a manuscript gets bogged down.

No one Afrikaans publisher specialises in the field of commissioned books to the same extent that The Reader's Digest does in English. Quite a number of general publishers have however often commissioned books on local history, company history, historic buildings, and so on.

Commissioning also plays a large role in the presentation and design of Afrikaans books. Whereas the manuscript itself may not be commissioned, the publisher will commission a graphic artist to design the book. The artist then takes on the responsibility for the overall layout, the cover design, illustrations used, and so on. Afrikaans cookery books have developed a certain visual identity largely through the work of a number of well-known commissioned artists, of whom Etienne van Duyker is probably the best known. This kind of commissioning is one of the most important mechanisms in publishing, as the nature of the commission—the "brief"—must take into account various marketing factors. If the brief is not properly thought through, the author may see his or her excellent book flounder as a result of poor jacket design, inappropriate jacket illustration and confusing or unsuitable text layout.

Packaging

A few local Afrikaans publishers (Ukelele and Blommaert are probably the best known) have come into existence who will handle the production of a manuscript on behalf of the author. They provide only rudimentary editorial assistance, and deliver the printed product to the author/client, who has to take the task of distribution on his or her own shoulders. There are many pitfalls in this branch of general publishing—not so much for the publisher as for the client. Quality control does not extend to the contents of the book, and marketing depends on the know-how of the client. But if the packager has experience of publishing, this approach may suit the needs of some authors. Packaging of this nature is often—revealingly—referred to as "vanity publishing".

Points of interest to would-be authors

Afrikaans publishers tend to grant advances on the sale of new publications only to authors with a proven track record. The amount granted is directly in proportion to the expected income from the sales of the book; the astronomical advances granted in the US and UK are foreign to Afrikaans publishing.

When an author enters into a contract with an Afrikaans publisher, he or she will find that a clear distinction is made between sales to the normal book trade and sales to book clubs (the latter is much lower). Poets and authors of short stories who contribute to anthologies will find that their remuneration is in accordance with a set of guidelines formulated by the Afrikaanse Skrywersgilde together with the Afrikaans publishers in the early eighties.

The future

It is too early to tell what influence coming changes in the educational system will have on Afrikaans publishing, but one can generalise and say that Afrikaans general publishers are optimistic about the future. The resounding success of Leserskring has opened up the Afrikaans market over the last decade, inspiring the CNA to concentrate on Afrikaans books to a larger extent than in the pre-Leserskring days. As a result the CNA experienced enormous growth in the sales of Afrikaans books, leading to the establishment of a new section, Category 42, devoted to the sale and promotion of Afrikaans books. The programme started with 42 participating CNA branches but within a year the number of branches involved had to be doubled.

With Afrikaans fiction selling extremely well, with titles on cookery, gardening and life skills doing even better, and with the enormous growth in the field of mass-market books for children, the future of the Afrikaans book looks rosy indeed. Controversial issues such as the official status of Afrikaans, Afrikaans in education and the use of Afrikaans on television and radio have overshadowed the fact that Afrikaans books are selling in larger quantities than ever before, and that there have recently been more Afrikaans general publications produced than ever during the apartheid years.

Once Afrikaans publishing has shaken off the unnatural circumstances that have influenced publication in the language since 1948, it will be able to compete more aggressively for the attention of Afrikaans-speaking people within the framework of a normalised system. One of the central issues facing Afrikaans general publishers is whether they can reach the previously disenfranchised black and coloured people who regard Afrikaans as their first or second language, and who will in the next decade or so enter the world of literacy, whilst at the same time great care must be given to retain as readers those Afrikaans-speaking people who gravitate towards English, the lingua franca of the country.

6

Publishing in African languages

Dumisani Krushchev Ntshangase

Publishing African languages can be divided into publishing *in* African languages and publishing *on* African languages. Publishing in African languages refers to that body of works which is printed in book form and is written in an African language. Publishing on African languages refers to that body of works which is printed in diverse forms on subjects pertaining to African languages. While the former will be in an African language, the latter may not necessarily be. This distinction is crucial to our understanding of the activities involved in African languages and publishing.

Publishing in and on African languages is less than a hundred years old. Pioneering works in the last quarter of the 19th century in African languages were mainly missionary-driven. These included translations of the Bible, translations and the writing of sermons, hymns, songs and other activities related to Christian religion. Later publishing came to incorporate the translation of "colonial literature" of writers such as Bunyan and Rider Haggard. This resulted in the establishment of missionary publishing houses like Lovedale, Mariannhill and Morija.

By the start of the 20th century publishing in African languages took a commercial turn. With the establishment of commercial publishing houses and university presses, the interest in African languages expanded from the religious sphere into other areas. Presses like the Witwatersrand University Press and its African Treasury List, Mariannhill Missionary Press, Lovedale Missionary Press, Morija Press and others published mainly novels, poetry anthologies and drama-plays in African languages. (I prefer the term drama-play because performance literature in African languages is mainly written to be *read* rather than written to be *performed.*)

Today, publishing in African languages is one of the largest and financially most viable enterprises within the educational publishing industry. Very little though has changed in terms of the areas of publishing. Publishers still concentrate on novels, drama-plays, poetry and short story anthologies, and language books (generally known as textbooks).

Most works *on* African languages are academic books describing the structural composition of African languages and other elements relating to both the languages and their speakers, and are based on research. This area has not as yet become financially viable locally as it still reaches a very small market of intellectuals, but internationally it has a bigger market and can be financially viable. The main disciplines in this field are various subjects within linguistics, ethnology, anthropology, sociolinguistics and other humanities disciplines. The main publishers were initially British and French (the latter mainly in the case of Sesotho and Venda, which had a strong French missionary influence) and locally the missionary and university presses. However, recently commercial companies have begun publishing academic books with a limited circulation.

What are African languages?

The term African languages is a rather unfortunate historical term. It refers to a diverse group of related and unrelated languages and does not mean much more than the geographical description it carries. African languages can be described as those languages whose origin can be traced to Africa. Though this includes KiSwahili, a mixture of African languages and Arabic, most Africans would exclude Afrikaans, even though its origins are similar to those of KiSwahili and clearly identify the geographical location. This exclusion of Afrikaans is political and is the result both of Afrikaner nationalists excluding themselves from Africa in the past, and of the African nationalists denouncing the former's cause.

In South Africa there are nine recognised African languages:

- **Zulu** (spoken in the southeast and the largest group)
- **Xhosa** (spoken in the south and the southwest, and the third largest group)

- **Tswana** (spoken in the west and western central area and in Botswana)
- **South Sotho** (spoken in the south-central area and in Lesotho)
- **Northern Sotho** (spoken in the northwest, and the second largest group)
- **Venda** (spoken in the northeast and in parts of western Zimbabwe)
- **Tsonga** (spoken in the northeast and in western Mozambique)
- **Ndebele** (spoken in the east and in southern Zimbabwe)
- **Swati** (spoken in the east and in Swaziland)

Some of these languages are similar in structure and syntax. Zulu, Xhosa, Ndebele and Swati are grouped as the Nguni languages. They have major features in common and are mutually intelligible. Tswana, South Sotho and Northern Sotho are grouped as the Sotho languages. Tsonga and Venda are mutually unintelligible to each other and to the other groups.

There are many other languages spoken in South Africa that are not recognised. Languages like Sepulane (spoken in the east) and many other "dialects" of the officially recognised African languages are spoken by many people. However, speakers of these languages invariably learn the dominant language of their immediate environment or the recognised dialects.

In addition, Khoi languages are not recognised in South Africa. Though many people of Khoi extraction no longer speak Khoi languages but have adopted Afrikaans, these languages are still found mainly in Namibia and the southern and central parts of Botswana. It can be said that most Khoi languages underwent language death.

There are also urban languages that are not officially recognised, such as Tsotsitaal and various forms of Iscamtho. It must be stressed that research into African languages is far from complete and still remains a major preoccupation of academics both within South Africa and beyond.

The study of "dialects" and interlanguage relations both at structural and communicative level will interest writers who write mainly academic works. With the increased interest in sociolinguistic studies, publishing houses such as the Witwatersrand University Press and David Philip have published academic books on African languages based on recent research. There is also a growing cross-border and trans-oceanic networking with academics in African languages who have published financially viable books and journals. These have mainly been published overseas by companies such as Basil Blackwell, Newbury and others, and American and British university presses.

The market

Publishing for a market in and on African languages presents interesting options. The main areas of publishing are in language books, novels, drama-plays and anthologies of short stories and poetry. There should be a strong market for newspapers and magazines and multimedia options, but this has not as yet been adequately realised. Emerging areas of interest are African languages as second languages, where publishing should surpass English first language publishing. Second language publishing will require linguistically graded reading materials, language teaching materials, reference works (library books) and will rely on newspapers and magazines as resource materials.

Other emerging areas are tourism, health, commerce, industry, and lexicographic and terminological works. In the future there will be a need for pocket-size manuals for tourists with keys to essential and courteous communication in restaurants and other service agencies. These can be very useful and with proper marketing may yield good returns. Government-related agencies will require books on, for example, basic health care for health workers. There is a need for industry-specific manuals, e.g. building, mining, forestry, banking and general services. Dictionaries and terminology books are expensive and as yet difficult to market, but with careful project management dictionaries can be financially viable.

Small soho-type houses have taken up this challenge and are currently starting to publish in these areas. These books have the potential to be distributed by the major retailers—not only can they be seen as "exotic" but they also provide a breath of freshness in an otherwise predictable industry.

Currently, technical publishing is not viable in African languages. Neither are books on computers, tertiary mathematics and science, farming, leisure, natural history, coffee-table books, lifeskills, politics and current affairs. There is simply no market for such books at present, although the need may arise in the future.

The writer

Most writers in African languages have been teachers or college and university lecturers, owing to the narrowly concentrated market of the education system. Recently, there have been major developments in the pool of writers in African languages.

Not only have new writers emerged, after almost thirty years of domination by the same writers, but more and more Black writers who formerly wrote mainly in English, are developing an interest in writing in African languages. Writers such as Gomolemo Mokae, who writes in Tswana, have brought a new respectability to writing in African languages. Other writers who have gained prominence wrote their books in Britain and the United States but have published their books in South Africa. Writers such as Nhlanhla Maake and J.C. Buthelezi are examples. Maskew Miller Longman has taken the lead in bringing a new dimension to publishing fiction in African languages, and other companies will follow.

These developments are significant because the state of book publishing in African languages was previously very static. Writers in all the African languages showed a predictable pattern in their writing and made no attempt to experiment with different ideas. The themes in literature were stale and repetitive.

This situation was due to a lack of training and the politics of the country. The work of the above-mentioned writers has introduced new topics into African languages. For example, African language fiction used to avoid topics such as politics.

The apartheid system which established language boards (homeland-attached government structures created to develop African languages and recommend books to be prescribed by the education departments) also aimed at exposing readers to works that glorified the state. This political role of the language boards resulted in stifled thematic development. In the end writing was almost totally restricted to members of these boards, known to publishers as "contacts". This inevitably led to corruption in the prescription procedures. With the establishment of the Pan South African Language Board we hope that things will change.

Writers in the future will have to experiment with ideas. There is no formula for literary success. Writers must find their own style and experiment with a wide selection of themes and topics. Books in African languages should deal with real human experiences and should present clearer character portrayal, sensitive to political, racial, ethnic and gender issues. The emphasis should be on literary rather than didactic value. While the bulk of the market still remains educational, there will be critical approaches to reading which will test books according to their social, aesthetic and literary value.

Female writers in African languages have not featured much up to now and will have to be encouraged to submit their books for publication.

Writers of language books must realise that new methodological approaches are needed. While language books will be very important for the schooling stage, a more critical awareness of the diverse methodologies and greater social sensitivity will be vital in the acceptance of books by both publishers and users.

Most publishers acknowledge the fact that many African writers have no computer or typewriting skills and are therefore willing to accept handwritten manuscripts in African languages. However, authors should be encouraged to learn to use the available technology—not only does it make their writing more accessible, it also reduces the time required to prepare a manuscript for publication. The golden rule in publishing is: submit a legible manuscript to the publisher.

In the next few years attempts will be made to establish schools or centres for the teaching of creative writing skills. These centres will be linked to tertiary institutions or run by NGOs and will provide publishers and the market with a new breed of adequately trained writers. The publishing industry should also take up this challenge to develop not only African languages but also creative literature in South Africa.

Publishers and booksellers

The most important group, as far as African languages are concerned, are the educational publishers. Publishing in African languages is mainly linked to the education system, so most publishers rely on the needs of the education department rather than on the consumer market. Prescribed books for the school syllabi form the biggest market for African languages, therefore most books in African languages are school textbook and prescribed literature books. Many publishers are active in this field: Educum, Nasou, Via Afrika, Kagiso, Juta, Maskew Miller Longman, Shuter & Shooter, Heinemann, Hodder & Stoughton, J.L. van Schaik, Oxford University Press, University of South Africa Press, Rhodes University Press, Witwatersrand University Press, University of Natal Press, Vivlia, Struik, Reach Out, Ravan Press, David Philip and Macmillan South Africa (see *Directory of South African Publishers* for more details of publishers).

Among tertiary publishers that publish books on African languages are Via Afrika, Witwatersrand University Press, Oxford University Press, Fort Hare University Press, University of South Africa Press, University of Natal Press, Rhodes University Press, Heinemann, Juta, David Philip, Maskew Miller Longman, Kagiso, Penguin Books and many overseas publishers. There are other publishers who publish tertiary books on African languages but they do not regard this as an important part of their publishing activities.

Unfortunately African languages have as yet little importance in trade or general publishing. This is a negative spin-off from apartheid education, and a result of the negative downgrading of the status of African languages. The situation is changing as a result of the political transformation but it remains to be seen whether trade publishing will expand to include African languages. While companies such as Human & Rousseau and Tafelberg have published extensively in Afrikaans fiction, they have not as yet ventured into African languages. There are small independent publishers who have done important work in reaching the market. They have mainly concentrated on African languages as second language. An author will have to rely mainly on word of mouth, as most of these publishers usually do not survive long in the industry. One publisher of note in the Johannesburg area has been Marilyn Wood.

Mainstream booksellers do not usually keep books written in African languages. Most booksellers who stock books in African languages are educational publishers who also operate as booksellers, such as Juta, Via Afrika and Nasou. The dominant retailers like CNA-Gallo and Leserskring/Leisure Books do not generally distribute books in African languages. Some independent booksellers such as Adams and Sasavona distribute books in African languages.

The future

With the political change in South Africa, the potential growth of African languages and publishing is still a matter of speculation. South Africa now has eleven official languages (nine African languages, English and Afrikaans). This new situation will change the attitudes of speakers of various languages towards other languages, but it remains to be seen whether this policy will elevate the status of African languages to the point where they become used as languages for wider communication. Publishers and writers have to ensure that the production of materials in African languages is at least equal to that of English and Afrikaans. If not, the political implications will be serious.

Some key areas will not, at least in the foreseeable future, be viable for publishing in African languages. Areas such as encyclopedias and comprehensive dictionaries, general interest books, coffee-table books, scientific, academic and professional books, bibliographies, wildlife and travel books, and functional do-it-yourself books are not areas of immediate growth. Areas related to government and society and books on tourism, multilingualism and multiculturalism, skills training and service are starting to develop and will continue to grow. Children's books and second language books are the major growth points in this field. Up to now the new areas that may open up in African languages have not as yet been tapped by publishers. Despite that, publishing in African languages in South Africa is the most extensive in the entire continent of Africa.

7

Educational publishing

Kate McCallum

In its narrow sense, "educational" publishing refers to publishing for schools; more broadly, it refers to material published not only for schools, but also for tertiary education, adult education, literacy teaching—in fact, to any material used in an educational sense, whether this be in a formal or informal learning and teaching situation, or self-instructional. Few educational publishers in South Africa these days restrict themselves entirely to publishing only textbooks for schools, and most cover some or all of the range, developing expertise in particular areas.

There is a far broader range of educational material published than most people realise, some of which crosses over into other areas of publishing such as general publishing. (For example, much of the literature prescribed at secondary school level consists of books published initially for the general market, like Margaret Craven's *I Heard the Owl Call my Name*.) The categorisation publishers give their books depends largely on whether they are sold through educational, academic or general bookshops, or through other distribution outlets.

The following range of material is published for schools, in some or all of the 11 main languages spoken in South Africa:

- core textbooks: for all school subjects at all levels; usually produced in a series; for examination and non-examination subjects; for teachers' use only or for pupils' use, or as supplementary classroom sets;
- workbooks;
- language series: these may consist of language books, readers, teachers' guides, wall charts, cassette tapes, games, all of which can be used as separate items or as part of a scheme;
- reading schemes: usually to teach reading in a particular language;

- supplementary readers: sometimes supplementary to a particular language course; frequently "stand-alone" to provide extra reading material for classrooms; usually carefully graded in terms of vocabulary and language structures;
- prescribed books (literature prescribed from Standard 5 upwards): novels, short stories, plays, poetry, mixed genre anthologies;
- teachers' guides: for all subjects;
- supplementary books: additional books which a teacher may choose to use in addition to the core textbook, for example, books on media studies for senior secondary students in the English classroom, books about study skills, enrichment materials;
- children's large-format hardcover fiction and non-fiction: usually at primary level, for classroom and school libraries;
- reference books: for example, dictionaries, atlases, or any reference material for classroom and school libraries.

Much of this material is sold through specialist educational bookshops, although some academic and general bookshops stock material which they think might appeal to the general public or to individual purchasers (for example, study guides). The purchasers are the state (through centralised or decentralised purchasing), and pupils (private purchasing).

In addition to educational books published for the formal learning sector, there is an increasing body of material published for the non-institutional, non-formal and informal learning sectors. It consists of:

- pre-school material: fiction and non-fiction; school readiness material for use at home and in edu-care organisations;
- educational material for home use by parents and children: for example, language games, maths puzzles, games developing cognitive skills;
- literacy material;
- adult education material;
- self-instructional material, for example, the "Teach Yourself . . ." series.

It is worth noting that although much of this material exists in English, there is a great deal being quietly published in other

South African languages, which may not necessarily be visible and on display in urban bookshops.

As can be seen from the lists above, "educational publishing" is defined largely by the purposes to which the material will be put, and further defined by publishers according to the distribution channel it follows. For many publishers it is the areas of sales, marketing and distribution which define the range of educational publishing they undertake. Some choose to cater for educational bookshops alone; others attempt to find alternative distribution channels for their material. The decision tends to be based on the size and spread of the publisher's sales force and agents.

Writing educational material

It is not surprising, when one looks at the range of material produced, that most authors and editors of educational books tend to be ex-teachers, who apply their experience and knowledge to the material produced. Generally, a writer of educational material ought to have the following qualifications:

- an intimate and academically sound knowledge of her or his subject;
- familiarity with the various syllabi in use and the methodologies advocated for teaching them—as well as those not advocated;
- experience of classroom practice—invaluable for taking into consideration the range of abilities in a classroom, the aids available to rural teachers, the physical circumstances of many classrooms, as well as the amount of material a class can realistically cover in a given period of time;
- a knowledge of appropriate language levels and the language ability of the intended reader;
- a knowledge of the development of cognitive skills, and ideas as to how these can be taught in various subjects;
- an ability to write clearly and concisely, particularly for expository text;
- an ability to create imaginative and enjoyable material;
- a knowledge of visual literacy: how text and illustration work together on the page to convey meaning.

Such a perfect beast as the writer described above seldom exists, which is why many educational publishers turn to teams of writers (three to five is a workable number) to ensure that such a range of skills is present in the team and evident in the material produced.

Enlightened educational publishing

Planning the perfect team to write the perfect material is one thing; dealing with the realities of political, educational, bureaucratic and financial constraints is another. On the whole, an education system tends to get the quality of books it deserves by the way it structures, interprets and examines the curriculum, by the way it "allows" books into the system and into schools (most education departments operate an approved list of books, to which publishers make submissions), and by its purchasing policies.

Despite these constraints, and the severe financial consequences for non-compliance, it has been and is still possible for educational publishers in South Africa to produce innovative and exciting material that interprets the curriculum in fresh ways. They can also take the initiative in producing experimental material that ends up influencing planning for future curricula. Surprisingly enough, although it tends to be the more enlightened education departments who permit experimentation, pioneering work has been done in some of the most conservative and traditional of the education departments. An example of this is the material produced by the Molteno Project.

This kind of innovative publishing is exciting, if risky. Many do try it, since the most satisfying form of educational publishing is the kind which is both pioneering and successful. Publishers interested in this kind of publishing face the perennial problem of judging where to pitch the material—10 years ahead of its time, five years ahead of its time, or for the moment? Too far ahead may result in financial losses, since no one is willing either to approve or to buy the material, but catering for the status quo may make material seem dated within a few years.

To produce good textbooks for schools, a publisher needs at least three years from the release of the new syllabus to its implementation in the classroom. This allows time for writing, editing, design, production, trialling, rewriting, submission for approval, printing, marketing to schools, ordering and supply. In practice this seldom happens, with publishers often being given only six months to produce books. This is the major reason why poor quality books emerge. Another contributory factor is the way in which the submission system is applied. When the system is fair, informed, open and free of corruption, better quality books result; when it is closed, nepotistic, corrupt, suspicious and more concerned with price than high standards, poor quality books result.

At the time of revising this edition (February 1996) much has changed in the formal educational publishing sector, since the market itself has been changing rapidly. Seventeen different education departments with individual policies, interpretations of syllabi, approved lists, and purchasing policies, have been integrated into nine provincial education departments, but it is yet to be determined whether real power will lie with the provinces or national education. An originally diverse and fragmented market had allowed a diverse and thriving publishing industry to develop.

Any move towards a more centralised system will inevitably reduce the number of "niches" available, and therefore the number of publishers. Since all publishers use various parts of their publishing programmes to subsidise others, this will have an impact on publishing in the rest of the industry.

Another major factor in the development of educational publishing is future language policy, which will have an impact on the range of publications in the various languages. It may well be that a system of subsidisation develops in order to ensure that the numerically smaller languages, where publishing is not economically viable, receive adequate attention and development.

It remains to be said that simplistic generalisations about a complex industry ought to be ignored. It is true that the standard of educational publishing has not, on the whole, been high in South Africa, largely because of the nature of the political and educational system which has given it impetus. However, it is equally true to say that there has been some extremely exciting, innovative work. High quality books have been published quietly in difficult circumstances and in what many consider "closed" markets. It is true that there has been corruption and malpractice in many areas of the interface between educational publishers and departmental officials; it is equally true that many education departments and publishers operate ethically and without resorting to corruption and bribery. It is possible to make a living honourably in educational publishing.

It is as well to bear in mind that in educational publishing, educational principles and business principles co-exist in a symbiotic relationship: one cannot exist for long without the other. Commercial publishing houses might put their duty to shareholders and employees ahead of their duty to education, while non-commercial publishing houses might put education first; but both, in the end, have to ensure that commercial and educational requirements are met. There are as many educationists as business people in educational publishing. In some publishing houses, one or the other type may predominate; in the best, there is a balance between the two. As someone once said, "The first duty of a publisher towards an author is to remain solvent!"

South Africa's history of a segregated education system with gross inequalities in state expenditure per capita on education, with maladministration, and an alarming deterioration in the quality of education provided, has not been one to be proud of. What is urgently needed are good materials to help create the kind of education that will empower the country—materials that are non-racist, non-sexist, instil democratic principles, are educationally sound, appropriate and relevant, and at affordable prices. There is a lot to be done in educational publishing.

Choosing an educational publisher

Choosing an educational publisher for your material is much the same process as for any other publisher:

- know what you want in a publisher;
- find the right publisher for you and your material.

The directory in Part 5 of this book will tell you who publishes what kind of book, but bear in mind that few are purely "school" publishers; many overlap into other areas, and will therefore be able to market your book in those areas. Some are educational, academic and general publishers, with sales forces operating in all three broad market spheres. All will send you a free copy of their catalogue for inspection, which is a useful way of seeing the range of publications. Going to a bookshop to examine a particular publisher's books is a further step in assessing whether the quality and content of their publications match your intentions. Unfortunately public libraries have not stocked a full range of educational books in the past, so they are not as good a source of information on educational books—although this is starting to change.

Just as there is no such thing as a perfect author, there's no such thing as a perfect publisher: some are stronger in one or more areas than others. These are some of the criteria on which you might like to base your final choice, not necessarily in order of priority.

- **Reputation.** What is the publisher's reputation among the general public, booksellers, educationists, academics, and internationally? Does it have a good reputation in the areas important to you?
- **Service.** How does the company treat its authors? Are the staff professional, knowledgeable, courteous, honest, ethical, obsequious to the point of dishonesty, great "lunchers" but poor editors, or known for sharp practices in the trade? Are they willing to tell you both the strong and weak points of your work? Are authors treated as part of the team, and consulted or informed on matters such as the format, design, cover, publicity material? Are they strong on editorial but weak on sales, or the other way around? If you can, contact one or two authors on the company's list for their views.
- **Editorial knowledge, expertise and contribution.** Do the editorial staff (publishing director, commissioning editor, desk editor) understand educational principles, your subject, what is happening in the educational market? Do they offer suggestions for the improvement of the manuscript? Do you feel you could learn from your association with them?
- **Marketing expertise, ability and network.** What is the size of the sales and marketing force? Do the representatives visit educational, academic or general booksellers? If the book has an international market (unlikely for an educational book), does the publisher have international marketing links? What kind of promotional activities does it undertake? Is the author expected to assist with marketing? What will this involve?

- **Financial terms offered.** Will you receive an outright fee or a royalty? (A royalty is always preferable from the author's point of view, if you have faith in the long-term viability and success of your book: the author's and the publisher's interests are then closely linked to the same risks and rewards.) Is the royalty based on the published price or on the net receipts? (The latter is more common these days. The term refers to the money received by the publisher after discounts have been given to retailers. In educational publishing, where a 30 per cent discount to educational bookshops is the norm, a royalty of 12 per cent of published price is the same as 17,25 per cent of net receipts.) Advances are very seldom given in educational publishing, since educational publishers aim only to break even in the first year of the life of a book, and to make a profit in the subsequent seven years of the life of a book. See Chapter 15 for a more detailed discussion of royalties.
- **Speed of production.** How fast and how well can the company produce your book? Is the lead time reasonable? Since publishers usually have full publishing programmes planned a long time in advance, how soon can your book be slotted in, and what priority will be given to it? A smaller publisher might well have an advantage over a larger publisher at the editorial stage, in that they're more flexible and can move faster. However, a larger publisher can offer a larger sales force when it comes to marketing extensively and comprehensively. Using freelancers can help to speed up the editorial process.
- **Quality of publications.** Does your idea of quality match the publisher's? Do they publish books that you consider to be of an acceptable standard? Will they do justice to your book?
- **Size and stability.** The advantage of a small publishing house or a one-person operation may be exceptional service and attention. There will probably be a few carefully selected books in production, and the publisher will be devoting all his or her time to these. The disadvantage of a small company is that it is vulnerable, dependent on a single individual (who may become ill, emigrate, or sell the company), on that individual's having the full range of skills (editorial, design, production, sales and marketing, finance, distribution), as well as sufficient capital and cash flow to be able to pay suppliers and royalties to the author.

The converse is true of larger publishers: you and your book may feel lost among a hundred other books in production and you may not receive so much attention (depending on the individuals you deal with). However, there will be greater financial and human resources (particularly specialists in their fields) devoted to your book, with back-up if required.

- **Ethos or "fit".** This is possibly the most important criterion of all, and a highly subjective area. Do you feel comfortable with the private and the public persona of the publisher? Will you be proud to be associated with the company? Are the individuals with whom you will be working people whom you can trust and with whom you can build a good working relationship? Ultimately, these can only be personal decisions.

Educational publishing differs from general publishing in a number of ways: it's less glamorous (brace yourself for the fact there will probably be no launches or interviews in the newspapers), it's more long-term on a greater number of books (be prepared to revise your work at regular intervals—some series run for ten to twenty years—and to help run training courses if these are required), but it generates a steadier income if your book sells well.

The one exception to this is literature for the classroom, which is something of a wild card in the educational system. For example, an anthology of short stories which is produced specifically for the formal educational market may have exceptionally low or no sales for the first few years of its existence or its entire existence; if and when it is prescribed, it could sell anywhere between 5 000 and 30 000 copies, with top-up stock being re-ordered each year.

8

Tertiary-level publishing

The tertiary market includes universities, technikons, teachers' training colleges, private colleges such as Damelin, and technical colleges. Together they form a market segment that is quite distinct from the schoolbook market. The major difference is that textbooks for schools are normally approved and prescribed on a centralised basis by a selection committee, whereas books at tertiary level are normally prescribed either by individual lecturers or by individual departments within institutions. For this reason the tertiary market has a completely different dynamic from the school market; all the publisher's energy is focused on the lecturing staff at these institutions, since they are both the providers (authors) of published material and the main consumers who determine which books are going to be used in class.

Whereas locally produced books have for years made up the staple of textbooks provided at school level, tertiary level education has been dependent upon imports, initially from Britain but since the Second World War increasingly from the United States. South Africa is not alone in this. American textbooks have over the past 50 years conquered markets all over the world, even in non-English speaking countries. With their enormous resource base and large print runs, American companies can create books and other educational materials with which publishers anywhere else in the world find it hard to compete.

After 1985, American books lost a great deal of market share in South Africa because of the cultural boycott imposed by many of the major American publishing houses. They had been forced into the boycott in their turn by pressure from local and state school boards. American books became very expensive and sometimes difficult to obtain, although they never actually disappeared from the market. After the new democratic dispensation was established in South Africa, the big American companies returned. One after another giants such as McGraw-Hill, Prentice-Hall, Times Mirror and International Thomson set up sales networks in South Africa, in most cases not with a view to publishing in South Africa but to re-establish their overseas product in this market. The notable exception so far has been International Thomson, who decided to enter the market not only as distributor but also as a publisher by buying out the academic division of Southern Book Publishers.

All these companies market their American books in this market at specially low prices. The heating up of competition has led to artificially low prices in the South African academic textbook market (not that students will agree with that statement!), but with the continuing weakness of the rand against the dollar it is doubtful whether such low price levels are sustainable.

Over the last 30 years or so local publications have made major strides into the import-dependent tertiary market. No breakdown of market shares is available, but I would guess that about a third of all tertiary books sold in South Africa are local books—that is, a third of the number of copies sold, not a third of the number of titles sold. For whereas the number of academic books published locally each year is not great (probably no more than a few hundred), they tend to be aimed at the lower levels of the more popular subjects, with the result that the large number of copies sold is out of proportion to the number of titles published. To give you some indication of how disproportionate this ratio is, bear in mind that in excess of 100 000 titles are imported each year for consumption at tertiary level.

Choice of subject

Which subjects are targeted by local tertiary-level publishers? Publishers follow two basic criteria: first, there must be enough students in the subject to justify a reasonable print run, and second, there must be a need for local content in the subject.

Let us examine these two points more closely. Chapter 17 discusses the economics of publishing, and the fact that reasonable print runs are needed to sustain a book, otherwise the book becomes too expensive for the market (see pages 138–142). What is a reasonable print run? In a tertiary context, a minimum print run is probably about 2 000 copies. Most publishers would not want to print stock to last more than two years at the most because of the financing cost involved. That means that a particular title has to sell about 1 000 copies a year to be barely viable. A simple analysis of the tertiary market will show that there are not many subjects with enough students to buy so many books. They will tend to be the more popular subjects at undergraduate level. That is therefore where local publishers will concentrate their effort.

Now for the matter of local content. Subjects like medicine and engineering tend to be universal in their principles; moreover, books for these subjects are complicated and expensive to produce, often requiring expertise and resources which simply do not exist in this country. For this reason not many books are published in these subjects locally. However, in the arts, humanities, business sciences, social sciences, education, nursing and similar subjects there are not only large markets available, but also experts capable of writing textbooks. There is also a great need for local content. A book on human resources management, for instance, needs to contain details of industrial-relations practice and labour legislation in this country which no imported book can provide. The ultimate example of the locally specific book is a legal textbook. Since virtually no other country in the world uses our Roman-Dutch law system, South Africa is totally dependent on its own publishers to provide legal textbooks.

Local publishers of tertiary textbooks tend to be less specialised than in other countries because of the tiny size of the market; nevertheless, there are companies that do have certain clearly discernible strengths or focus areas. For example, Butterworth and Juta are well known as publishers of legal books, International Thomson and Juta as publishers of business science books, David Philip and Oxford University Press as publishers of books on political science, and so on. The catalogues of the various academic publishers are easily available, and a cursory glance at the table of contents will show any prospective author in which areas the publisher is active.

How the tertiary market works

My comments here are specifically relevant to universities, but the system used for other tertiary institutions is very similar.

A university publisher has sales representatives and manuscript scouts (commissioning editors) who regularly visit the various campuses around the country to introduce new material, to persuade lecturers to prescribe their titles and to look for possible manuscripts. Some publishers have a system whereby representatives bring in leads on any forthcoming manuscripts, which are then followed up by the commissioning editors. Competition in this market is strong, and some publishers are aggressive in their drives for new authors. Once a book is published, sample copies are sent out for comment to all relevant departments, in the hope that the book will be prescribed if found suitable.

How does the university publisher decide which textbooks to publish? Normally a great deal of marketing is done before the publishing decision is taken, because an individual publisher will not usually have enough expert knowledge to assess the content of the book. He or she is therefore reliant on others to judge the suitability of the material—in practice, lecturers in the same subject discipline at other universities. If enough of them approve of the book, it will be prescribed in sufficient numbers to warrant publication. If there is no such interest, or if the student numbers are too low, the book will simply not get published.

Because of these constraints, the University of South Africa (Unisa) and larger residential universities such as the Universities of the Witwatersrand and Pretoria are the sources of most textbooks. This is not necessarily because they have the best authors but because they have the largest departments and the largest number of students. It might not be the best system in the world, for it does lead to the publication of some second-rate material. Unlike in the United Kingdom, for instance, merit is not the sole criterion used in deciding which book to publish for universities in this country. On the other hand, it is the only practical way to get anything published, and despite the system a great number of good textbooks are produced. The weaker ones will die an early death in any case—they are removed from prescribed lists as soon as a particular lecturer moves on if they have no real merit.

Problem areas in tertiary publishing

One of the recurrent themes in tertiary-level publishing is the endless argument among universities (specifically lecturing staff), students, booksellers, publishers and importing agents regarding the availability of textbooks in bookshops at critical points of the academic year. The system that delivers books to the student in the bookshop is a complicated one, particularly where the book is an import. There are frequent breakdowns in the system which may lead to a student having to sit an exam without having been able to get hold of a textbook.

Although universities are quick to complain, they are in many cases the culprits themselves, since they often fail to provide complete and reliable lists of prescribed books in time for the next academic year. This problem is more specifically related to book imports rather than local publishing, where sufficient stocks of books are normally readily available, so we do not need to dwell on it.

A feature of publishing in the tertiary market is that many authors play publishers off against each other by holding an "auction" on a particular manuscript and asking various publishers for tenders. The fact that these authors ask for tenders shows that they have no conception of the working relationship between a publisher and an author; they are confusing publishers with printers. Often an academic will give his manuscript to the editor who makes the most outrageous promises at auction. Once the contract is signed and the book in production, it is very difficult for the author to keep the publishing house to such empty promises, made under pressure of competition.

If a university textbook is successful, it will probably need to be revised every three years or so in order to stay current. The author should be aware when giving a manuscript to a publisher that this is not just to be a one-off affair (a one-night stand, as it were) but the start of a long-term commitment. A successful book can easily go into half a dozen or even a dozen new editions over 20 years. With each new edition the author has to deal with the publisher almost as intensively and continuously as if he were publishing the book for the first time. A good relationship between publisher and author is therefore exceptionally important in this area.

Multi-author panels are common for tertiary-level books, by the very nature of the material. The relationship between a publisher and two or three authors can be complicated enough, but in the case of a large panel of 20 or 30 people it becomes impossible. It is then necessary to appoint a managing editor from amongst the authors (sometimes several editors). The task of the managing editor is to co-ordinate work, set deadlines, get contributors to write to the correct length with similar terminology, references, systems and headings, and so on. The managing editor will be the main link between authors and publisher and become a conduit through whom manuscripts and proofs for corrections are channelled. He or she will normally be compensated for the extra trouble by an extra share of royalties.

Photocopying

Photocopying is the single biggest threat to tertiary publishing in this country. It is common on all campuses, amongst both department staff and students, and has been steadily undermining tertiary publishing for years. It deprives the publisher of sales and the author of royalties. Photocopying is such a disincentive that soon some publishers may decide to spend their time and money in other markets.

Problems with photocopying, copyright and the infringement of intellectual property rights are certainly not limited to South Africa. They occur world-wide. South Africa is a signatory of the Berne Convention, and our Copyright Act of 1981 follows the guidelines of the Berne Convention. All books published in this country as well as all books imported into this country are protected by our Copyright Act. Penalties for infringement are very severe but can be difficult to enforce in practice.

Publishing as an industry is of course dependent on respect for intellectual property. No one in their right minds will keep on producing material if it is immediately hijacked by others with no compensation paid. How the publishing and academic communities solve this problem in the coming years will to a large extent determine the fate of tertiary publishing in South Africa.

Changing demographics

The traditionally white profile of the South African student has been changing over the past 20 years, and in another 20 years white students are likely to form only a small percentage of the total student population. These changing demographics have major implications for the tertiary market. For instance, they are having a significant effect on the language in which books are published. For obvious reasons Afrikaans universities have been more keen than English ones to create local material for use by their students, with the result that a large number of the textbooks published were in Afrikaans. Since most other students prefer English as a medium of study, Afrikaans has been losing ground steadily and will probably continue to do so in future. That has certainly been the trend at "bilingual" universities such as Unisa, but even major Afrikaans campuses like Stellenbosch and Pretoria now have a significant proportion of English students.

What about African languages? Although there is far greater emphasis now on African languages than in the old South Africa, it does not seem as if anybody is seriously contemplating using any of the African languages as a medium of instruction at university level. It is therefore unlikely that university textbooks, apart from language studies, will be published in African languages.

Changing demographics affect far more than language. With a greater number of disadvantaged students arriving at universities, there is a greater need for material that is easily understood by such students, especially since they suffer from the double disadvantage of studying in a second language and of coming from a poor educational background in many cases. The discussion on reading levels in Chapter 22 is very relevant here. A great deal of money is spent by universities on bridging courses and the upgrading of student skills, but virtually no attention is paid to upgrading the written communication skills of the lecturing staff. (These skills are often weak to begin with.) It is a feature of academic writing in this country—especially in the social sciences and education—that books are often unnecessarily complicated and unreadable. Lecturers do not write such textbooks for their student audience, as logic would dictate, but to impress their peers in the faculty.

I would like to quote academic and author Alan Clements, Motorola Professor of Computer Science at the University of Teeside. He was discussing what he called the "dog-food syndrome" of publishing as follows:

> Dog food is designed by people, but eaten by dogs. Books are written by academics, produced by publishers, reviewed by academics, but read by students. I bet no publisher ever sends manuscripts first to students to see if they understand them.

Neither, for the record, does any academic.

Imported books are not a great help here either. If they come from Britain or the United States, they are written for an audience whose first language is English. American books written for "freshman" level in the United States still have a reading level beyond that of the average first-year student in South Africa. What we need is locally developed material that is systematically rewritten to communicate in the most effective way possible with the target audience. Few such books exist at the moment; in fact, the debate about this issue has not really started.

Price

In the end, however, the biggest issue facing tertiary textbook publishers in this country is price. It is impossible to talk to a student, lecturer or anyone who is at all involved in tertiary education without the subject of high prices coming up.

At one level, high prices are a reality. It is a fact that over the past two decades printing prices have been escalating steadily, the value of the Rand has been deteriorating against the currencies of the countries from which we import books, and together these two factors have forced up the price of books. Of the two factors, the weakening of the Rand is the more serious, since price levels are generally set by imported books rather than local books, which tend to be cheaper. What can we do about this? Unless inflation and the consequent weakening of the Rand can be eliminated from the South African economy, there is not much that can be done. If the Rand keeps on getting weaker, imported textbooks will continue to escalate in price.

Do the same conditions then apply to local books? Not necessarily. Since the product can be varied, it should in principle be possible also to exert greater control over prices. However, that would require more co-operation among all stakeholders than seems likely at present. There are two possible ways of making local textbooks cheaper: either use cheaper technology and materials or undertake larger print runs.

Cheaper technology

Many academics feel that the answer to reducing book costs must lie in cheaper technology and cheaper paper. Not true. In many cases paper quality is already very close to rock bottom and, anyway, using the cheapest possible paper only makes a difference of 5 per cent to 10 per cent to the selling price. As far as technology is concerned, nobody has so far been able to come up with an improvement on the printing process. Photocopying at this stage is not an economic alternative, except on very small print runs.

A new technology known as "image printing" has been developed recently that makes it possible to print directly from a digital image, obviating the need for film and plate, and allowing smaller runs to be done economically. The technology is, however, still very new to this country and has yet to prove itself in the market place.

A lot of people put great store on Desk Top Publishing (DTP). Yet DTP is really a misnomer, since it refers not to any form of publishing but to a different way of typesetting (see Chapter 16, pages 136–137). It is true that DTP can be faster and more efficient than traditional typesetting, but publishers who have switched over to DTP systems have so far found the savings to be elusive, not least because they have been forced into purchasing expensive computer equipment that needs constant updating and maintenance. In any case, typesetting forms only a small part of the total production cost, which in turn is only a small part of the total costs of the publisher (see Chapter 17). Once again the effect on the final selling price is likely to be negligible.

This is not to say that all such means of reducing prices should not be considered and investigated. What bothers me about these and similar proposals is that they imply that there is some *deus ex machina* (presumably in the form of the State) that can somehow come up with cheaper and better technologies than the free market has been able to. The greatest incentive to publishers to explore all these possibilities is competition, and there is certainly no lack of competition in the tertiary market. If a cheaper way of producing books can be found, it will be found.

It also needs to be added that such an innovation is unlikely to be found in our country in the first place. If there is some technological breakthrough that will allow cheaper reproduction, it is likely to come from one of the major industrial countries and to be established in that market first.

Print runs

There is another element that is far more important and that everyone seems to lose sight of in this debate. It is the question of print runs. If you read through the chapter on costing (Chapter 17) you will see how miraculously prices can be reduced by simply increasing a print run.

It must be remembered that the printing process is only really efficient for large print runs; the larger the run, the more efficient and cheaper the process. Since we have no technology available to replace printing at this stage, we are forced to follow the logic of printing efficiency. To get cheaper books, we need to print more.

The difficulty in doing that, is of course, that you can only print more copies if you can sell more copies. And you can only sell more copies if more lecturers are willing to co-operate, if more departments, faculties and universities are willing to get together to agree on syllabi and on which textbooks to prescribe. As long as every institution reserves the absurd right to use any title from anywhere in the world, our market will remain a small and fragmented one that leads to short print runs and consequently to high prices.

Perception of prices

There is, however, another component to the "high price syndrome" that I would like to point out, and that is that students and staff perceive prices to be high and continually increasing even when they are not. Twenty years ago when I was calling on campuses, at a time when the Rand was 10 times as strong against the Dollar as it is now, the greatest complaint I faced in trying to sell American books was that they were too expensive. We had endless complaints about the prices of our books. In retrospect those complaints were laughable—the books were ridiculously cheap compared to today's prices. However, people believed that they were high.

The same phenomenon has occurred over the last decade. There were periods of a year or two when the value of the Rand did not vary much against that of the Dollar and the Pound, and in those years the prices of imported books remained virtually static. However, the fact that books had stopped increasing in price did not have the least effect on students and staff, who simply kept on complaining that book prices were increasing so rapidly.

Recently, with the return of the major American publishers as discussed before, prices have remained remarkably stable, and are in fact very low compared to the prices of those same books in the United States, but again, the fact that American books are sold here at specially low prices seems to have made no impact on the perception among students that textbooks are unaffordably expensive. Also, the erratic behaviour of the Rand does not bode well for book prices.

High-level academic publishing

I have tried to limit myself so far to a discussion of textbooks for tertiary institutions. True academic publishing is not the same as textbook publishing. There is a huge industry in the UK and the United States that is involved in the publication of academic work—monographs, advanced studies, professional books, and so on. In this regard university publishers play a major role.

Academic publishing remains the poor cousin of South African publishing. We simply do not have the market to support publishing of this type on any scale. Some universities do publish academic works (the university presses of Witwatersrand, Natal, UCT and Unisa for instance, as well as Oxford University Press), and there are a number of academic journals dealing with specific disciplines in which research material is published. By and large, however, the academic is limited in what he or she can publish locally. This may be one reason why local academics so often try to put new research material into what are supposed to be first- or second-year textbooks. The two elements are usually not compatible.

In some cases an academic who wishes to publish research work needs to go overseas to find a book publisher interested in taking on the work. This is a pity, but most of the smaller economies in the world are in exactly the same position.

Getting a tertiary textbook published

If you want to write a textbook for a university or technikon course, the likelihood is that you are a member of the lecturing staff at one of these institutions. In that event you are probably familiar with some of the reps and editors who visit your department. You can either work through them, or simply look up the main publishers in this field in the directory in Part 5, and write to them or phone them.

It is, however, useful to understand what it is such companies would want to know from you. Look at the questionnaire shown in Figure 8.1. This is typical of the questionnaire a tertiary publisher would want you to complete in order to have a clear idea of what your project is about. You may pre-empt the publisher by condensing this information into a concise form and sending him or her that information with your first communication about the project.

Apart from that, there is no real difference in the way you would choose and approach a tertiary publisher, or in the way you would prepare an academic manuscript. The general guidelines given in this book (particularly in Chapter 12) should meet all your requirements.

The future

Some areas of academic book publishing are under threat from electronic publishing. This threat particularly applies to high-level reference works. Indeed, it seems possible that the university library of the future may be an on-line facility rather than a physical space with books on shelves.

However, there is no indication so far internationally that CD-ROM or the Internet will actually replace textbooks. Indeed, in South Africa this is highly unlikely, since the greater proportion of our student population are unlikely to have access to computer facilities on a regular basis.

PROSPECTIVE AUTHOR'S QUESTIONNAIRE

Please return this form to: The Academic Manager
XYZ Publishers
P.O. Box 3103
HALFWAY HOUSE 1685

Would you like to publish a book?

Name: ....

Work address: ....

....

Telephone number: ....

Subject of manuscript: ....

....

For what course (name and level): ....

....

Prescribed market envisaged (student numbers, where and when):

....

....

....

Competing publications: ....

....

Why your work is better: ....

....

....

....

Stage manuscript has reached (planning, halfway, etc.): ....

Extent of manuscript (in number of words): ....

Extent of illustrations: ....

Date when manuscript will be complete: ....

Date when book should be published: ....

Figure 8.1: Sample author's questionnaire for prospective author of tertiary textbook

9

Book club publishing

Mike Jacklin

There are various types of book club distributors in South Africa. Not all of them publish books: most book clubs (for example Leserskring/Leisure Books) only distribute books which they purchase from established publishing houses. They promote titles available from publishers by means of catalogues published at regular intervals. Members of the club either accept the club's main choice, or select another book from the catalogue.

However, another type of book club has long been popular in South Africa: the type that publishes its own books and functions without a catalogue. These publishers need books in various categories to feed their thousands of book club members every month. This provides great opportunities for new writers and illustrators to get published.

Book club publishers tend to specialise in certain areas such as children's fiction and non-fiction, novels and religious books, and they require new titles every month to keep their clubs running smoothly.

Although some book club books sell readily into the general and library market, book club publishers are subject to certain constraints: they publish a book per month for every category of member for whom they cater. In the case of children's books they sometimes publish every book in English and Afrikaans. It follows that there is great pressure on such publishers to produce books on time and that they have to work to a very tight schedule.

Let us consider some other constraints:

- Club members pay a fixed monthly fee, so the publisher is limited to a certain number of pages per book. It is not economical to the book club publisher to publish one book of 48 pages this month and a book of 60 pages next month. Book club members will also object to receiving a thinner book than usual.

- For the same reason book club publishers are limited with regard to the format (size) of their books. They also have to bear in mind that they have to use standard packaging materials, since all their books are sent out by mail.
- Every book club has a set pattern and formula. The members who subscribe to a particular club insist on having a book of that particular pattern and formula. Book club publishers therefore have to restrict their choice of genres: if for example a monthly package consists of a story book, a non-fiction book and an activity book, he or she cannot simply slot in books from other genres.
- Some books have to be rejected because they do not lend themselves to translation into the second language in cases where a book club caters for both English and Afrikaans. For example, where word play forms an integral part of the story, or in the case of poetry, it is difficult to translate such material without losing the flavour of the original.

Authors intending to submit manuscripts to book club publishers have to bear all the above constraints in mind.

Although book club publishers are almost by definition restricted with regard to format, genre and so on, it does not follow that the quality is lower than those of books published in the conventional way. In fact, members are prone to pull out of the book club if they receive a book which is not in line with the normal standard of work produced by that book club, so the publisher has to be extra careful in what he does.

While South Africa has a long history of book club publishing, with many clubs being formed and going out of business over the years, especially in the Afrikaans language market, there are two major current publishers that dominate the market.

The one is Knowledge Unlimited (Pty) Limited which was founded by Daan Retief. Daan Retief established the Daan Retief Kinderklub in 1972 for an Afrikaans readership. So successful was the club that another one for English children, The Young People's Book Club, was created in 1982. Membership of the two clubs grew phenomenally, and quality improved to such a high standard that the Katrina Harries Award of the South African

Institute for Library Information Science for the best illustrated children's book was received several times, as well as awards by the ATKV. The clubs form part of Knowledge Unlimited which is now a joint venture between Mike Jacklin and Time Life. Based in Midrand, the company has diversified into a number of book, music and video distributorships but has maintained the children's publishing division. In 1995 over 60 children's books were published including several from local authors and illustrators. Many titles are translated and published in English, Afrikaans, isiZulu, isiXhosa and Setswana.

The other main book club publisher is J.P. van der Walt and Son, which started operating in 1941 as Springbok Biblioteek, which became Keurbiblioteek in 1946. In 1956 Eike-Boekklub was started, in 1972 Treffer-Boekklub, in 1980 Romankeur, and in 1983 Winkel oor die Pos. In 1983 Uitgewery Bezuidenhout was taken over, and in 1985 President-Boekklub.

The five book clubs in this company annually publish 60 popular novels in Afrikaans, but in addition the company now publishes many other books on any imaginable subject, including children's books, educational books, academic books, recipe books, books on art and self-improvement, history and even crossword guides.

Although the company is now a general publisher across a wide range, it is still a leading publisher of popular novels in book club form. These include romances, mysteries, detective and adventure novels of about 60 000 words aimed mainly at female readers.

A feature of book club publishing is that authors normally receive a one-off cash payment for the manuscript instead of royalties.

10

Publishing overseas

There is one category of book for which you should not bother to approach a South African publisher, but should instead try to get a publisher in the United Kingdom: popular fiction in English. The possibility of getting a popular novel published in South Africa is remote (although not impossible). You would also not be reaching the world-wide English-speaking audience you probably have in mind. You may be better off not going to the South African branches of major British publishers, either. They tend to be strong on selling UK product but weak in acting as scouts for the British editors (my apologies to the few exceptions).

The thing to do is to find yourself a literary agent in London who will get your book placed with a suitable British publisher. A literary agent is a person who acts as conduit between authors and publishers in markets such as the United Kingdom, where there are so many authors and publishers that it is impracticable for them to liaise directly with one another. Despite the title, literary agents handle every type of book, not only literature. Most general books in the United Kingdom go to publishers through literary agents, but literary agents do not operate in the educational field.

Do not attempt to go to an American publisher or literary agent, for they are unlikely to take much notice of you. As far as publishing goes, the English-speaking world is divided into two major markets: the United States on the one hand, and Britain and the Commonwealth (including South Africa) on the other. A convention exists whereby British publishers do not sell books directly into the American market, but sell the American rights to an American publisher instead. The reverse also applies: the American publisher will sell UK and Commonwealth rights to a British publisher.

Since South Africa traditionally forms part of the British market, it follows that a South African author is more likely to get published in the United Kingdom than in the United States. If the book is successful in Britain, American rights will be sold on to an American company by the British publishers. This convention has come under pressure recently with the creation of transatlantic mergers such as HarperCollins and Viking-Penguin, which operate across the world, but it is still strong enough to ensure that most internationally selling South African authors get published in the United Kingdom. (South Africa is in any case far more of a known quantity in Britain.)

To find a literary agent in the United Kingdom, consult *The Writers' and Artists' Yearbook*, published annually by A.&C. Black, or *The Writer's Handbook*, published annually by Macmillan. The latter book has a very useful section on literary agents. It is worth quoting the introduction to this section in full:

> **Making an unsolicited approach to a literary agent**
>
> Any active agent is on the look-out for new talent. It's their seed corn. Fostering and encouraging new talent is an important part of their work. Furthermore, no reputable agent charges a reading fee and authors should never agree to pay one. This system allows an agent to react as briefly or as fully to new work as he or she likes. So don't expect a detailed report as a matter of course.
>
> Most importantly, before approaching an agent you must have completed the work in a draft you are happy with. No agent wants to see a draft you plan to rewrite; and no publisher will commission an unknown author to finish a book.
>
> Agents, however, do have other work to do. So to save their time and yours, follow this simple procedure. Write—don't telephone—to one agent at a time, sending a brief covering letter addressed to the agent concerned. Too often authors send out photocopies addressed "Dear Sir/Madam" so it's obvious all the agents in this book are being approached at the same time. These go straight into an agent's bin. (Do you answer all the circulars that come through your letter-box?) This letter should state who you are and any writing experience (especially professional work such as journalism); and the names of the publishers (if any) who have already declined the work you are submitting. Don't write a blurb. Your novel may potentially be the best since *Gone With The Wind*, but let it speak for itself.

Secondly, send two sample chapters and a synopsis of the rest of the work, together with a note of its length. This should be the first chapter and another (not necessarily the second). It's no good sending only a synopsis as it gives no idea of how you write. All work submitted must be typed double-spaced and on one side of A4 paper only.

Finally, send return postage (and a stamped post card if you want an acknowledgement). Agents can't be expected to subsidise a service they are giving free. They are not the copyright extension of the Citizens Advice Bureau.

Always keep a copy of any material submitted—don't rely solely on registered post or recorded delivery—and allow at least a month for a response.

Distribution overseas

When it comes to overseas distribution of a locally published book, be realistic in what you can expect from a South African publisher. South African educational books, whether at school or university level, rarely travel well out of this country. Non-fiction titles on specifically South African topics become obscure when read out of context. A literary work by a person who is not famous is unlikely to find a taker among overseas publishers. Even South African branches of international publishers may find it difficult to interest their colleagues in other countries in local books, if the topic is too parochial. If it is a title of universal interest, they are likely to want to publish it themselves.

There are some South African publishers, particularly of non-fiction, that exhibit regularly at international rights fairs such as the Frankfurt Book Fair, which takes place in October each year in Frankfurt, Germany. They have networks of overseas publishers and distributors with whom they can work, provided they have a suitable title. However, these are few and far between. By and large, if you go to a South African publisher you are likely to get effective distribution in Southern Africa only.

Co-publishing overseas

Some books lend themselves to international co-publishing more readily than others. Such a book needs to cover a topic that can travel, is not too parochial, and must be of very high quality.

In co-publishing, another publisher in another country buys an entire edition or print run of a particular book from the South African publisher. This is different from a distribution arrangement, where the overseas agent only distributes smaller quantities of the South African edition. An overseas co-publisher will normally publish the book under his own imprint, and will treat it in every way as his own publication. Conversely, many titles "published" in South Africa are in fact not local books at all, but co-published editions bought in from overseas publishers and published under the local publisher's imprint.

A great deal of international publishing takes the form of co-publishing these days. This is particularly true of books printed in full colour, where the costs are so high that only massive runs done simultaneously for a number of different countries and different languages make the books affordable to a publisher in any particular country.

A new breed of publisher, known as a "packager", has even emerged. A packager does not sell books in the normal way to booksellers; instead he only sells finished books to publishers, who in turn sell them to booksellers. No South African publisher is really a match for the large international packagers such as Dorling Kindersley or Colour Library. Many packagers use their own in-house authors and illustrators to create books.

11

Self-publishing

Monica Cromhout

The possibility of self-publishing has probably crossed the minds of most authors at least once. Those authors whose work has been published previously might wonder whether there is more money to be made, more rapidly, by publishing their own books instead of working through a publisher. Would-be writers often find it difficult to find a publisher. From the South African publishers' point of view the decreasing number of readers and book buyers makes publishing an increasingly risky business, and they are becoming more cautious than in the past. As a result, a growing number of writers find that self-publishing is the only possibility open to them.

The advent of the computer technologies of word processing and desk-top publishing, together with developments in printing and binding processes, makes this option more viable and accessible than ever before. Throughout the history of publishing there have been authors who have successfully—and unsuccessfully—published their own works.

The purpose of this chapter is practical rather than philosophical. The debate that rages around the concept of self-publishing, challenging and stimulating as it is, will not be addressed here. We will aim, rather, to provide the author who is seriously contemplating self-publishing with concrete guidance and realistic advice about what can be an exciting and rewarding process.

Numerous factors affect the success or failure of a self-published book, such as identification of the market for the book, the pre-publication planning, and the ability of the author to remain objective about the quality and saleability of his or her own work.

What is self-publishing?

A self-published book, in the context of this chapter, is one where the author, or an individual, rather than a publishing company, carries the responsibility for the financing of the book, as well as for other aspects such as production and marketing. Author-publishing is also known as "private" publishing.

It is important to understand that the term "self-publishing" implies a total publishing process that embraces the writing of the manuscript, the editing, correcting and proofreading of the text and page proofs, the design and production of the book, and finally the storage, marketing, promotion and selling of the book.

From the outset the author-publisher needs to be fully aware of the costs, the pitfalls, difficulties, dangers, and the responsibilities involved in publishing a book. It is a business venture into which the author should enter with a clear understanding of all the implications—as is the case when entering into any kind of new business.

Publishing one's own book can be a joyous, exciting and stimulating process that opens the door to new experiences. A careful, cautious and responsible approach can ensure this result.

Advantages and disadvantages of self-publishing

Like any other human activity, self-publishing has certain pros and cons that are worth considering. Let us first consider the disadvantages:

- **Prestige.** Acceptance of a book by a publisher carries prestige. The obvious implication is that the book is worth publishing. On the other hand, finding a publisher, especially for a first book, can be a difficult, frustrating and time-consuming experience.
- **Quality.** Major publishers have access to professional expertise, and the editing and proofreading should be of high quality. An amateurishly produced book published by the author might look home-made.
- **Marketing.** Publishers have standing and credibility in the market place, and a developed infrastructure to sell and publicise books.
- **Financial risk.** Perhaps the greatest advantage of using a publisher is that he or she then carries the high financial risk that is always attached to any publishing activity.

- **Objectivity.** If you do not subject yourself to an outside judge, you run the risk of putting rubbish on the market because you might not be critical enough of the quality of your own work.

On the positive side, there are certain advantages to publishing your own work:

- **Speed.** If you publish a book yourself, you can devote all your attention to it and get it onto the market in a short space of time.
- **Control.** You as author have control of the publishing and production process, and the appearance and design of the book.
- **Profitability.** The return an author gets from publishing his or her own book is better than the return in royalties he or she is likely to get from a publisher, provided of course that the book is successful in the market place. The income earned by the author will also accrue much quicker than royalties, which are typically paid once a year in arrears.

Pre-requisites for successful self-publishing

The author should have a precise understanding of what he or she hopes to achieve with the publishing venture. If he or she for instance hopes to make money, then the book must have a large and accessible potential market, and there must be adequate capital available to launch a strong advertising campaign. However, the author may merely want to have the work in print for posterity and may not be interested in making any money out of the venture.

Author-publishers must cultivate an entrepreneurial flair, must have courage and be creative, and have a capacity for sustained and independent effort. They must have the ability to plan, and stick to the plan, and to cope with stress and setbacks. They must also be open to feedback and advice, and be willing to adapt and learn from mistakes. In addition, they should display a healthy self-understanding and objective awareness of the dangers of a sensitive ego, and be aware that over-enthusiasm for one's own book may result in an unrealistic belief in its marketability.

There must be capital available for investment in the origination and production of the book, and also in its promotion and marketing. Be aware of the fact that publishing is a risky business and that you might not be able to recoup your capital outlay on the project.

The proposed book must have a clearly identifiable market that can be defined precisely. It is not good enough to say that your market is the "general public" or the "intelligent layman" or any equally vague and ill-defined entity.

Self-publishing is a business venture, and new author-publishers have to go through a steep learning curve. To speed up the learning process, they should become involved in all aspects of the writing, publishing and bookselling world. This involves reading books on the subject, attending workshops, joining associations and groups, and subscribing to relevant publications.

What to publish

Any kind of book could of course in theory be published, but one has to be realistic about the market potential of the different genres. The following pose a high risk to the self-publisher:

- **Fiction (novels and short stories)** is very difficult to sell.
- **Poetry** is written by many but bought by few. Best to do small runs for family and friends.
- **Children's books** mostly fall outside the reach of the self-publisher because the illustrations need to be in colour, making it far too expensive for a private publisher to produce.

Other books lend themselves far more readily to exploitation by individuals:

- **How-to and self-help books** are probably the best bet for the author-publisher. The topic defines the market, which can therefore be targeted more easily.
- **Informative books.** Depending on the information, these may work well, especially if they are topical.
- **Life stories and biographies** can be quite successful and can be creatively marketed.

A general rule is to stay away from books that require full-colour treatment and have a high design content, since these invariably cost a few hundred thousand Rand to produce.

Important considerations

Once you have decided to publish your own book, there are a number of decisions and choices that must be made as you work through the publishing process.

- **Why do you want to publish your book?** If you believe that your book is a road to wealth, you are on the wrong road. Abandon the project, and try another way to generate money. If, however, you wish to experience the pleasure of having your work in print, or believe that you have a message or information that is worth sharing with others, or you want to leave behind your own story, and will be happy to at best cover costs, and provided you are not afraid to risk the possibility of losing the money you invest, it is worth continuing.
- **How much money, time and effort are you prepared to invest?** The amount of money you invest will impact on the quality and quantity of the book you publish, and the amount of time and effort you give to marketing will largely dictate the financial success of the book.
- **Who will buy your book?** Where are the potential readers? How will you let them know about your book? What channels of distribution will you use to reach them, and how much will they be prepared to pay for your book?
- **Who will you use to print your book and how much of the work are you able to do yourself?** You can work directly with a printer near you who is able to print books, or you can use the services of a support publisher who specifically offers a service to author-publishers. A support publisher may be hard to find, but they are on the increase as technology makes it more possible for individuals to gain expertise in the broad range of processes that make up the publishing process. Be careful, however, of using someone who does not have as much experience and know-how as you need.
- **Who can you approach for the best advice and support?** A printer is unlikely to be in a position to offer support and advice regarding your manuscript, the design of the book, and its marketing. He will give you exactly what you want, but is usually not in a position to guide you. You, the

author, can manage well provided you have the necessary skills, knowledge and contacts.

- **What should your book look like?** The amount of money you invest will largely dictate the look of your book. Visit a bookshop and examine current designs. The design of the book should be inviting to the eye. Your reader should not be daunted by blocks of tight, tiny text locked within narrow margins. If you need to cut costs by reducing the number of pages in your book, cut the number of words rather than squeezing the margins or reducing the font size. Allow enough leading between lines. Bear your reader in mind—as much as you did when you wrote it—while you plan the design of your book. Magnificent prose will not bear the strain of poor layout.

Costing the book

You should be aware from the outset how much can be invested, and possibly lost, in self-publishing a book. It is also important to understand how the costs are made up, and that you will get what you pay for. A book produced as economically as possible will look and read like a cheap book. Try to achieve the highest quality possible with what you have.

The cost of self-publishing is affected by the—

- length of the book, i.e. the number of pages;
- print run—the more copies you print, the lower the unit cost;
- type and quality of the binding, paper, cover material, dustjacket, etc.;
- cost of copy-editing and proofreading;
- type of illustrations used: photographs, line drawings, etc.;
- use of colour—every extra colour used increases the cost of the book.

As a rough guide, the most economically produced, 100-page, folded and stapled book with a single-colour, unvarnished cover, edited and proofread by yourself, could cost around R10–R15 per book for 100 copies, while 100 copies of a hardcover, stitched book of the same length, with text edited and proofread by professionals, could cost anywhere up to R200 or more per book. As a self-publishing author, therefore, you must cut your cloth according to what you have, and negotiate at every stage.

Also consult Chapter 17 in this book on how a book is costed.

Preparing your manuscript

Once your book has been published and is out in the market place, it cannot be taken back. It lasts for a long time, so get your text right the first time. Develop the habit of placing a guard on your ego, and do not let it run away with you. Ask honest and expert people for an evaluation and for suggestions, and be prepared to listen and act accordingly.

Obviously your book must be well written, readable, and meet the minimum standards of good style, grammar and editing. Get your facts straight. Do not skimp on research and accuracy. There are numerous books and courses available to assist in the writing process, which will not be dealt with in this chapter. When typing your work on the word processor, use the simplest format, without underlining or using bold, italics or paragraph alignment. Be meticulous about re-working and polishing your manuscript before submitting it for typesetting. Use another pair of friendly eyes to proofread. Any corrections to be made at page-proof stage cost money!

You will find *Part 3: How publishing works* and *Part 4: How to prepare a manuscript* in this book very useful.

Marketing and selling your book

No matter how good your book may be, and regardless of its price, the market will not rush to buy it if they do not know about it, and are not continuously reminded of it. Bringing your book to the notice of your buying public could, and should, become a way of life. Start networking and speak with confidence about your work.

A marketing plan must be drawn up even before you publish the book, and must include a definition of who your potential buyers and readers are. What are their age, race, sex? Where do they live and work? What language do they speak? How well do they read? How much will they be prepared to pay? How will they hear about the book? The marketing plan should also include events, dates, venues, media contacts, promotional materials, review copies, interviews, paid advertising, order forms, etc.

Read books about the specifics of drawing up a detailed marketing plan, and apply that knowledge to the marketing of your own book, adapted to your budget. There are also books specifically about the marketing of books, and the Publishers Association of South Africa offers a course in book marketing.

You can also consider starting a mail order business, with your book as your first product. You may add more of your own books in the future, and could expand to other products. The more books you have out in the market, the higher your income. Read books on the mail order business for ideas and guidance.

There are many potential outlets for your book apart from bookshops:

- **Non-book trade outlets** such as curio shops, nurseries, sports shops, craft markets. The number of potential outlets are endless, but depend on the specific nature of your book. Think creatively about the appropriate display of your book.
- **Groups and associations.** Find and use appropriate mailing lists, and distribute promotional material and order forms to the members.
- **Libraries.** These are major book buyers in South Africa.
- **Book catalogues.** Look out for them and make inquiries about having your title included.

But before you even attempt to sell your books through the above outlets, you have to bring them to the attention of the public. There are a number of marketing strategies you can employ to achieve that:

- **Book reviews** are an accepted and valuable way to let the public know about the book. You have to submit copies of your book together with a covering letter to those publications in which you think a review should appear.
- On the **last page of your book** you can put details of the price and ordering procedures for other books you may have published.
- Offer to give **free talks** and run workshops where possible. Always have copies of your book on hand to sell.
- **Press releases** to the media can be very effective, especially if they are professionally done and you know people in the media. Make yourself available for **interviews** on television and radio, and in newspapers and magazines.

Responsibilities of the self-publisher

Anyone entering the world of publishing as a producer of books carries a responsibility to create the best quality of book possible. This applies particularly to the quality of the information and the written text. Reducing the quality of paper or binding may be excusable, but not poor quality of writing style, grammar, proofreading, and of course, accuracy.

Self-publishers are responsible first of all to themselves, and then to other self-publishers, all of whom are aware that they face an uphill struggle to establish the credibility of privately published books. Unfortunately the damage to the cause of self-publishing of one sloppily produced book far outweighs the positive impact of one perfect book. If you plan to have your book out in the general market place, it should *not* look sloppy or home-made. You do not necessarily need to spend a great deal of money, but you do need to devote extra care and be open to advice and criticism.

There are two legal requirements linked to publishing. You have to acquire an ISBN (International Standard Book Number) for each book you publish, and submit a complimentary copy of the book to each of the country's five legal deposit libraries. The State Library in Pretoria can provide you with details of both ISBNs and legal deposit libraries. Bar-coding is not a legal requirement but many bookshops (including the CNA) will not purchase any books without bar-codes. A serious author-publisher may also want to consider registering as a VAT vendor.

In the end it is the author-publisher's attitude and capacity for sustained effort that will lead to success. Launching into self-publishing is an investment in a life experience, rather than a money-spinning opportunity. Be prepared to face with confidence and openness the vestiges of prejudice against self-publishers that still exist. Do not pretend to be anything other than an author-publisher. You have the right to publish and be proud of your own work, in the same way that any artist has the right to create and promote his or her own work.

Part 2

How to find the right publisher

12

How to choose and approach a publisher

You will have realised by now that books can all be classified into broad categories (general, school, and so on), and that your approach to a publisher is going to be determined to some extent by the type of book you want to get published.

Choosing a publisher

Once you are clear about the category to which your proposed book belongs, you can consult the directory in Part 5 of this book to see which publishers operate in that field and find out some basic details about them.

The next step should be to visit as many bookshops and libraries as you can and to look very carefully at the products of the various publishers displayed there. Also scrutinise catalogues from likely publishers. Match up what you have in mind for your book with what those publishers have produced in the past. Look at the prices, dust-jackets, formats and any other features that spring to your attention to make sure that this is a publisher you will trust to handle your work. (You may like to refer back to Kate McCallum's advice on choosing an educational publisher in Chapter 7, pages 60–63.)

Make a list of likely publishers. Approach them one after the other. There will always be the temptation to contact all of them simultaneously, but resist that. If you do approach more than one at a time, be honest about it and tell them that that is what you are doing. Otherwise you may make yourself very unpopular.

New writers of poetry and short stories who have not been published before often find it difficult to get their work accepted for publication in volume form. A way around this is to try to have their poems or short stories published first in a literary journal or magazine. (See Chapter 3 for a more detailed discussion of literary magazines.) Local libraries will probably carry a selection of these magazines, or may be able to provide the names and addresses of others. Once writers of poems and short stories have established a name for themselves through publication in magazines, journals and newspapers, it is then that they should consider approaching a book publisher with their work.

The publishing proposal

It is important to put together a publishing proposal at the earliest stage possible, before you actually write the full manuscript. It could save you from writing a book nobody wants. By submitting a proposal at an early stage, you can get comments from publishers which will enable you to adjust your work in line with market expectations. (Of course, the word "write" at the start of this paragraph, really means typing or, preferably, keyboarding into a word-processing system.)

You will increase your chances of getting published and save everyone concerned a great deal of time if you can put together a package consisting of the following:

- A short covering letter with details of the book, its market and yourself.
- A one-page general summary of the book's range and contents.
- An assessment, as realistic as possible, of who are the potential buyers of the book. Stress the major markets, not the fringe markets.
- A short summary of the details of competing books in this field.
- A detailed outline of the contents. Either give sub-headings under the chapter headings or describe the contents of each chapter in a few lines. The outline must be such that the structure and development of the book are immediately obvious.
- Details of the length of the manuscript (number of words, if possible), the number and kind of illustrations, and what stage you have reached in preparing the manuscript.
- A short description of your own qualifications and experience relevant to the writing of this book. Also provide details of any previous books you may have written.

Before you send in a proposal, phone the publisher and establish which person in the company is the correct one to send the material to. Send it, and then be patient. Commissioning editors are notoriously over-worked and you do not want to spoil your chances of going with a publisher of your choice simply because you could not wait for a little while. Only chase up the publisher after a reasonable period has elapsed.

Assessment and follow-up

If the proposal is of interest, the publisher will probably ask for sample chapters or the complete manuscript should that be available. It may also be useful for you to visit the publisher in person, or to do a presentation (but never undertake this before agreeing it with the publisher first and making an appointment).

It is at this stage that the commissioning editor will begin the process of assessing the quality of the work as well as its sales potential. You may be asked to cut or expand certain sections, or to accept that you can have only a certain section in colour instead of the whole book in colour as you wanted. The commissioning editor may also at this stage refer to other experts in the field to get an opinion of the proposal.

In the case of educational or tertiary books, the decision to publish may depend not so much on what you have written but on whether the book is accepted by an education department or prescribed for certain institutions. In this case you should expect a commitment from the publisher only once he or she has had the opportunity to get a commitment from the educational department or universities concerned.

It is possible that the publisher may come back with a counter-proposal for the book that is so far removed from what you had in mind originally, that you may want to go to another company. Remember, no two editors will have exactly the same response to a particular book. A book that is rejected by one company may be quite acceptable to another. Do not become disheartened too soon. Most successful authors have had books turned down, many several times. And most editors curse themselves for turning down books that subsequently became bestsellers. But if the publisher does not want a manuscript, don't try to bully him or her to accept it. Forced marriages never work.

Only once you have had a clear negative response from your first publisher should you approach the second on the list, and so on. If in the end you can find no publisher at all, you may want to consider self-publishing. But be careful: if no publisher wants the material, it may not be commercially viable. Publishers normally provide three things which few authors have access to themselves: the financing for a project, the technical know-how to create a presentable book, and the marketing infra-structure to sell the book. Think seriously whether you could overcome the obstacles in all three of these areas.

Whatever you do, do not print a book on credit. It is better to wipe out your life savings than to be bankrupted by a print bill you cannot pay.

If you are in the happy position of having found the right publisher for you, who has agreed to publish your book, you should ideally enter into a contract as soon as possible. The publisher's contract is discussed in detail in Chapter 15.

13

How a publisher decides what to publish

One important thing to understand about publishing is that it is an enormously risky business. A new title is a new product, often launched on the market without any prior market research, since publishing the first edition tends to constitute the market research in many cases. To get some idea of the risks involved in publishing—especially in general publishing, where the publisher is not assured in advance that a certain number of students will have to purchase the book—let us consider the process a publisher has to go through in publishing a major new title.

In the first place, developing the book is likely to take at least a year or two. The project will then tie up editorial and production time for a year while in production. The total cash outlay, excluding overhead cost, might run to R300 000 for an important full-colour title. The publisher has no guarantee whatsoever that any copies will be sold at the end of the day. The publishing company, and not the author, will normally carry the full financial risk involved. The publisher will therefore not commit the company to a project unless convinced that there is a need in the market-place for it.

Publishing expertise

Just how does a publisher know that a need exists for a particular book? Any publisher who has been in business for a while will have built up a certain expertise, and will have gathered historical data on which books have worked for the company and which not. If a book on birds, or South African cookery, or rugby has been successful for the company in the past, the publisher is going to be more kindly disposed towards a similar type of book. If it is a brand new idea, he or she is bound to be more careful.

There is a great lack of market information in this country. Few statistics are available as to which books sell how many copies in which markets, what sort of people buy what books, and so on. A publisher is therefore enormously dependent on "gut feel". Gut feel, of course, is just another term for experience. This experience might be either that of the individual person or that accumulated in a company.

The gaining of experience in any field presupposes a measure of specialisation and focus. It is therefore not surprising that each publisher will tend to have an area or various areas of concentration. He or she may concentrate on gardening and cookery, or on natural history, or on social sciences, or whatever the case may be, rather than being all things to all people.

This is a very important consideration for the prospective author. Remember, you want not only a publisher who will accept your book, but an effective publisher who will understand what the book is about and be able to maximise sales. Just as you would not go to a butcher to have your shoes repaired, you would not go to a schoolbook publisher to have your book on South African cookery published. You will rather go to a publisher who has the expertise needed to publish decent cookery books, as well as a marketing mechanism to ensure that your book achieves the widest possible distribution.

It also needs to be said that publishing companies are organisations made up of people who sometimes publish books for irrational and even downright bizarre reasons. Be careful not to land with the wrong company simply because it is willing to accept your book. Make sure that the book is in line with the mainstream of their publishing and that they have the expertise needed to handle it, in terms of both editorial and marketing knowledge.

A business like any other

A publishing house must be run as a business. It has salaries and creditors to pay, it needs to persuade the bank to advance money for development, and it needs to provide its shareholders with a return, otherwise they invest in another business. All publishers, even ones that set out to be non-profit-making, have to get a return from most of their books, or else they will not survive.

Even a small number of wrong publishing decisions can bankrupt a flourishing company.

In any case, a book that does not sell is a useless object. It clutters up the shelves of a warehouse and brings nobody any joy. A year or two later its uselessness is recognised and it is thrown away or turned into pulp.

A fallacy prevalent among would-be authors is the idea that a publisher has some moral obligation to publish a certain book, regardless of whether it has any sales potential. It is difficult enough to get a return from books that have a clear market, are well priced and well distributed. Much better to avoid adding to the mountain of unsold books that are produced all over the world every year.

The publishing decision

To optimise your chances of getting a book accepted by a publisher, try to put yourself in that publisher's position—ask yourself the type of question he or she would be asking and try to provide rational answers in advance. Table 13.1 gives some indication of questions a publisher is likely to consider when assessing a book for publication. Some publishers complete highly complex forms of this type and will not publish a book that does not reach a high enough total score. Other publishers may have no formal system at all to help them make the publishing decision.

What most are likely to do before they finally make up their minds is an initial costing or budgeting exercise on a project, to see whether it is financially viable. The methods used vary from sophisticated computerised accounting operations to simple sums on the back of a cigarette box. All the same, the final decision is still likely to be a subjective judgement to a greater or lesser degree. For this reason, an author should not despair if his or her manuscript is not accepted by the first publisher to whom it is submitted. If your work really has merit, some or other publisher is going to realise it.

Educational books

With educational books—at school or tertiary level—other criteria apply. The most important questions the publisher will ask in this case are likely to be:

- How many students study this subject?
- How well does the book meet syllabus requirements?
- How likely are we to get this book adopted as a prescribed text within an institution or education department?
- How strong is the competition the book is likely to face?

APPROPRIATENESS	Does it fit in with present list?	YES/NO
	Does it represent a new direction we want to expand into?	YES/NO
COMPETITION	Does a similar book already exist?	YES/NO
	If so, is ours an improvement?	YES/NO
SALES	Is there a market for the book?	YES/NO
	Will we be able to sell the print run in the first 18 months?	YES/NO
	Can our sales force sell the book?	YES/NO
RISK	Will the production cost be high?	YES/NO
	Will it take more than a year to earn back the cash outlay?	YES/NO
PRICE	Can we do a high enough print run to get to an acceptable unit cost?	YES/NO
	Is the price of this book significant?	YES/NO
	Are we likely to be able to produce this book competitively?	YES/NO
PRODUCTION	Can our production department cope with this book?	YES/NO
FINANCE	Is the book likely to strain our financial resources?	YES/NO
FINALLY	SHOULD WE PUBLISH THE BOOK?	YES/NO

Table 13.1: Questions the publisher is likely to consider in assessing a book for publication

The method used to decide which titles to publish is therefore likely to be quite different. It is less a matter of judging what the market will like and of "gut feel" than a question of how many students are likely to use the book.

The decision-maker

Which person in a publishing company actually makes the decision regarding what books to publish? The answer to this question depends very much on the structure of the particular company. In a small concern it is likely to be the chief executive. In a larger company, there may be an editor who specialises in a certain field. In most companies it is likely to be a committee decision to some extent.

It is, however, possible to generalise and say that there is usually one person in a publishing company who is the prime decision-maker. That will probably be the person who actually reads the manuscripts and makes a recommendation to publish (to the manager, to the board, or whatever). This person is usually called an editor. The correct name is in fact "commissioning editor", although the word "publisher" is also often used in this country to describe such a role.

The term "commissioning editor" gives a clue to the method used by most publishers to acquire new books.

Commissioning

There seems to be a widespread perception amongst the public that a publisher is a person who reads manuscripts that are submitted by authors, decides whether they are good enough to publish or not, and then gives them to a printer to print. This is a misconception. Most manuscripts are in fact commissioned for a specific purpose by the publisher. Very few final manuscripts received through the mail ever get published. This is because it is unlikely that an author working away in isolation will have a clear concept of what the market needs or wants. That is the publisher's main function, namely to act as conduit between an author and the market.

Most books that are not commissioned will grow out of material submitted by authors, but this material will seldom be used in the form submitted. A proposal from an author might trigger an idea, but the resultant book may be quite different from what the author intended in the first place.

Inexperienced authors generally underestimate the creative role played by the publishing company, and specifically the commissioning editor, in the process of writing a book. A good commissioning editor will direct the author in his or her writing, warn against pitfalls in the road ahead, help the author to meet deadlines, and generally offer encouragement in what is after all a very lonely job. Really good books are normally the result of a close relationship between a commissioning editor and an author. If they respect one another's contribution to the process of making a book, the results can be impressive.

The changing face of publishing

Publishing is an industry that is prone to continual acquisitions, reorganisations, mergers, and so on. That is true not only in this country but all over the world. You may therefore find that the small independent publishing company which impressed you so much when you did your first book is now part of a huge conglomerate when you do your second. Staff changes are also common. The commissioning editor you start off with might depart for greener pastures halfway through the book, or may be promoted sideways or into a position where he or she can no longer be of value to you as author.

These are the risks of the trade; like life itself, nothing is ever static. The intelligent author will try and remain abreast of the latest developments in the company he or she deals with.

14

The people you deal with

If you are an author writing for a publishing house, you are likely to be in contact with the following people at various stages of the publishing process.

Commissioning editor

A commissioning editor (who may alternatively be called a sponsoring editor, acquisitions editor, publisher, publishing director or just editor) is the person in a publishing company who:

- scouts for new authors;
- liaises with existing authors;
- thinks up new projects;
- negotiates contracts;
- assesses the quality of manuscripts;
- generally builds up a list of titles in a particular market niche.

Clearly this person is pivotal in your relationship with a publishing company. Not only is this the person you deal with initially, whose recommendations will lead to your manuscript being accepted or rejected or who may come back to you with proposals for altering it, he—or more likely, she—is going to remain your main contact with the company throughout the life of your book. She will be the one to keep you informed of the progress of the book, send you proofs to read, jackets to check and so on, and who will eventually hand you the finished product.

However, the relationship does not end there. The commissioning editor is likely to remain your main link with the publishing house after publication of the book. She will probably keep you informed of sales (or lack thereof) and will (you hope) eventually discuss with you reprints and new editions of the work. This is likely to be an important relationship, so it helps if you can establish a rapport with your commissioning editor.

Copy-editor

Copy-editors are also known as desk editors, sub-editors or production editors. They are the people who turn messy manuscripts into legible books. They edit books in such a way that the reader will find them easy to understand, that the author's errors are eliminated, and that the typesetter will know what to do with the manuscript. These days "manuscripts" are more likely to come in the form of floppy disks or stiffies, and the copy-editor is as likely to do editing on screen as on paper. Whether on screen or paper, the job remains the same: creating order from chaos.

Many authors (particularly academics) feel that their work does not need editing. Surely they know how to structure material, how to be grammatical, and so on. But any publisher will tell you that every manuscript does need copy-editing. No author, not even the most experienced, is capable of delivering a perfect manuscript. The reason for this is not far to find: people are to a greater or lesser extent blind to their own errors.

So what does the copy-editor actually do? She (virtually always she) checks that the structure makes sense and that arguments are clear; that terminology is suitably explained; that illustrations are correctly placed, clear and useful. She corrects grammatical and spelling errors; eliminates repetition and ambiguity; checks references and footnotes; makes sure that all chapters, headings, sub-headings, figures, tables and so on are correctly numbered; and generally crosses the t's and dots the i's throughout the manuscript. Whereas the author is of course responsible for the creative work in the book, the fresh eye of a good copy-editor will spot all sorts of minor problems.

The copy-editor may be on the publisher's staff or may be a freelancer. In either case, at some stage the author is likely to have to spend some time with her sorting out queries and being forced to face his or her own inconsistencies and carelessness. It can be a humbling experience. However, good copy-editors will never make their authors feel stupid—just safe in the knowledge that they will be saved embarrassing errors.

Production staff

The role of a production manager in the publishing process is to arrange quotes, deadlines and schedules with typesetters and printers, to control the whole production process and to check the quality of the product. He or she is also responsible for the costing of the book. A designer, who may be a freelancer or someone working within the production department, will decide on typefaces and other visual aspects of the book and mark up the manuscript for the typesetter.

Whether you as author deal directly with any of the production people will depend a great deal on the structure of the company and on the nature of the book you are writing. The more complex the book from a production point of view, the more likely you are to have to work closely with production people.

The people working on the production side of a publishing house tend to be highly skilled, technically. This has advantages and disadvantages. The advantages are obvious: you certainly want your book to be put together by experts who understand what it is all about. The disadvantage is that production people, like computer experts, often speak a language of their own that is unintelligible to the layman. In most companies you will never work directly with the production people; the commissioning editor or the copy-editor will act as go-between between the author and production.

Publicist

Companies that publish for the general market will often employ a person who may be known as a publicist or public relations officer, whose function it is to bring your book to the attention of the media. (This function might be carried out by the marketing manager in a smaller company.) The publicist will line up interviews with newspaper and magazine journalists, arrange radio interviews, and generally work towards bringing your book to the attention of the general public. If you are a shy or retiring person, you may find this part of the job a heavy burden to bear.

However, many authors find it is the most exhilarating part of publishing. This is where you are given the opportunity to prattle on about your favourite obsession.

A good publicist is a person to be treasured. She (once again women predominate in this position) has to be able to sum up your personality and your product and match them up with the correct media vehicles. Many of the best authors are relentless self-promoters. This may make them difficult people to work with but is valuable when it comes to getting book reviews and editorial comment. Authors should, however, not attempt to take over the publicity function themselves, even in cases where they are well connected in the media. They should rather co-operate with the publicist and fall in with a carefully designed publicity plan.

Marketing people

Ultimately you want your book to be read by as many people as possible. This is only possible if the publishing company possesses a sufficient sales and marketing infrastructure. The person you are most likely to work with in this area is the marketing manager. He or she is responsible for working out a marketing plan for the book, for launching the book on to the market and for overseeing the various sales activities needed. Normally the marketing manager will welcome any suggestions from the author and, indeed, many authors become important outlets for their own books.

There are two possible areas of friction between the author and the marketing department that you should be aware of. The first is the launch party. Many authors want big and expensive launch parties; they firmly believe that their books will not sell without such a celebration. This is a myth. The major function of a launch party is to make an author feel important. Its secondary function is to keep up the profile of the publisher within the book trade. A launch party will not normally attract coverage from the media. Most journalists would much prefer to have an in-depth interview with an author, rather than attend a cocktail party after hours.

Having said this, there are of course books that are of such a nature and for which the market is of such a type that a good launch party will benefit them hugely. If there is a party, it should be done properly, with no holds barred.

The other area of friction is what I would call "my local CNA syndrome". Almost every author I have ever known has phoned up at some point to tell the marketing department that their book is nowhere to be found in the local CNA. The implication is that the publisher's marketing leaves much to be desired.

What the author should bear in mind is that no publisher has any power over a bookseller. A bookseller will stock only what will sell in the immediate neighbourhood. Even when a chain like the CNA takes the book, it will not necessarily stock the title in all its stores—it will only stock it in those stores where it is likely to sell. Of the hundreds of branches in the CNA chain, only 30 or so in the major centres are really important bookshops. Neither the CNA nor any other bookshop is going to change its system of distributing books for the sake of the author who lives in Wakkerstroom or Pofadder. Do not expect your publisher to put a gun to a bookseller's head and force him to stock a book.

A final word of caution: do not, repeat, do not pester all the bookshop managers in your vicinity every time your book is out of stock for a few days. They do not take kindly to it, and might deliberately avoid restocking your book if you make too much of a nuisance of yourself.

Part 3

How publishing works

15

The publishing contract and royalties

Please note that in the following chapter, the author is referred to as "she" and the publisher as "he", rather than the more clumsy "he or she" in every case. Of course the publisher may be a woman and the author a man, or both may be women or both may be men.

Most publishers have standard contracts which set out the basic agreement with an author and procedure to be followed in the publication of a book. It is to the advantage of both author and publisher to sign an agreement as early as possible. The author will then have the reassurance at an early stage that her labours will not be in vain and that if her manuscript needs amendment, the necessary input from the publisher can be obtained early on. From the publisher's point of view, it enables him to plan ahead and budget well in advance. Beware of a publisher who refuses to enter into a legally binding contract.

While most publishers work with a standard agreement, many of the clauses are negotiable. If the author feels strongly about a particular point, she should not hesitate to raise it with the publisher. Neither should she hesitate to object to anything she finds unacceptable, or to query anything she does not understand. There will be some clauses on which a publisher would refuse to negotiate because they contain principles that are simply too important to compromise. What is important is that the parties should agree to a contract they are both happy with. Sometimes it is better for one of the parties to walk away from the agreement rather than tie herself down to a contract she is not comfortable with.

What follows is a discussion of a publisher's contract on a clause by clause basis. The sample contract examined here is the standard one used by Southern Book Publishers. Contracts issued by mainstream publishers in South Africa are much alike. They may not contain the exact same clauses, but the same or similar principles will be contained in any author's agreement. It also needs to be said that the agreements used by most South African publishers do not differ in any substantial way from those used in the major publishing countries of the world.

1. **Publisher's undertaking.** The publisher shall produce and publish the work at his own risk and expense within a reasonable time after the delivery by the author of the complete typescript or disk acceptable to the publisher and ready for the press.	Please note the following: • The publisher clearly undertakes that he carries all financial risk in the venture. • Many authors object to the term "reasonable time", but remember, if you insist on a specific publication date or period the publisher will in turn insist on specific deadlines for each stage of the process in which the author is involved. The point is that the publication period depends not only on the publisher but to a large extent on the author herself.
2. **Right to publish.** The publisher shall have the exclusive right to produce and publish the work and any subsequent edition or translation thereof throughout the world.	This clause amounts to a temporary cession of the author's copyright to the publisher. The following points are important: • The rights ceded are not only for this edition but also any subsequent edition. • If this clause remains unchanged, it gives the publisher control of all translations of the work.
3. **Translation into another language.** If a translation is done into any other recognised language used in the Republic of South Africa, a separate agreement between the publisher and author shall be prepared for such translation; alternatively the publisher may commission someone to do	This clause specifically deals with translations into any South African languages, and is not to be confused with translation into foreign languages.

the translation and deduct the translation costs from any royalties due to the author, unless another arrangement is made to which the parties mutually agree in writing.

4. **Competing works.** The author shall not arrange for the publication, other than by the publisher or with his agreement in writing, of any abridgement or expansion of any substantial part of the work, or of any other book of a nature likely to compete with the work, or of other books in a series if this work should form part of a series.

This clause is absolutely essential to protect the publisher's rights. Without this clause the author would be at liberty to supply essentially the same material to two different publishers to produce competing books. Normally, however, the publishers have no objection if material from the book is used in other forms that do not compete with the book itself. For example, a chapter in a university textbook might also be published as an article in a scholarly journal. The journal presents no competition to the book sales and does not detract from them so the publisher cannot suffer any damage as a result. The acid test here is whether any sales are lost.

5. **Subsidiary rights.** The publisher shall have control of all subsidiary rights arising from the work, and shall pay the author 50% (fifty per cent) of all sums received by the publisher for such rights. Subsidiary rights include, but not by way of limitation, serial and extract rights, foreign language translation rights (other than as specified in clause 3), motion picture, radio and television rights, book publishing rights leased to another publisher, anthology and quotation rights and the right leased elsewhere to reproduce the work or any part thereof by sight or sound or a combination of both, or electronically.

The clause covering subsidiary rights here is quite compact. In many publisher's contracts this particular clause would cover a number of pages and different percentages might be specified for each type of right. For instance the author might earn 30 per cent on serial rights, 70 per cent on video rights, etc. If the sale of such rights is a serious possibility, it is worth negotiating this particular clause in detail. With most books published in South Africa, however, subsidiary rights do not play an important part and that is why this clause is kept as simple as possible.

6. **Author's copyright.** The copyright of the work shall remain the property of the author, who hereby empowers the publisher to take, in the author's name but at the publisher's expense, any action, legal or otherwise, that the publisher may consider necessary to protect his rights under this agreement.	The publisher needs to be granted the right to prosecute people who infringe the copyright of the work, for instance by photocopying a textbook for use by university students.
7. **Copyright notice.** The publisher undertakes to include the necessary copyright notice in the work and any reprint or new edition of the work.	
8. **Control over format.** The publisher shall control the format of the work and of its jacket. While the author will be consulted where it is reasonable to do so, all decisions regarding the production, publication, copy-editing, typography, illustration, advertising, price, title, revision, reprint, print run and terms of sale of the work shall rest with the publisher.	Many authors are not happy with this clause, since it seems to place total control of the work in the publisher's hands. In practice, most publishers do consult the author on every aspect of the book's production and sale, otherwise the author is not likely to remain in that publisher's stable for very long. Few publishers will be willing to compromise on this clause, which is designed to protect them from the idiosyncrasies of the type of author who, for example, insists that her talented niece of fourteen should do the cover design.
9. **First refusal rights.** The author agrees to submit her next manuscript to the publisher for consideration to publish. The publisher shall be allowed a period of three months from receipt of the manuscript to consider the suitability of the new work; if the publisher decides not to publish the work, the author will then be free to offer it to any other publisher.	While a first refusal right clause is very common in the standard agreements of South African publishers, there is normally no great pressure on the author to agree to this. If the author does not feel comfortable with this clause, she should simply scrap it.

10. **Royalties.** During the legal term of copyright of this agreement the publisher shall pay to the author on all copies of the work sold, the royalties set out below. All royalties shall be calculated on the net receipts (i.e. the published price minus trade discount) of the work.

Please see the notes at the end of this chapter regarding royalties (pages 123–125).

(a) On all copies sold, except as specified in (b) and (c) below, a royalty of _______ divided as follows: _______________

____

(b) In the event of an edition of the work being specially printed for another publishing company outside the publisher's normal domestic market of Southern Africa, or on copies of the South African edition of the work sold for export outside the publisher's normal domestic market of Southern Africa, an export royalty of 10% (ten per cent).

(c) In the event of the publisher selling a quantity of books at bulk discount to a book club, a book club royalty of 10% (ten per cent).

The reason why lower royalty rates (normally 10 per cent of net price) are payable on book club and export sales is that these sales require far higher discounts than are usual within the book trade. A normal book club discount will be in the region of 68 per cent, and a normal export discount will be in the region of 65 per cent. It is immediately obvious that the publisher makes precious little money out of this deal. Neither can the author expect to receive too much.

This raises the question: why bother at all? The reason we bother with book club and export sales is that they enable the publisher to increase his print run, thereby reducing the unit cost of the book and therefore the retail selling price. Quite often major publications are only made possible through bulk book club or export deals which enable the book to be sold at a reasonable price through the local bookshops.

(d) Where a sliding scale of royalties is paid, the scale will start anew with each revision of the work.

The scale of royalties starts anew with each revision of the work because the publisher will reincur all the same origination cost (such as typesetting and design) in the case of a new edition as he did with the original book.

11. **Date of royalty payments.** Accounts shall be made up annually to March 31st, delivered during the following July and settled by cheque or its equivalent with the accounts, provided that payment for amounts due because of sales of the work has in fact been received by the publisher at the time of paying royalties to the author.

Some publishers in South Africa pay royalties twice a year, but once a year is more common. It is very difficult to get a publisher to vary this date, since that throws out his accounting systems.

12. **Review and inspection copies.** The publisher may at his discretion present copies of the work to the media, to lecturers or to other persons or organisations through whom advantageous publicity or adoptions may be gained. Copies of the work so presented shall not be reckoned as copies sold.

13. **Author's copies.** The author shall on publication receive six presentation copies of the work and shall be entitled to purchase further copies for personal use at the normal wholesale price. If more than one author is involved the number of presentation copies shall be six in total, except where there are more than three authors, in which case each author shall receive two copies of the work. The author shall be entitled to two presentation copies of any subsequent edition of the work.

Author's copies are solely for the author's personal use and should not be confused with promotion copies. The publisher will normally supply promotion copies free of charge to reviewers and other "useful" people.

14. **Remaindering.** Where copies are sold off as remainders at more than cost, the publisher shall pay the author 10% (ten per cent) of the

Some authors get upset when their books are remaindered (sold off very cheaply to reduce stocks). Remember, publishers will only remainder a book net receipts from such sales. Where copies are sold at cost or less than cost, no payment shall be made to the author.

once they have given up completely on selling the book at the normal price. There is a need for a clause such as this, otherwise the publisher will be compelled to keep the stock in his warehouse for ever.

15. **Author's warranty against plagiarism, libel and obscenity.** The author hereby warrants to the publisher that the work does not violate any existing copyright and that it contains nothing obscene, indecent, or of a defamatory or libellous nature. The author indemnifies the publisher against loss, liability, injury or damage caused to the publisher or any other persons from whatsoever cause or howsoever arising, including but not limited to any breach by the author of the warranty. The publisher reserves and the author accords him the right to alter the text of the work as may appear appropriate for the purpose of removing any passage or statement therein which in the publisher's discretion or on the advice of his legal advisers may be considered objectionable or actionable at law.

This clause is self-explanatory.

16. **Publisher's liability for loss or damage.** The publisher is not liable in any way for the loss of or damage to typescripts, disks, illustration materials, photographs, transparencies or the like. The only exception is colour work lost or damaged on the premises of the Publisher.

It is normal for publishers to insure colour photographs and artwork for an amount to be negotiated with the author, but not other material.

17. **Extent and form of typescript.** The author shall supply the typescript on double-spaced A4-size sheets of 300 words per page, typed on one side only. Alternatively the author shall provide a computer disk or disks of the manuscript, together with a hard-copy print-out thereof. The typescript shall consist of the following:

(a) A maximum of ______ words.
(b) A maximum of ______ black and white line illustrations.
(c) A maximum of ______ black and white photographs.
(d) A maximum of ______ colour transparencies.
(e) A maximum of ______ colour plates.
(f) A maximum of ______ maps.

Note that only maximums are specified and no minimums. For some bizarre reason all authors tend to produce too much material. This is the publisher's attempt to pin down the author to an agreed-upon extent.

18. **Deadline.** The author undertakes to deliver the complete manuscript of the work, including illustrative material, ready for the press on or before the following date: ______________19_____
In the event of this condition not being fulfilled, the publisher shall be at liberty to decline to publish the work, in which case this agreement shall become void, but the author shall not be at liberty to publish the work elsewhere without first offering it to the publisher on the terms of this agreement.

Deadlines work best when they are set down by the authors themselves. Most authors run slightly over the deadline in practice, but having deadlines is psychologically important. The main purpose of this clause is to prevent the publishers from having to publish a book that may be hopelessly out of date by the time the author finishes it.

19. **Quality.** If the quality and content of the work as evidenced by the typescript and the illustrations are in the opinion of the publisher not

The purpose of this clause is to protect the publisher against rubbishy manuscripts. It does not mean the manuscript has to be absolutely perfect in of a sufficient standard to justify the publication in that form, the publisher may elect either:

(a) To decline to publish the work, in which event he shall send written notice of his decision to the author within three months of receiving the typescript and illustrations, and whereupon the publisher shall have no further obligation to the author in terms of this agreement; or alternatively

(b) To request the author to revise the work into such a proper form as may be reasonably required to make it publishable in the publisher's opinion.

every way, merely that it has to be in line with what was initially discussed.

20. **Copyright material.** Any fees paid by the publisher for the use of copyright material in the work shall be charged against and deducted from any sums due to the author.

In practice there could be considerable negotiation around this clause, depending on the type of book. In the case of anthologies, this clause becomes a critical one.

21. **Illustrations.** If the publisher and author agree that illustrations are needed in the work, the author shall supply for the publisher's use, with the written permission of the copyright holder, free of charge and copyright fee, suitable photographs, pictures, diagrams, line drawings, maps and other material for illustrating the work. Such materials supplied by the author shall remain her property and shall be returned to the author after publication of the work, if so required. Where the publisher

The question of who is responsible for illustrations and who should pay for them is subject to a great deal of negotiation. Much depends on the kind of book. In the case of a photographic coffee-table book, for instance, it is clearly incumbent upon the author to provide the photographic material. In the case of an academic book with some flow diagrams, however, it is quite normal for the author to provide rough illustrations and for the publisher to have these drawn at his own cost. Again the golden rule is: negotiate a fair deal for both parties.

arranges for the preparation of such illustrations on the author's behalf, the publisher is hereby empowered to charge the cost of such illustrations against royalties due to the author.

22. **Reading of proofs.** The author shall read and correct proofs of the work as required by the publisher and shall return them to the publisher within a reasonable time of their receipt.

See the note referring to the phrase "reasonable time" in Clause 1.

23. **Author's corrections.** The publisher may deduct from any sums due to the author all costs of author's alterations to proofs (except corrections of printer's errors).

Take careful note of this clause! Under its terms the publisher is at liberty to penalise the author for any corrections she makes at proof stage that are not due to printer's errors. If you ignore this clause, you may find yourself with no royalties left at the end of the day, and with no one to blame but yourself. Most publishers build in a penalty clause of this type, to stop the author from rewriting a manuscript at proof stage.

24. **Index.** The author agrees to supply the publisher with an index, or bear the cost of having one compiled, if in the opinion of the publisher an index is desirable.

With powerful word-processing programs freely available, the question of indexing is less of a problem than it used to be. Also see the discussion of indices in Chapter 25.

25. **Disks.** If the author provides the work in the form of disks, she will also provide hard copy to go with it, and the author hereby warrants to the publisher that her disks are virus-free.

26. **Subsequent editions.** The author agrees to edit and revise, if necessary, every subsequent edition of the work. In the event of

In the case of books that are likely to have a long life, such as dictionaries, it is essential to talk through the implications of this clause. The "author" in the author failing, or by reason of death or otherwise being unable to edit or revise the work or supply material as required, the publisher is hereby authorised by the author to employ another person to supply new material and to deduct the cost of such employment from the royalties payable to the author.

this case might be a large panel of people, some of whom may retire, die or whatever by the time future editions need to be prepared. It is important that everybody has a clear understanding of the implications of this clause, since it can severely affect the future estate of the author.

27. **Termination of agreement.** If the publisher fails to comply with any of the provisions of this agreement within three months of receipt of written notification from the author to remedy such failure; or if an order is made for the liquidation of the publisher, whether provisionally or finally (other than a voluntary liquidation for the purpose of reconstruction only); or if after the work has gone out of print the publisher has not within twelve months of a written request from the author issued a new edition or impression, then the author shall be entitled on written notice to terminate this agreement without prejudice to any claim which the author may have either for monies due or damages.

The termination clause tends to be very similar in most commercial contracts. Make sure that your agreement with the publisher does spell out in what circumstances the agreement may be terminated.

The rest of the contract is mostly the normal legal gobbledegook to keep the lawyers happy.

A note on royalties

To the author, the royalty clause is undoubtedly the most important clause in the contract, since it spells out what compensation she will be entitled to receive for her work.

Royalties are the normal form of payment used by publishers the world over. They force the author to some extent to share in the risk of the publication, and bind the author to the publisher with a view to future revisions. Royalties also have a great advantage for the publisher in that they do not become a cost unless the books are actually sold. The advantage to the author is that it is possible to earn far greater amounts of money in the long term from a royalty agreement than from a one-off payment. This is particularly true if the book is a real success.

The author should make sure that she understands exactly what is implied by "royalties on the net receipts", or the alternative, which is "royalties on list" or "published price". In our company (Southern Book Publishers) we pay royalties on the net price of the book, that is the retail price less VAT and less discount to the book trade. However, some publishers pay royalties on the list price, i.e. the actual retail selling price of the book (less VAT). The tendency has been in recent years increasingly to pay royalties on the net price of a book. This trend is caused partly by the fact that retail price maintenance has been declared illegal in this country, which means a bookseller can sell a book at any price he fancies in the shop. The whole concept of a retail selling price is put in doubt if it can vary from shop to shop.

To the author it does not really matter whether royalties are paid on list or net, as long as she understands what she is getting. Table 15.1 sets out a comparison: an author who is paid a royalty of R10 on a R100 book could be receiving various percentages of royalty depending on whether the royalties are paid on the list price, a net price with 30 per cent discount (typical of an educational book), and a discount of 40 per cent (typical of a book for the general market).

The actual percentage of royalties varies enormously according to the type of book and from one publisher to another. My own estimate would be that a generally accepted average for the industry would be in the region of 15 per cent of the net price of the book.

I am often asked the question, "Does it really pay for an author to get a book published? Does she get enough money out of it?" That is a bit like asking, "How long is a piece of string?" In a country with as small a book market as ours, the average author should not expect to make too much out of royalties, although

	Royalties paid on list price	Royalties paid on net price (30% discount)	Royalties paid on net price (40% discount)
List price (selling price less VAT)	R100	R100	R100
Average discount		30%	40%
Net price		R70	R60
Royalty percentage	10%	14,3%	16,5%
Royalty in Rands	R10	R10	R10

Table 15.1: A comparison of royalties paid on list and varying net prices

there are some authors who earn a great deal—mostly writers of textbooks, especially school textbooks. There are, however, very few people indeed that can make a full-time living out of writing books. It is in essence a part-time hobby, and the returns are often not in proportion to the amount of time and effort put into the task.

It is also true that many people write books not primarily to earn money but because they want to see their names in print. Some are not interested in money at all, but simply want to share their thoughts with a wider audience. Most publishers would, however, agree that whereas many authors write for the love of their subject, there are few things that motivate authors over the long term to the same extent as money. In this authors are no different from anyone else.

16

The publishing process

The publishing process is a long drawn-out affair that commonly takes from six to nine months. Many first-time authors are surprised and dismayed by the length of time it takes to get a book on the market. This chapter briefly describes all the procedures involved; once these are understood, it becomes easier to understand why the process takes so long.

Figure 16.1 is a diagrammatical representation (flow chart) of the conventional publishing process (conventional as opposed to DTP, which will be discussed further on in the chapter—see pages 136–137). It may be helpful to refer to this diagram as the various stages are discussed.

Assessment and revision of project

The key person on the publisher's side in this part of the process is the commissioning editor. In this stage the author submits an outline or a manuscript, which is subjected to scrutiny and comment (as has been discussed in previous chapters). He or she revises, cuts or expands the material, and resubmits it until all parties are satisfied that the manuscript contains what it should.

The manuscript

Please bear in mind that the term "manuscript" is commonly assumed to include all illustrative matter as well as preliminary matter such as the introduction, table of contents, and so on. If the book is of a photographic nature, then photographs form part of the manuscript.

Many authors hand in part manuscripts in an effort to save production time. Whereas time pressures often force the publisher to accept the manuscript in sections, it is much better

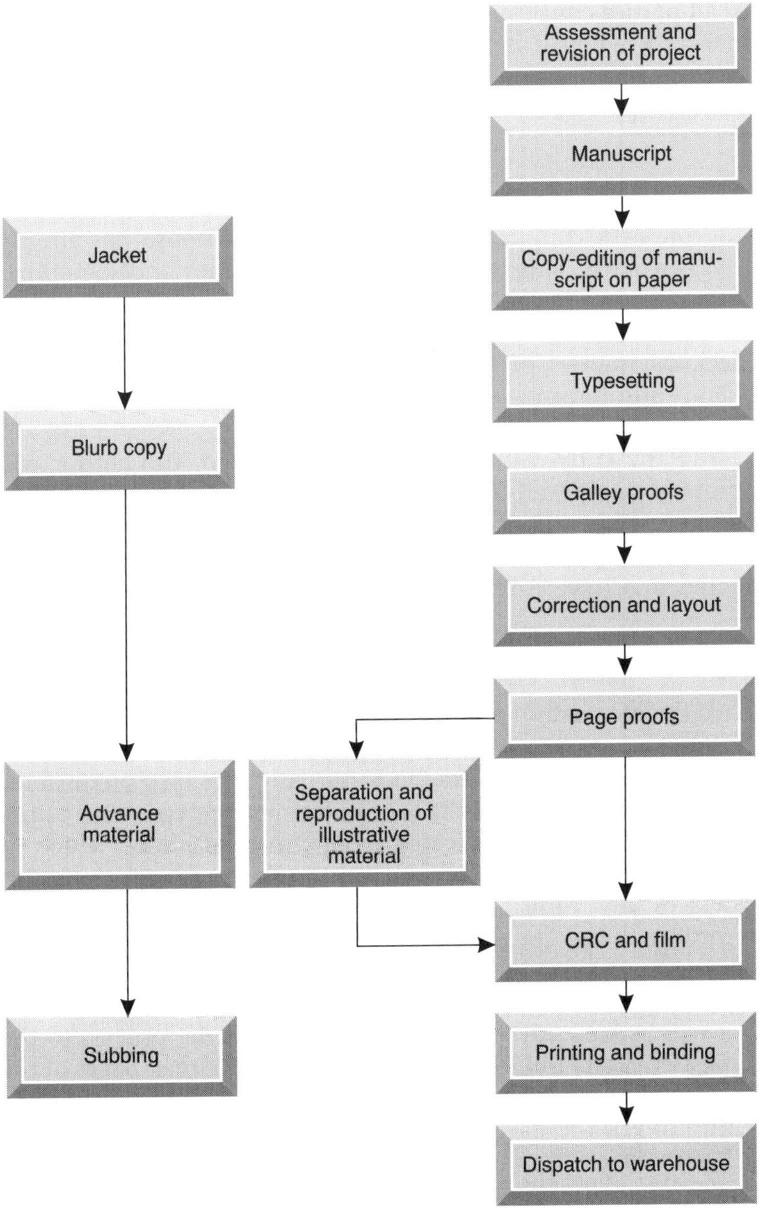

Figure 16.1: The conventional publishing process

for all parties concerned if the manuscript is in its complete and final form when it is handed over. It makes the job of a copy-editor so much easier and can save a lot of time and hassle later on in the process.

Copy-editing

The role of a copy-editor in the publishing house has already been discussed. This is the stage at which minor and sometimes not so minor details are sorted out by a copy-editor who goes through the manuscript with a fine-tooth comb. The editor will check on matters of content, style, grammar, spelling, consistency, numbering—generally on the aspects discussed in Chapter 23 of this book.

After the copy-editing process is completed, the author will normally be allowed the opportunity to check and comment on the editing. At this stage there will often be a lengthy session where the copy-editor and author will get together to sort out queries that have arisen from the editing process.

Typesetting

Once the copy-editor and author have agreed on the final details of the text, and the manuscript has been marked up for a typesetter by a designer, the book formally goes into production.

In conventional typesetting an operator retypes the entire manuscript onto a dedicated typesetting machine which is capable of producing book-quality work in a wide range of typefaces and fonts. The typesetter will set the book strictly according to the designer's instructions with regard to type area, spacing, type sizes, indentations, and so on.

Unless you have a specific knowledge of typography and layout you will be well advised to leave this part of the process to the publisher. Many publishers will have a few specimen pages of the book typeset and show them to the author for approval before continuing.

Typesetting normally takes two to three weeks but this could be much longer in cases where the text is larger or where the material is very complex, such as books on mathematics, computer science or chemistry. The typesetting process will be speeded up if you attach to your manuscript a list of unusual symbols or difficult tables used in the book.

Galley proofs

The typesetter will supply the first set of proofs for checking in the form of galley proofs or galleys. Galley proofs are photostats of long sheets of text not yet divided into pages; illustrations do not appear in them. The author will receive a set of galleys to proofread. You will ease everybody's task if you become familiar with the standard proofreader's marks used in the printing industry (see Chapter 24).

Now that the manuscript has been converted to type, many authors are seized by an irresistible urge to rewrite the book. Do resist this urge, or suffer the consequences—most publishers' contracts contain heavy penalties for what are known in the trade as "author's corrections" (see page 122). The cost of author's corrections increases as the book nears completion, so if you have to change anything in the proof stage, do it on galley proofs rather than on page proofs (see pages 182–184 for notes on proof correcting). Remember, effecting a few corrections on one page may turn out to be far more expensive than typesetting that entire page in the first place. You will of course not be penalised for correcting errors committed by the typesetter himself. That is the point of reading the proofs.

The publisher's proofreader will normally read another set of galley proofs at the same time. Before the galley proofs go back to the typesetter for correction, the two sets will be collated and a master set of corrected galley proofs created to send to the typesetter to work from.

Page layout

After correcting the galley proofs the typesetter will proceed to create pages. If the book is straightforward, the typesetter will go straight to pages by simply breaking the type mechanically at page-long intervals. The more complex the material, the more important it will be for the typesetter to have some plan or diagram to work from. Often the publisher's designer will provide a rough paste-up or detailed page plan for the typesetter to follow.

Once the pages have been laid out, photostats are run of these. These photostats are known as page proofs.

Page proofs

The page proofs go through the same process as galley proofs: the author reads a set, the publisher's proofreader reads a set, then the proofs are collated into a master set, which is sent back to the typesetter for correction. A set of page proofs is also used to compile an index, because at this stage page numbers are known.

Depending on the accuracy of the typesetter's work, the willingness of the author to refrain from rewriting his or her book at page-proof stage and the complexity of the material, further sets of revised page proofs or selected pages may be required. These might or might not have to be checked by the author again, depending on the circumstances. In the final stages, many corrections are checked by the editor without involving the author.

CRC and film

The final version of the pages is commonly known as CRC (camera-ready copy), which is transferred photographically on to photographic film. From the film, printing plates are made, which are wrapped around the cylinders of a printing machine.

Printing and binding

Books are printed in sections of 16 pages at a time on one sheet (sometimes it might be eight or 32 pages per section). The sections are folded in a folding machine in such a way that the page numbers follow one another correctly. The sections of the book are then placed in sequence to make up the book, sewn together and trimmed.

The final process in manufacturing the book is binding, where the cover board (which has in the mean time been printed separately) is drawn and pasted on to the body of the book. (Don't confuse the terms "cover" and "dust-jacket"; the former is an integral part of the book, whether hardback or paperback; the latter is a loose removable paper flap.)

This explanation of the printing and binding processes is grossly simplified, but to do justice to the subject would require another book, and the topic is not really of great importance to the author.

Dispatch to warehouse

It is important for the author to realise that a considerable period might elapse between the printing and binding of a book and its delivery into the publisher's warehouse. The physical distances involved can be considerable. Most South African publishers print their books in Cape Town, and stock of newly printed books may take a number of days to reach a warehouse in Johannesburg. Some books are printed in Hong Kong or Singapore, and may take a month or more to reach the warehouse.

Jacket design

While the inside of the book is being produced, the jacket design proceeds along a parallel line (see Figure 16.1 again). The jacket will be put together by a professional designer, very often a freelancer. Most publishers will consult extensively with the author regarding the design of the jacket and will make an effort to accommodate the author's wishes. The designer will provide some kind of rough visual which has to be approved. Often a cover gets redone several times, and even then the last version may be amended extensively before approval is granted.

The cover design is enormously influential in the sale of the book, especially if it is intended for the general market. For this reason it is common to obtain approval of the final cover not only from the editor and the author, but more importantly from the sales and marketing division. They are after all the people who have to present the book to the outside world and in many cases the only visual item they have to work with is the jacket cover.

Blurb copy

Blurb copy is what publishers call the description of a book and its author on the jacket. Where the book has a dust-jacket, it is common to have the description of the book on the front flap and the description of the author on the back flap. Where the book has a paperback, or a drawn-on cover that consists of a stiff board with a jacket pasted onto it, the blurb copy will normally go on to the back of the cover.

It is common for the publisher to ask the author to prepare the basic material for the blurb copy, and for the copy then to be rewritten by an editor or publicist in a way that will appeal to the public.

Subbing

A month or two before the publication of the book, the publisher's representatives will do the rounds of booksellers to "sub" the book, using the dust-jacket and possibly other attractive material from inside the book (such as colour plates, interesting drawings, a dummy of the book, the content page and so on). Subbing (which is short for subscriptions) refers to the soliciting of orders from booksellers in advance of publication. The idea is that when the book finally arrives in the warehouse, there should be a number of orders waiting from booksellers. These orders will then be executed simultaneously so that the book appears in bookshop windows all over the country at the same time.

That is the theory. In practice, books do not appear in all the bookshop windows at the same time, partly because of the enormous distances involved in dispatching materials from the publisher's warehouse to far-flung booksellers and partly because some booksellers have lengthy internal procedures to complete before the books actually appear in individual bookshops in a chain.

Production and lead times

Having looked at the individual stages in the production of a book, it may be easier to understand why the process takes as long as it does. The time it takes to produce a book leads to so much controversy in publisher-author relations that it calls for more detailed discussion.

Let us start by looking at an "average" book. We will assume that it is of a standard format and runs to about 300 pages, that there are some line drawings in it and some tables, that it is printed inside in black only and that it has a four-colour cover.

An average production schedule

If you were to approach the "average" production manager (if we can have an average book we might as well have an average production manager) with a request to draw up a production schedule for this "average" book, he or she is likely to come up with something like the following:

Book production time estimate sheet

Assessment of manuscript	
Editorial assessment	1 week
Design assessment	1 week
Discussion and manuscript update by commissioning editor and author	1 week
Specimen setting	1 week
Total for assessment	4 weeks
Production schedule	
Copy-editing	4 weeks
Author's checking of editing	2 weeks
Final editing and mark-up for typesetter	2 weeks
Typesetting	3 weeks
Proofreading of galleys	3 weeks
Collation of galleys	1 week
Production of revised galleys	2 weeks
Checking of revised galleys	1 week
Paste-up	2 weeks
Page make-up	4 weeks
Checking of page proofs	2 weeks
Creation of index	1 week
Producing revised pages	2 weeks
Checking revised pages	1 week
Creating final pages	1 week
Creating film	2 weeks
Checking film	1 week
Printing, delivery and release	6 weeks

This gives a total of 44 weeks, or 10–11 months.

The above is a conservative estimate of the time needed for such a book, but not excessively so. (If the book were printed overseas, for example, the delivery time could be much longer.) Most authors would be appalled if they were faced with such a production schedule. It is true that in practice most books of this "average" size and content are more likely to take six to nine months than a full year to produce.

Reducing production time

As we will discuss later, using a DTP system can speed up the whole process considerably, but only if the author can refrain from rewriting his or her book at proof stage and if the publisher's editorial and production departments are fully geared to DTP.

To cut down on production time in the conventional publishing process, you have to be very specific about which steps you eliminate or shorten. Let us take a look at one or two possible stages.

We allow four weeks for editing. This assumes that there is an editor available and capable of doing the job immediately. Unfortunately manuscripts do not come into a publishing house in neat sequence. If the publisher produces 48 titles a year, the manuscripts do not come in as four titles per month—they are likely to rush in a dozen at a time in one month, with four desert months thereafter. It follows that if a publishing house has only four editors available (who could theoretically handle four manuscripts per month quite easily) they are going to be drowning at certain times of the year, and some manuscripts will simply have to wait until an editor has the time to pay attention to them. Using freelance editors may help ease the logjam, but they are not always instantly available either.

The same principle applies to the other stages of production. It is no problem to proofread galleys in three weeks and collate them in one week if the staff are available. However, if the proofs of four or five titles land on a proofreader's or editor's desk simultaneously, something is going to suffer.

The author may also have problems with timing. It is virtually impossible to plan for authors to receive proofs for reading only at times when they are readily available. Like other people, authors are involved in numerous activities such as marking exam papers or meeting other deadlines. At certain times the proofs will simply have to wait until the author has time to look at them. If the author loses a couple of weeks before he or she can read the proofs, those two weeks have to be made up for somewhere else or the schedule will suffer.

Put together all the titles that are being published simultaneously within a medium-sized publishing house (bringing out say, 100 titles per year) and you can begin to imagine the amount of scheduling and re-scheduling that a production manager has to do to be able to bring out books on time.

Underlying these problems is the fact that, just as manuscripts are not received in neat little bunches each month, books cannot be published that way either. In general book publishing there tends to be a clustering of books towards the end of the year for Christmas, which means those books have to be out by September/October; in educational publishing new books have to be ready for the start of the academic year, in time for a new syllabus, and so on.

Production time often becomes an issue because a book's publication date is coupled with such a specific event. If the event is, say, Christmas or the beginning of an academic year, it will obviously be significant for the sales of the book. However, linking publication with an ephemeral event such as a particular conference is often simply not worth the effort. Authors must always bear in mind that by insisting on short-cuts in the production process, they may damage their book. Short-cuts usually lead to errors, and the author has to weigh up what is most important: a really well-produced book or speed of production.

Authors sometimes feel that the production of a book is taking unreasonably long because they look at their book in isolation, without taking into account that the publisher has to juggle dozens or hundreds of titles together in the production process. This lack of understanding on the author's part can lead to disputes, or to a particular publisher being shunned by an author.

Nevertheless, it must also be said that authors sometimes do experience undue delays on the side of publishers. Publishers, like authors, are not always competent. If you feel you are being short-changed, do not hesitate to complain to someone in authority in the publishing house.

Desk Top Publishing (DTP)

The publishing process can be significantly simplified by using a Desk Top Publishing or DTP system. DTP can generate text, illustrations, tables and so forth on computer and organise these into columns and pages. The advantages of a DTP system are greater freedom of design and greater speed, greater flexibility of page make-up and of manipulating text and illustrations. In handling complex material DTP has, however, certain limitations which makes it impossible to use for certain types of books.

In comparing the DTP process with the conventional publishing process, it is noticeable that certain steps are either left out or simplified. Compare Figure 16.2 with Figure 16.1. The project still has to go through the same process of assessment and revision, but instead of a typed manuscript or typescript, the author hands in a disk (although he or she is still expected to hand in a hard-copy print-out of the manuscript as well).

Instead of editing on paper, the copy-editor now edits on a screen directly on to the disk supplied by the author. A "clean" disk (that is, free of grammatical and other errors) is then produced which can go directly into a DTP program on a computer. The data on the disk is manipulated within the DTP program to create layouts and pages. Normally the galley proof stage is missed out completely when using a DTP system. The first proofs seen by the author will be page proofs. The author should be restrained at this stage from rewriting the book at page proof stage, otherwise all the advantages of using DTP will be cancelled out.

From here on the stages followed by the project are much the same as conventional typesetting. Such differences as do exist are so technical and complex in nature that they should be of no concern to the author.

In recent years most authors have switched over to providing manuscripts on disk, normally produced on a word-processing program such as WordPerfect or Microsoft Word, which are now the most commonly used programs, and most publishers have switched over to DTP to a greater or lesser extent. Authors are strongly advised to do all their work on disk. It is likely that in future all publishers will insist on a manuscript in disk form.

The whole industry is still in a process of transformation. Many of the top designers, for instance, are far more comfortable working with paper on a table than working with DTP material on a screen. Similarly, a great many experienced copy-editors are happier editing on paper than on screen. The trend is, however, clearly towards greater use of DTP technology and that will no doubt continue in the future.

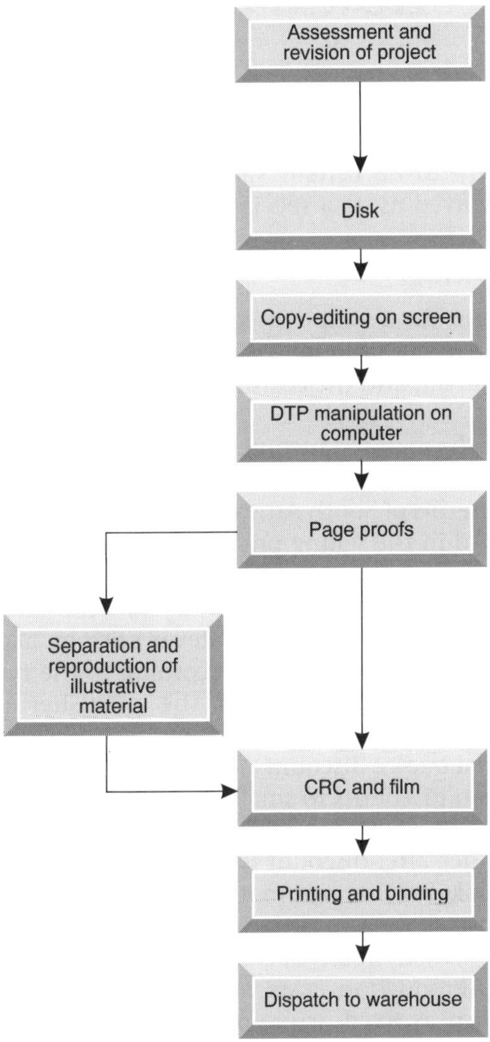

Figure 16.2: The DTP publishing process

17

How a book is costed

Not all publishers follow the same formulae in costing a book, but there are likely to be certain similarities. Let us examine the principles involved using a specific example.

A sample costing

Figure 17.1 sets out a simple income statement for a particular book. The title in question here is a full-colour book intended for the general market, and the costing shown is a real one for a real title.

Let us work through the income statement from the top down, commenting on each line:

1 and 2. In terms of South African tax legislation, VAT needs to be included in the selling price of the book. Please note that there is no reason for the bookseller to stick to the selling price proposed by the publisher; by law the bookseller has complete freedom to sell at whatever price he likes.

3. Discounts to booksellers vary according to the type of book sold, the outlet sold to and the publisher concerned. Discounts on general books are higher than discounts on educational books; discounts to large chains like the CNA are higher than discounts to smaller shops. An average of 40 per cent discount on a book of this type is normal.
4. The net price after discount is the income the publisher gets for the book. For that reason it is commonly used as the price on which to base a royalty. Note that the income that the publisher actually receives is only about half the retail price.

6, 7 and 8. Production costs can be classified as origination (also known as fixed or pre-press cost) and print and bind cost (also known as press or variable cost). Origination cost refers to all the costs incurred in order to create the product.

Print run: 5 000 copies

1.	VAT-inclusive price:		R100,00
2.	Less: 14% VAT:		R87,72
3.	Less: Discount to booksellers (average 40%)		R35,09
4.	Net price after discount		R52,63
5.	Costs:		
6.	Production		
7.	Origination	R12,00	
8.	Print and bind	R11,69	
9.	Total	R23,69	
10.	Royalty (15% of net)	R 7,89	
11.	Total	R31,58	
12.	Less: Total costs of		R31,58
13.	Less: Gross profit		R21,05 (40%)
14.	Less: Overhead of		R14,21 (27%)
15.	Less: Write-down provision of		R 1,58 (3%)
16.	Profit before interest and tax		R 5,26 (10%)

Figure 17.1: A simple income statement for a specific book

These commonly include the cost of copy-editing, proof-reading, typesetting, colour processing, film, illustrations, corrections, and so on. Note that this cost remains the same regardless of how many copies are printed. Print and bind cost vary with the number of copies printed. The actual Rand cost of a print run goes up with the number printed, although the unit cost might come down.

9. Note that in this case the selling price of the book is 4,22 times that of the production cost and 8,55 times the printing and binding cost. Most publishers arrive at an estimated selling price (excluding VAT) by multiplying the production cost by between four and five times. To the uninitiated this sounds outrageous, but as you can see in this figure, production cost forms only one part of the total cost of the book.
10. The royalty here is based on the net price of the book, i.e. R52,63. (As mentioned in Chapter 15, some publishers also pay royalties on the selling price of the book.) The 15 per cent on net used here is normal for this type of book.

13. The gross margin of 40 per cent used here is again quite normal for the first printing of a book like this. In publishing terms it is on the low side. The publisher will have to get the "average" margins higher than this to survive. There may, however, be numerous reasons why publishers would accept lower margins for specific titles. It may, for instance, be only a small print run of a title that they hope to sell in large quantities later to education departments, or it may be a book that they believe will have a long shelf life, and on which they hope to achieve a higher gross margin once the book reprints and the origination cost falls away.
14. The overhead cost of 27 per cent in this case is an estimated one. The real percentage will vary from company to company, and from one type of book to another.
15. Many companies build a provision for writing off a portion of the book's value into the costing. That does not mean that they expect to have to write off stock equivalent to the value of 3 per cent of sales for this particular book—it rather means that that is the *average* percentage they provide for in the case of all books. Some books sell very well and reprint quickly, therefore not incurring any write-off cost, while others fail dismally and have to be written off completely. The percentage used here is therefore an average for that particular publishing house, and would depend on its history of write-offs. Three per cent of sales is a formula that is commonly used.
16. Note that the profit before interest and tax obtained by the publisher gives a lesser income than the profit obtained by the author through royalties. Interest is a very real factor, since the publisher has to finance the publication either by borrowing money at current interest rates, or by foregoing interest if the book is financed from cash reserves. And tax, of course, is unavoidable to a company showing a profit.

The effect of print runs on unit cost

Let us look at Figure 17.1 again. If we assume that the print run is not 5 000 copies but 15 000, what effect does this have on the cost price of the book, and therefore on the selling price?

In the first place the origination cost on 5 000 copies was R12,00 per copy, therefore R60 000 in total. However, bear in mind that origination costs are fixed—that is, they are the same whether you print 10 copies or 10 000 copies. In this case the R60 000 in origination costs are now divided among 15 000 copies instead of 5 000. The result is that the unit origination cost for this title is now R4,00 instead of R12,00, although it is still exactly the same book.

The print and bind cost is also bound to come down if you print a higher quantity, although not as dramatically as the origination cost. In the case of this book the print and bind cost is likely to come down from R11,69 to something like R8,00. If we add this R8,00 to the R4,00 of origination cost, we find that the total production cost is now R12,00 instead of R23,69. If you now apply the same ratio between production cost and selling price that we applied in Figure 17.1, namely 4,22, we find that the selling price of the book is now R50,64 instead of R100,00.

This seems miraculous: we are still publishing exactly the same book. All that has changed is the number of copies we print, yet the book is now selling for half the price originally calculated.

Obviously a publisher cannot simply increase print runs *ad infinitum* to get to a lower unit price. If too many copies are printed, they do not all sell, or they take far too long to sell out. The capital outlay will also be greater. Most publishers will try to print for no longer than eighteen months. If this period is doubled to, say, three years before the books sell out, the financing cost of keeping all that stock in the warehouse increases to such an extent that it cancels out the advantages of a low unit cost achieved via a large print quantity.

This then is the central dilemma of publishing: whether to print a large number of copies, thereby achieving a low unit cost and low selling price, or whether rather to print a smaller number of copies and thus reduce the risk. There is a debate around these issues within a publishing house on every single title published.

Many authors believe it is always good to reduce a selling price, and that any book will sell more copies if it is published at a lower price. That may be true of some books, but certainly not of all books. The sales of a popular mass market book will increase if the price is reduced substantially, but many books fall into categories that appeal only to certain parts of the reading public. Let us take for example a botanical work on the flowers of the Cape. If it is a serious botanical work, it is only going to appeal to those people seriously interested in botany. Let us assume that there are 5 000 such people in the country. It will then make sense to print, say, 6 000 copies of this book, 5 000 to sell to these people, plus 1 000 for libraries.

Conversely, if you were to publish a popular field guide to the flowers of the Cape, your potential readership would be infinitely greater. Virtually anyone with a reasonable income and some spare time to drive around the Cape might be interested in such a work. In this case you will obviously sell far more copies if the book is cheaply priced.

The gearing effect of print run explains why some small books are incredibly expensive while other massive, very lavishly illustrated ones sell cheaply. Print run, not size or extent or complexity, is the first determinant of the price of a book. This rule applies everywhere in the world. It is a simple function of the mechanics of printing.

18

Paperback versus hardback

There is a general perception amongst consumers in South Africa that books are priced very high. Many publishers would argue that this can be seen to be false if you compare the price of a book with the price of a restaurant meal, an evening at the movies, and so on. It is a futile debate, in my opinion, because whether or not people are correct in their perceptions, they are going to vote with their wallet: if they believe a book is too expensive, it will not be bought in quantity. No amount of logical argument is going to change the consumer's mind on that point.

A great number of books never see the light of day in South Africa because publishers turn them down on the basis that they will be too expensive to sell. This might be because of the innate nature of the book (huge amounts of colour, complex layouts, or whatever) or it may be because of a lack of potential readership, or a combination of both.

Many authors believe that the way to get the price of their books down to an acceptable level is to have them printed in paperback instead of hardback. The assumption is that paperback books will always be cheaper than hardbacks. This is not necessarily the case, and to understand why, we need to examine the history of the paperback book. Paperback binding was first thought up by Penguin Books as a marketing concept, and gained ready acceptance after the Second World War. So successful has this marketing concept been worldwide that the public simply assumes that a paperback equals low cost. However, it is essential to understand the underlying mechanism involved.

The mass-market paperback

This is a distinct type of book, always printed to a specific small format that fits into mass-market shelving in chain stores. It is mostly fiction, always aimed at the popular market, and nearly always a derivative of existing books. In the English-speaking world it is essentially a phenomenon of publishing in the United Kingdom and the United States, although their products are of course also exported into this market.

What happens is this: an author writes a book, which is first published in hardback by a publisher in the true sense of the word, i.e. a business that takes risks with a new product. If the title is successful, the paperback rights are then sold to a paperback house, which is essentially not a publishing house but a marketing organisation. It is true that the paperback is cheaper, partly because of a smaller format, less expensive paper and cheaper binding, and so on. However, the determining factor in the price is the print run. A book that had an initial run of 3 000 or 4 000 copies in hardback might be republished in paperback in quantities of 50 000 or 100 000. Because of the economy of scale (and also because royalties paid to authors on paperbacks are lower than on hardbacks) the price comes down dramatically.

Paperback publishing developed along those lines in the decades after the Second World War. In the past decade many hardback and paperback houses merged, so that the difference between hardback and paperback publishers has become less marked, and we have also seen the appearance of the "trade paperback", which is sort of half hardback and half paperback.

If we examine the situation in South Africa (as opposed to the UK and the US) we will immediately see that there are no such paperback publishers in South Africa. All our mass-market paperbacks are imported from the UK, and a few from the US. The reason for this is not hard to find: since mass-market paperbacks depend on economy of scale, they need a far bigger market-place in which to operate than South Africa is capable of offering. Paperbacks published in the UK are sold not only there but in Europe and all over the Commonwealth. This allows an economy of scale which would never be possible in one country, not even a country with a reading population the size of Great Britain.

Other types of paperback publishing

Having said that there are no mass-market paperback publishers in South Africa, the fact remains that a large number of books are published in this country with paperbacks, also called limpbacks or softcovers. These are not true mass-market paperbacks. In many cases the books have not been published first in hardback; in fact, it is often a toss-up whether a book should be published in hardback or paperback. There is no change in format, the quality of paper and the print run are still the same, and so on. The only difference is a piece of cardboard that is pulled round the book to provide a hard cover.

It follows that under these conditions there cannot be a major price difference between the hardback and the paperback of a book; the difference will be the cost of that piece of cardboard. The reason why so many authors believe that their books can be published very cheaply is because they confuse true mass-market paperbacks imported from the UK with softcover books printed in this country (or elsewhere) that do not enjoy any particular advantage in print quantity.

The public perception of paperbacks as being cheap has been further strengthened by the use made of paperbacks by large American publishers of university textbooks. The system that has developed in American textbook publishing is as follows: a large, very lavish edition of the book in hardback is done for the American market first. These Mercedes versions of the book are commonly referred to as "domestic hardbacks" by American academic publishers.

Using the same material, the publishers then publish another, smaller edition of the book in paperback for the market outside America. These versions are commonly known as international student editions, or ISEs. Because they use existing origination and because they are printed simultaneously for a large number of countries there is considerable economy of scale and the prices are much lower than those of domestic hardbacks. Most American university textbooks used in South Africa are ISEs, although the domestic hardbacks may have to be bought in the case of less popular courses where ISEs are not available. In recent years some American publishers have stopped producing ISEs and have instead simply produced run-ons of their American hardback editions, which are then sold more cheaply overseas than in their domestic market.

A third edition of the same basic American text might be printed in a Third World country such as India. These editions, which are printed on the cheapest of papers and bound in the least sophisticated way, are known as Third World editions and are only available in Third World countries. They are for instance unknown to South African audiences because the American publishers would not allow their importation into a country such as South Africa where they would rather sell the ISE editions.

The use of cheaper paperback ISE editions as university textbooks combined with the phenomenon of mass-market paperbacks coming to South Africa from the UK have together produced a perception in the public mind that paperbacks are cheaper. Do not, however, expect your book—of which only 2 000 or 3 000 copies may have been printed—suddenly to become miraculously cheaper simply because the cover is paper instead of board.

Reducing the cost of books

A lot of time is wasted in this country in discussions on trying to bring cheaper books to the masses. The way to do it is not to invent cheaper production methods or print on cheaper paper, but to increase print runs. If you increase print runs, the price will take care of itself. If you cannot produce reasonable print runs, nothing in the world will make the price of the book come down. For instance, printing a book on the cheapest of cheap paper instead of very good paper might make a change of 5 or 10 per cent in the cost of the book, nothing more. There is no point in spoiling a good book by using inferior paper if the end result is that people refuse to purchase the book because it is printed on such poor quality paper.

Part 4

How to prepare a manuscript

19

How to prepare text

Physical preparation of the text is important, both with a view to getting the manuscript accepted by a publisher, and to minimise error and confusion once the manuscript actually goes into production.

Manuscripts are presented in one of two ways: as a typescript, i.e. actually typed on a typewriter, or increasingly as a disk from a word-processor, with an accompanying hard copy. Let us consider both types of preparation.

Preparing a typescript

Type on one side only of A4 paper, allowing wide margins on both the left and the right side. Use double-line spacing throughout the typescript. Not only the main text, but also quotations, notes and bibliographies should be typed in double spacing, to allow room for amendments by the copy-editor. A page of typescript typed up in this way would normally present about 300 words per page, an average of 10 words per line and a total of 30 lines on a page. Such a page is easy to convert into a number of words, which is important for the publisher's production department when they cast off the number of pages the final book will make.

Text that is to be printed in italic type should be underlined in typing, while bold type should be indicated by a wavy underline. Any handwriting in a manuscript, e.g. for mathematics or words not in roman characters, should be neat and legible. Corrections should be made by striking out the matter to be corrected with a single line, and writing the new copy in between the line corrected and the line above.

The first line of a new paragraph should be indented five spaces; do not leave extra space between paragraphs unless you intend a line space to appear in a printed book. Begin a new page for a new chapter. The pages of the typescript should be numbered consecutively in the upper right-hand corner. Never hand in an unnumbered manuscript—if the pages get confused, it is difficult and time-consuming to get them back in the right order.

Avoid illegible and unsightly scribblings on the typescript. Do not write extra paragraphs into the margins. Type late additions on separate sheets (use whole sheets even if the addition is quite small, for small pieces of paper are apt to get lost). A page added late may be numbered, e.g. 25a, but in that case please make sure that there is a note of warning on the previous page that 25a should follow. If a whole page is deleted, say page 33, the previous page should be double numbered 32/33 to avoid breaking the sequence.

The typesetter will need the typescript in loose sheets, so if you clip or staple the sheets together, make sure that they can easily be undone. Send the original to the publisher, but always keep a carbon or photocopy of the typescript in case it gets lost.

Preparing a disk

These days most manuscripts are prepared not on typewriters but on a word-processing program on a personal computer. Make sure that the program you use is one that can be accessed by the publisher, or that can interface with his equipment. Safe programs are WordPerfect and Word, which are the most commonly used in South Africa these days, but there are at least half a dozen other programs that should present no problem in conversion. It is useful to send in sample material on disk to the publisher at an early stage to make sure that your material can be "read". The same applies to any illustrations that might have been done on a drawing or other program. You do not want to put in months of work only to discover that no one can access the material in the end.

Always provide hard copy to go with a disk. The hard copy should conform to all the requirements set out above for typescripts; for instance it should be double-spaced, have large margins, each page should be numbered, and so on.

A publisher might handle material in one of several ways. One common method is to do the copy-editing on the hard copy, and hand that back for the author to do the final corrections on the disk. Far more common these days, however, is for the copy-editor to edit the material straight on disk so that it is immediately convertible into a DTP program. The main drawback of this method is that it makes it difficult for the author to check the copy-editor's changes before the book goes into production, since he or she has to check the edited manuscript sentence for sentence against the original manuscript. Not many authors do that very thoroughly. Alternatively, the publisher might be able to provide the author with a red-lined printout, that is one which indicates in each case both the original text and the copy-editor's corrections.

Once a disk has been copy-edited, the text will be transferred on to a photo-typesetting or DTP system. The typesetter will insert instructions on layout and typefaces and produce page proofs.

Some dos and don'ts when preparing a disk

Accuracy and consistency are very important when you (or your typist) prepare a disk for a publisher. Note especially the following:

- Always leave a single space between words.
- Do not justify the right margin of any lines, even if your machine has the capability.
- Leave only one space after all forms of punctuation, including a full stop.
- Do not use bold type in the text where italic is the norm in books.
- Do not use a carriage return at the end of a sentence.
- In abbreviations such as *e.g.* no additional space is required in the middle, but a space should be left in *p. 60* and similar references, and between initials, e.g. *A. B. Smith.*
- Do not divide words at the end of a line, since an unwanted hyphen could be retained if the text is rerun through a typesetting machine.
- Be consistent in the way you represent a dash, and make sure it will not be confused with a hyphen.
- Type complicated tables on separate pages and gather them together—it is unlikely that they can be converted to DTP. They will probably have to be typeset in a more conventional way.
- Avoid using tabs, special fonts and excessive formatting.

Copyright permissions

South Africa is a subscriber to the Berne Convention. In terms of our Copyright Act of 1981 no one may reproduce a substantial portion of an existing published work without first obtaining the permission of the copyright holder. When exactly do you need to obtain permission, and whose responsibility is it to do this?

Let us first deal with whose responsibility it is. There will normally be a clause in your author's contract that specifies whether you or the publisher will be responsible for obtaining copyright permissions. If the responsibility is yours, you should start writing to the copyright owner at the earliest possible stage, since it can take a long time to get the necessary permission.

When exactly are you required to obtain copyright permission? In South Africa copyright subsists for 50 years after the author's death, or if the work was not published during his or her lifetime, 50 years after first publication. In European countries this period is 70 years. Unpublished work remains in copyright permanently.

The Copyright Act compels you to obtain copyright permission whenever you use a "substantial part" of a written work. "Substantial" refers not only to the length of the extract, but also to its importance. Thus copyright permission will be needed if you quote a poem that consists in its totality of two lines.

The meaning of a "substantial part" has not been tested in South African courts. No one can therefore say with certainty exactly how long an extract needs to be before permission is required. A guideline that is widely used is that a single extract of up to 400 words of prose (or a series of extracts, with comments interposed, up to a total of 800 words, of which no single extract exceeds 300 words) is permissible, or not more than 40 lines of poetry, but in no case more than a quarter of the complete poem. It should be stressed that the Copyright Act itself does not prescribe a specific number of words and the whole matter is open to interpretation.

Remember, it is important always to acknowledge the source of a quotation, figure, photograph or whatever it is that you are using, regardless of whether you actually need to apply for permission to reproduce it. It is prudent also to apply for permission to reproduce any maps, plans, figures, and so on. Applications for permission are frequently more of a courtesy than an obligation, but there is no reason not to be courteous.

To obtain permission, you need to send a letter to the copyright holder. The only practical way of doing this is to send the letter to the company or journal that published the material in the first instance. See Figure 19.1 for a sample letter of permission.

100 Main Street
PARKHURST
2010

The Permissions Department
KYZ Company
Date

Dear Sir/Madam

I am at present writing a book entitled ____________________. It will be published by ________________________ (*publisher*) in (*hardback/ paperback*) in ________________________ (*date of publication*).

I would like to quote _____________ (*number of words*), starting on p________ and ending on p_________, from your publication _________ (*author, title, publication date*).

Please see the enclosed photocopy of the pages concerned, with the intended extract clearly marked.

I require ________________________ rights (*name geographical region, e.g. Southern Africa*).

The purpose of the book is ________________________________ (*student text, general trade, etc.*). The first print run will be _____________ copies.

The source will naturally be acknowledged properly. Let me know if this acknowledgement should take some special form. Also please let me know whether any fee will be payable.

Yours sincerely

Figure 19.1: Sample letter to obtain copyright permission

In practice it can be frustratingly difficult to reach the true copyright owner. A company might have ceased to exist or have been taken over or merged, and you could find yourself sending endless letters into a black hole. Sometimes you simply get no response despite your best endeavours. In such cases the publisher will place a disclaimer notice in the front of the book to indicate that every effort was made to find copyright holders, and to ask them to come forward. However, you must be aware that such a disclaimer should never be used unless all avenues to get hold of the copyright owner have been exhausted.

You may find that some publishers charge extravagant fees for copyright permission. It might then be more practical to substitute some other material although this may not always be possible (in the case of an important poem, for example). There is however no reason why you should simply accept extravagant charges. Write to the copyright holder, plead with him, if necessary exhaust him until he agrees to a lower figure.

It is extremely important to be quite clear from the outset whether you or the publisher will be responsible for picking up the cost of permissions. If the author is responsible for paying permission fees, the publisher will normally pay such fees as an advance to be deducted from the author's future royalties. In some cases (for example, poetry anthologies) the question of who picks up the tab for permissions—the publisher or the author—can be of crucial importance.

20

How to prepare illustrations

Three types of illustrations are commonly used in books: figures, photographs and creative artwork. Let us consider each type of illustration in turn.

Figures

Figures include diagrams, flow charts, graphs, maps and technical drawings in general. All drawings should be called figures and assigned numbers. The figure numbering sequence might also include maps and photographs, although tables are normally numbered separately. Figures are usually numbered in sequence by chapter, with the number also used in text references. For instance, the first figure in Chapter 3 will be Figure 3.1, etc. How the figures are treated by the publisher will depend on the form in which they are submitted. Any of the following are possible:

- The author provides roughs of each figure. Such rough drawings should contain all the wording and features required. The publisher then commissions an artist or draughtsman to do the final drawings, working from the roughs.
- The author may in certain cases provide his or her own drawings (for instance in a book on technical drawing). In such a case you should first send a sample to the publisher to make sure that your figures are suitable for reproduction, and that they are done to the correct size.
- Increasingly these days authors provide illustrations on disk, especially when these consist of graphs or other figures that are easily done with standard computer packages. In DTP typesetting, diagrams are often created as a virtual part of the text by the DTP operator.

You should discuss with your publisher which of these methods would be the best to use in your particular book.

Illustrations are normally provided separate from the typescript. If illustrations are to be captioned, provide a separate typed and numbered list of captions, with corresponding numbers in the text.

Annotations on figures are best drawn in by hand on photocopies, never on the original artwork; they will then be set and pasted in by the typesetter.

Photocopies of figures are often pasted into the typescript to indicate exactly where they should be placed. As with the main text, the main imperative when using annotations and captions is that of consistency. Make the style of labels consistent with regard to the use of capital and lower-case letters, roman and italic, type sizes, etc.

Simple maps can be treated as line drawings, but proper maps are best done by qualified cartographers.

A note of warning: reach a clear understanding with your publisher at an early stage about who is responsible for the drawing of figures, and for the cost thereof.

Photographs

Photographs might come from the author, a specially commissioned photographer, or the publisher (through a picture researcher who will collect the material from photo libraries or other sources). You always need permission from a photographer for the reproduction of photographs and might have to negotiate a fee with him or her.

For black-and-white photographs good prints showing a clear contrast in tonal values are best. Transparencies are usually used for colour reproduction. Photographs that have already been screened or printed in books or magazines are not normally suitable for reproduction.

It is useful, particularly when the book contains a large number of photographs, if you suggest relative sizes for reproducing them; for instance by numbering them 1 for large photographs, 2 for medium ones and 3 for small ones.

A complete list of captions should accompany the photographs. Always number photographs and put a corresponding number in the text. Whether the photographs finally appear numbered or unnumbered in the book will depend on whether there is a need for specific references to them in the text.

It is best to have a choice of photographs available for the same subject for the designer to choose from. The final choice will depend on the proportions of the photograph, the cropping needed, its position with other photographs on the same page, and generally on requirements of layout and balance.

Some dos and don'ts when handling photographs

Photographs should be handled with great care. If you are working with black-and-white photographic prints:

- do not attach paper clips to them;
- do not write on the back as this may crack the surface of the print;
- put each photograph into a separate envelope labelled with its number and caption, or put the details on an adhesive label that you stick on the back of the print.

If you are working with transparencies:

- put each transparency separately in a see-through folder;
- if you have to take a transparency out of the folder, handle it by the frame and never touch the trannie itself;
- stick a number on the frame of the transparency;
- keep a separate list of captions with corresponding numbers;
- ensure that the transparencies do not lie around at either the publishing house or the colour processor longer than is strictly necessary;
- prepare a list of transparencies before you hand them to the publisher. Detail any scratches or flaws in the transparencies and get the editor to sign that there are no others. This way no argument can arise later over whether marks were on the transparency when it was handed over.

Creative artwork

The term "creative artwork" refers to original drawings by artists of subjects such as people or animals. If you are an artist yourself or are collaborating with an artist, you need to show samples of your work to the publisher at an early stage to get approval, and also to get a brief on what sizes to use.

It is, however, more common for the publisher to commission an artist. In such a case the artist may need comprehensive references from you as author, in addition to detailed roughs or briefings. The leeway allowed an artist will depend greatly on the nature of the book. In the case of a children's story, for example, the number and size of illustrations might be left entirely to the artist, whereas in the case of a school textbook the artist will be closely briefed on exactly what is expected of him or her. Artwork is not normally numbered, unless it takes the form of plates.

An interesting recent development has been the emergence of computer illustration packages such as Corel Draw, which provide thousands of ready-made images. It is also possible these days to scan artwork into a computer, where it can be manipulated through elongation, adding shadows, superimposition, enlargement, reduction, etc. All the indications are that the simpler creative artwork in books will in future be done on computer programs. Finer artwork, such as illustrations of birds or plants for field guides, or illustrations for children's books, will continue to be done by artists.

21

How to structure a book

Once you have done your research and gathered your material together, you are faced with the task of giving structure to a mass of disparate information. Before you continue with the actual writing of the book, you need to consider the structural elements that are going to give shape to your work. These structural elements will arise partly from the nature of the book you are preparing, and will partly be based on the conventions of book publishing.

A brief analysis of most printed books will reveal that they basically consist of three major structural elements: preliminary matter, the main text and end matter.

Before we start with a detailed discussion of the preliminary pages, it would be useful to note two things: first, that books are normally printed in multiples of 16 pages (sometimes in multiples of 32 or eight) for technical reasons, and that this fact has important structural implications; second, that it is a rigid convention in book publishing that odd page numbers are always on the right and even page numbers are always on the left.

Preliminary pages

Preliminary pages or prelims are what we call the initial pages of a book that are normally numbered in roman rather than Arabic numerals (or not numbered at all). They contain the text that precedes the main text of the book. The prelims may consist of some or all of the following, depending on the type of book (see Figure 21.1).

- **French title** or **half title** (page i, therefore always on the right-hand side) normally shows the title of the book only, in fairly small letters. Not all books contain French titles—the page is often used as a device to make up a full 16-page section.

(i)	French title
(ii)	Blank page
(iii)	Title page
(iv)	Imprint page
(v)	Dedication page
(vi)	Blank page
(vii)	Foreword
(viii)	Blank page
(ix)	Preface
(x)	Blank page
(xi)	Table of contents
(xii)	Blank page
(xiii)	Acknowledgements
(xiv)	Blank page
(xv)	Introduction

Figure 21.1: Normal sequence of preliminary pages. Not all the prelim elements listed here are always used, and some less common ones (such as a list of illustrations or notes on contributors) have been left out. Some may well run to more than one page. Where that happens, the next prelim elements will normally again start on a right-hand (i.e. odd-numbered) page. Where the foreword and preface are very long, they may have to go after the table of contents.

- The next page (page ii, facing the title page) is normally left blank.
- The **title page** (page iii) provides basic details about the book: its title, sub-title, the names of authors or editors, possibly the name of the translator or illustrator as well as the publisher's name and/or logo.
- The **imprint page** (page iv also known as a **copyright page** or **title verso**) provides legal and technical details of the book. Prepared by the publisher, these should include:
  — the full registered name of the publisher
  — the publisher's address
  — the name of the copyright holder(s) and the copyright date

— the date of first publication and the printing history
— a rights clause reserving rights in the work
— the international standard book number (ISBN)
— details of the printer.

There may be considerable variation between the imprint pages used by various publishers, but they should contain the same type of details.

- The **dedication page** (page v) usually contains a short dedication to a person the author holds in high regard.
- A **foreword** (page vii) is usually written by somebody other than the author. Do not get someone to write a foreword unless it makes a real contribution to the book.
- The **preface** (page ix) is written by the author and sets the book in context. It is usually written from a personal point of view, in contrast to the introduction.
- The **table of contents** (page xi) can be condensed or extensive, running into a number of pages, depending on the type of book and the subject matter.
- The **introduction** (page xv) is normally longer than a preface and deals more closely with the subject matter of the book. If the introduction is really a part of the main text, it should rather be treated as a chapter and included in the body of the book. However, it is better to make it part of the prelim matter if it is likely to change with each new edition.

End matter

"End matter" is a term used for material that comes after the main text in the book. The end matter may consist of appendices, end notes, a glossary, a bibliography and an index, normally in that sequence.

- An **appendix** carries detailed or background information that is used to back up material provided in the main text, but which is kept separate to avoid disturbing the flow of the book. Appendices are usually associated with scholarly books and come in numerous shapes and forms.
- Depending on the system of reference used in the book, you may prefer to use footnotes, notes at the end of chapters, or notes right at the end of the book. **End notes** refer to notes that are accumulated at the back of the book. For details about the use of various reference systems, see Chapter 23.

- A **glossary** is a list of explanations of new or complex terms used in the main body of the text.
- The term **bibliography** is applied to a list of works referred to in the text. A bibliography is usually arranged in alphabetical sequence, but is sometimes divided up according to subject matter or by type of work referred to. The bibliography may include all works referred to elsewhere in the book or, in the case of a select bibliography, to a selection of the works used. It may also include works that are not in fact ever referred to in the text, but are relevant to the subject or recommended for further reading.
- The **index** is normally placed at the back of the book. Not all books need indices, and sometimes it is better to leave out the index than to produce a poor one. The space taken up by the index may vary a great deal, depending on the layout of the text, the number of sub-entries, and so on. To some extent the length of the index will be determined by whether there is enough space available to just fill a 16-page section. Indices are prepared at the page proof stage, and your publisher should be able to tell you then exactly how much space is available for an index, if you both agree that there should be one. Indices are normally compiled by the author, or by a specialist indexer if it is a very complex scholarly work. See Chapter 25 for more detail on how an index should be laid out.

Main text

There are a number of conventional methods of breaking up the thousands of words that make up the main text of a book into comprehensible and easily digestible units.

The first of these is the **section divider** or **part title**. The section divider is used to break a large book into several parts, usually called Part 1, Part 2, and so on. The section divider is of a larger order than a chapter heading. It is quite common for a section divider to start on a right-hand page as a heading on its own, with the following chapter within the section divider starting on the next right-hand page (note that chapters are numbered consecutively regardless of section dividers). Section dividers are normally only used in fairly large and complicated books.

The most commonly used device to break up the text into digestible batches is the **chapter**. Very few books do not have chapters. Even in fiction it is usual for the book to be broken up in this way, though the chapters in this case tend to have no real headings, except a number.

In any kind of educational or non-fiction book, chapters play an important role. It is worth spending some time getting chapter headings right; since they are listed in the table of contents, readers often use them as a guideline to what is in the body of the book. Interesting and catchy chapter headings can go a long way towards making difficult material interesting.

Chapters need to be well-constructed units, with a beginning and an end. Within the wider context of the book they need to lead logically from one to the other, be of a reasonably comparable size, and have the same or a similar internal structure. For instance, in a textbook it would be common for each chapter to start off with objectives, to have exercises interspersed, and to have a test section at the end, together with notes or references relating to the chapter.

The exact elements of each chapter in your book will be determined by the logic of the book itself. The important thing is to have *consistency* within and between each chapter.

Unless you are writing a work of fiction, the text within each chapter is likely to be broken up by **headings**. Headings serve not only to break grey blocks of type, but to make explicit the logic behind the way the material is put together. Restrict the level of sub-heading within a chapter to three at the most. Normally one or two levels will be sufficient. You should clearly distinguish the different levels, either by typing them in different ways or by putting an "A" in the margin beside the highest level, "B" beside the next level, and so on. It is in fact possible, by centring or setting to the margin in capitals or lower case, underlined or not, to achieve eight different kinds of sub-division, but more than three will add considerably to the expense and be apt to confuse the reader.

It is useful to number sub-headings metrically. For instance, in Chapter 6 you should number them 6.1, 6.1.1, 6.1.2, 6.2, 6.3, and so on. Even if you then delete this metric numbering, it helps to guide yourself. Many textbooks do in fact make use of this type of metric numbering, which is clear and logical, and makes it difficult to get confused.

It is poor style to have a heading with just one sub-head under it; for example 2.2, 2.2.1, 2.3. Also try to ensure that the style of headings is consistent with regard to capitalisation, centring, and so on.

Sometimes a heading is not part of the overall logical hierarchy of headings, but rather an indication that a particular type of text is to follow. Examples of this might be summaries or notes at the end of a chapter or section, or exercises or questions interspersed within the text. This type of flag heading will normally be treated in a different typographical way from the hierarchical headings, and may even be represented graphically.

Like headings, **lists** are frequently used to organise material within the main body of the text into a logical, orderly and clear representation of the information. Lists occur frequently in educational and technical books, but crop up in all areas of publishing occasionally.

Lists are greatly beloved by school textbook authors, often to the point where they kill all possible interest in the subject. It is a good principle to use lists sparingly. However, there are numerous occasions where a listing is needed to set out points clearly and avoid endless repetition. Remember that the guiding rule here, as in so much of the writing process, should be consistency. If you number your list, first use an Arabic one, then a lower case *a* in brackets, then a lower case roman numeral *i* in brackets, i.e. 1(a)(i). In many books numbering is simply dispensed with and replaced by bullets (round black dots), black squares, dashes or other typographical marks.

If you type each item in the list on a new line, make sure that you follow a consistent layout of indentation and spacing. Follow a consistent rule over the use of a capital or lower-case letter at the beginning of each item, and a full stop or semi-colon at the end. You could, for instance, use a capital letter and full stop for sentences, or alternatively a lower case letter and semi-colon for words or phrases. Two common ways of constructing lists are indicated in Figure 21.2.

Design elements

I will make no attempt here to go into any detail on matters of design, typography or layout, since that requires a book in itself.

Example 1:

How to structure a book

1. General

(a) Distinguish clearly between preliminary matter, main text and end matter.

(b) List all items that make up the prelim matter, e.g. title page, contents.

(c) List all end matter, e.g. bibliography and index.

(d) Set out the type of headings and lists to be used if the material requires it.

Example 2:

How to structure a book

▶ In general we should—

— distinguish clearly between preliminary matter, main text and end matter;

— list all items that make up the prelim matter, e.g. title page, contents;

— list all end matter, e.g. bibliography and index;

— set out the type of headings and lists to be used if the material requires it.

Figure 21.2: Two possible ways of treating text as listings. The supreme virtue to aim for in listings is to be consistent throughout the book.

This area is also the responsibility of the publisher rather than the author. If the author does not trust his publisher to handle these elements competently, he should probably be looking for another publisher.

However, there are a few points to bear in mind as you write a manuscript. One of the important things to think about is the size or format that would be suitable for the book you are writing. The choice of **format** is governed partly by conventions within book publishing, partly by the availability of certain sheet sizes of paper and printing machines, partly by what is economical in terms of paper size, and partly on what is traditional in each area of publishing.

This is one of the areas where it is useful to have a discussion with a publisher at an early stage, preferably before you are too far into your manuscript. If the book has special requirements, for instance maps or tables or calculations, these may determine the format right from the beginning and affect the way you put your manuscript together. Specific formats are sometimes needed for marketing reasons (such as the small format peculiar to mass-market paperback fiction); or in the case of a mathematics book, it might be impossible to have two columns in the book, because calculations will run too wide for each column; or maps might be used that require a certain minimum size for the annotations to be legible. There are endless reasons why certain formats should be used for certain books, and also endless constraints from the point of view of economy and practicality.

So, while authors should look around at an early stage to see what works and what does not work in other books of a similar nature to the one they propose to write, they must be reminded that not all the examples can be followed slavishly. A common mistake made by authors, for instance, is to look at American textbooks and expect a local publisher to follow the same type of textbook layout. In most cases this is simply not possible, because American book sizes differ substantially from local ones. For considerations of economy, local publishers cannot normally provide the wide margins that are commonly found in American textbooks, and that are indeed probably required for that market.

The number of **columns** used on a page may affect the way you write your material. The number of columns will depend on the complexity of the material, the age group it is aimed at, and so on. In smaller format books consisting of text only, such as most fiction or academic works, you are likely to find one column only. Books for children mostly use one column for the sake of clarity, and are also likely to have fairly large type. By late primary and early secondary stage, a larger format with two columns and smaller type may be used.

Multicolumns are very popular in glossy general books, which often have two or three columns in a large format that allows for varying shapes of illustrations to be easily fitted into it.

Other design elements that may affect the way you set out your book are the size of margins, the choice of typeface and size, the spacing between lines of text, whether the type is justified or unjustified, and so on.

In a book with great complexity of design, such as a field guide, it is common to work out a few pages of final layout and have them set up in type as specimen pages before the author actually starts writing the manuscript. This is necessary because such a book has a highly formal structure to enable the user to find material of a complex nature in as easy a manner as possible. In such a case the author will be required to keep rigidly to a certain number of words for a particular type of description, or a column of a certain number of centimetres for a particular type of illustration, and so on.

Paragraphs and sentences ultimately also serve to break up text into bite-size pieces. Again the length of paragraph will be dictated by the audience and the type of book, and the complexity of the material.

22

Good writing

Good writing requires both innate talent and a careful honing of skills over a number of years. It is clearly impossible to explain how to write well in one chapter. As is always the case with any creative activity, it is easier to point out pitfalls than it is to explain how to do it.

The first question to ask yourself is: who is my audience? What age group or level of sophistication is my book aimed at? Is the audience likely to be first or second language speakers, or a mixture of both? Is the book intended for formal education or for armchair reading? Is it meant to be read through in one sitting, or will the reader just refer to small sections at a time?

All these factors should influence the level of your vocabulary, the complexity of your writing, the illustration methods you use, and so on. Generally speaking, good writing is simple writing. This is not always true, but it is usually true.

Vocabulary

Keep your vocabulary as simple as possible. You could do worse than follow the advice of Fowler in *The King's English*. Fowler introduces his general section on vocabulary as follows:

> Anyone who wishes to become a good writer should endeavour, before he allows himself to be tempted by the more showy qualities, to be direct, simple, brief, vigorous and lucid.
>
> This general principle may be translated into practical rules in the domain of vocabulary as follows:
>
> - Prefer the familiar word to the far-fetched.
> - Prefer the concrete word to the abstract.
> - Prefer the single word to the circumlocution.
> - Prefer the short word to the long.
> - Prefer the Saxon word to the Romance.

These rules are given roughly in order of merit; the last is also the least.

Some basic rules of good writing

Confusion is the enemy of clarity and lucidity. Some simple rules will go a long way towards making inaccessible text digestible:

- When you explain a procedure, particularly a complicated one, break it down into its component parts, and go through it step by step.
- The shorter your sentences, the better. Do not overdo it, though. Too many short sentences in a row become staccato and boring, but too many subordinate clauses in a sentence interfere with understanding.
- Make sure that each sentence conforms to the rules of simple logic. For example, a sentence such as "Being dilapidated, he did not like the house," means the man was dilapidated, not the house. This kind of sentence structure indicates sloppy thinking and should be avoided. Unnecessary words clutter up your sentences and interfere with meaning. For example, "owing to the fact that" can be replaced by "since".
- Avoid clichés and hackneyed phrases, and beware of mixed metaphors, for example "It hit me between the eyes like a sore thumb".
- Avoid using too many abbreviations. If you have to use them, explain what they mean—you should never simply assume that the reader is familiar with an abbreviation.
- If English is not your first language, be particularly attentive to the correct use of prepositions, the article concord, word order, and sequence of tenses.
- Avoid the passive voice like the plague. It always weakens your statements and makes for tedious writing. So rather "I did the work" than "The work was done by me". Address your readers directly wherever possible.
- Avoid the use of qualifiers, especially "very". Let adjectives and adverbs speak for themselves: "Very beautiful" should be "beautiful"; "very nice" should be "excellent".
- Sometimes words are simply not enough. A photograph, drawing, chart or table may be needed to convey meaning.
- Most people find written text easier to understand if you use concrete examples to illustrate your point. When writing for

children, integration of text and illustration, simple grammatical structures, easy vocabulary and lots of dialogue and examples are needed to keep the child's interest.

Correct reading levels

One of the most difficult things the author has to come to terms with is that he or she may have to write for a specific target group whose understanding of written English leaves much to be desired. Most authors hopelessly over-estimate the reading ability of their audience. This is true generally, but more specifically in the case of instructional material such as textbooks.

Over the years many people have tried to find an objective measure of the readability of a text. This has led to the development of readability formulae, of which Gunning's is probably the best known. Gunning devised a ratio known as the Gunning Fog Index which uses average sentence length and percentage of hard words as the basis for a formula by which to judge the level of difficulty of a piece of writing.

To work out the Fog Index on any piece of writing, do the following:

- Choose a sample passage of no more than 120 words.
- Count the number of words and of sentences. Find the average sentence length (ASL) by means of the following formula:

  ASL = Number of words over number of sentences
- Count the polysyllables, that is the words of three syllables or more, to determine the percentage of hard words (PHW):

  $$\text{PHW} = \frac{\text{Polysyllables}}{\text{Number of words}} \times \frac{100}{1}$$

  Note that proper names, combinations of short and easy words, and verb forms made into three syllables by -es or -ed (such as *created*) do not count as polysyllables.
- To determine the Fog Index:

  Fog Index = (ASL + PHW) × 0,4.

The resulting figure is an indication of the difficulty of the writing. If the figure is 12, the work is written at the reading level of a student who has done matric (the 12 refers to 12 years of school). If the figure is eight, it is written at a Standard six level, and if the figure is 17, it is written at the level of matric plus five years tertiary education.

The lower the Fog Index, the easier to understand the passage. In South Africa many students who have completed matric do not have a reading ability of 12. The situation is further complicated by the problem of second-language users. A simple rule of thumb is to deduct 2 from the Fog Index for second-language users. In other words, where normally an index of 12 might be acceptable for matric students, it should be 10 in the case of second-language students.

To use examples outside the world of books, the *Readers' Digest* magazine is fairly consistently written at a level of 9, and *Time Magazine* at a level of 13. When we look at major authors, Henry James comes in at 5,84, Graham Greene at 6,64, Joseph Conrad at 8,13, James Joyce at 9,52 and Charles Dickens at 10,04. The gospel according to St John rates 7. The point in using these examples is to show that understandable writing does not have to mean simplistic or patronising writing: quite the opposite. Most really good writing is simple to understand.

Many people have difficulty in accepting that two such simple measures as length of sentence and number of polysyllables can actually indicate readability levels. Of course there are numerous other factors that influence readability, but it is amazing how consistent and reliable this simple index can be. Other indices measure factors such as the number of times the passive voice is used, the number of relative clauses in a sentence, and so on.

To do random checks of your own written material to assess its readability would be too tedious for words. Fortunately there are a number of computer programs available that check levels of difficulty. These programs evaluate the readability of a document by examining word and sentence lengths, vocabulary and so on, and by calculating how many years of schooling are needed to understand a document. There are numerous programs on the market. Some of the ones available are: *Grammatic 5, RightWriter, Correct Grammar, Evaluate, PC Style, Pass, Clear Cut, Styled* and *Maxiread.* The latest versions of most word-processing programs now also include readability measuring, in fact, several different measuring systems in some cases.

The only institution in South Africa that has done much to promote the idea of readability indices is the University of South

Africa. The Bureau for University Teaching at Unisa developed the Unisa Fog Index (UFI) that seems to work well in South African conditions, and also works equally well for Afrikaans and English.

There can be no doubt that one of the reasons so many students drop out of the school and university system is that they experience difficulties with language. These difficulties are often compounded by the readability level of the material provided to the student to study from. The prevailing attitude is that writing things in clear and simple English is equivalent to a drop in standards. That is nonsense. Good writing is always clear and simple. The result is that most academic books published in this country are filled with convoluted sentences and polysyllabic tongue twisters. This contrasts with the clarity of American textbooks, most of which are written to clearly set and understood readability levels.

The situation is worse at schools. The most cursory examination of school textbooks will show that there is virtually no correlation between standard taught and readability level. Often the readability level will even vary widely within the same book, in the case of multi-author texts. It is an aspect to which most South African authors, publishers and educational authorities are blind.

Oddly enough, it is in the general (as opposed to educational) publishing field that you find examples of well-written text with a low readability level. Authors of books such as gardening and do-it-yourself manuals take great care to write simply, in a way that the person in the street will understand, because they know that if they don't do so, their books will not be bought and used. Sadly the same does not apply to educational texts, where the poor student has no choice in the matter.

23

House style

"Style" in the sense that I am using it in this chapter does not refer to literary style, but to the more mechanical aspects of writing, such as consistency of capitalisation, spelling and hyphenation; agreement of verb and subjects; beginning and ending quotation marks and parentheses; numbers given as figures or written out; and similar matters.

The house style of a publisher is the style preferred by that particular company. A publisher might provide an author with a sheet or booklet setting out his house style and ask the author to follow it where possible. Alternatively, the house style might be imposed by the copy-editor when working through the manuscript.

Publishers vary in the degree to which they insist on a house style. Some are emphatic that everything published by their company should adhere to the same basic rules, while others will fall in line with anything sensible suggested by the author. Southern Book Publishers falls in between these two extremes: we prefer authors to follow our style, but if they have already written a book we will not insist on their changing a particular aspect (such as using double quotes instead of single quotes) to conform to our house style, provided they have applied their own system consistently.

Why does consistency matter so much? It matters because variations in spelling, hyphenation and other minor areas serve to distract and irritate the reader and obscure the story or argument. A prescribed house style is essentially a tool to ensure consistency in these matters.

What follows in the rest of this chapter is a concise version of the house style of Southern Book Publishers. It is by no means exhaustive, but it does cover the main points with which authors normally experience problems. A far more comprehensive reference that is widely used is *Hart's Rules for Compositors and Readers*, published by Oxford University Press. The *Oxford Dictionary for Writers and Editors* is another helpful guide published by Oxford University Press.

If you are working on a word-processing program, you can use the spell-checking facility, but please remember that many spell checkers check for American as opposed to British spelling, whereas we are supposed to follow British spelling in South Africa. Also useful are the various grammar-checking programs such as *Correct Grammar* or *Grammatic 5*. On some of these programs you have the facility to set the program to particular types of usage in line with house style. For example, it is possible in *Correct Grammar* to set endings to "ise" or "ize" depending on preference. However, at their present level of development, these programs are limited in their efficiency; use them to pick up simple errors but do not rely on them heavily.

Abbreviations

- Omit full stops in all abbreviations ending with the last letter of the abbreviated word (e.g. St, Mr, Mrs but Hon., ed.), in and after abbreviated points of the compass, after roman numerals when used in a sentence, and after the phrase "per cent".
- Use capitals without full stops for abbreviations consisting of capital letters (e.g. USA, RAF, ANC) and upper and lower-case, also without full stops, for acronyms that are pronounced as words (e.g. Unesco, Nato, Cosatu, Unisa).
- Omit the plural *s* after abbreviations unless they end with the last letter of the abbreviated word (e.g. yds but kg, mm for plural). Do not add *s* to foreign contractions whose plural may be formed in some other way.

Bibliography

- Entries in the bibliography should follow the same rules as those described for references (obviously without page references)—see pages 180–181. Initials and first names follow the surname whenever the surname forms part of an alphabetical list. In all other cases initials and first names precede surnames (e.g. in multi-author works).

- Works by the same author appear in chronological order, with multi-author works following.
- Indent turnover lines 1 em (12 points).
- Where many works by an author appear, a 2 em rule may be used instead of repeating the author's name. If this system is used, be sure to be consistent.

Capitals

- Capitals are used for proper names and for titles etc. attached to them.
- In natural history texts the scientific (Latin) names of families, orders, classes, genera—whether as nouns or adjectives—take a capital while species, subspecies, varieties and cultivars are lower case. Vernacular names should be lower case throughout (e.g. bat-eared fox, giant eagle owl), except when a proper name forms part of the animal's name (e.g. Pel's fishing owl).
- In names such as "Jan van der Merwe" use lower case for the intervening articles or prepositions, except where the first name is omitted (e.g. "It was Du Toit's turn"). Use capitals in, for example, Mr Du Toit, Dr Van Rooyen.
- In geographical locations or features both the name of the feature and the feature should have a capital (e.g. Orange River, Hartebeespoort Dam). When referring back to a feature like Victoria Falls, Oribi Gorge, use lower case (e.g. the falls, the gorge). When referring to more than one geographical feature, use lower case for the feature (e.g. the Bloukrans and Bushmans rivers). Note the difference between Southern Africa (political) and southern Africa (geographical).
- Pronouns referring to God should be lower case.
- The names of political parties take a cap (e.g. Communist Party) but not when used in a general sense for the policies/ideologies they adhere to (". . . their socialist leanings . . .").
- Adjectives and nouns derived from proper names do not take a capital when their connection with the name is remote (e.g. catholic taste, roman type, a biblical turn of phrase, but Victorian era, Biblical authority).
- Proper names prefixed should be lower case throughout: pre-socratic, anti-hitlerian, semi-freudian, etc.

- In headings either use lower case throughout (the first word and proper names have capitals of course) or start all important words such as nouns and adjectives with a capital.
- When in doubt whether to use a capital or not, use lower case. Never capitalise a word purely for emphasis.

Dates

- Dates given in full should be printed as 12 January 1891, without punctuation or ordinal abbreviation. When the year is not given the form should be the same: 12 January. If the day of the month only is given it should be spelt out (e.g. the twelfth). The definite article should not be used before full dates, except when they are spelt out (e.g. the twelfth of January).
- When the day of the week and date of the month are given they should be separated by a comma (e.g. Friday, 16 June).
- Where abbreviated, months and days of the week should be reduced uniformly to three letters, and have no terminal full stop (e.g. Mar, Wed).
- BC should follow the date and AD should precede it; both should be typeset in small capitals.

Definite article

The definite article in titles should be set roman lower case, unless it forms an essential part of the title: thus "The Netherlands" but "the Carlton Hotel".

Figures

- In ordinary text, numbers under 10 and all numbers in reported speech or dialogue, or an indefinite amount or period, should be spelt out. In text where numbers occur repeatedly, numbers under 10 may be used as figures. Numbers of 10 and above should be used as figures, except at the beginning of a sentence. Never start a sentence with a date or a figure. Spell it out or rearrange the sentence. Plural figures take *s* without an apostrophe.
- Set all **specific** weights and measures in figures, using the metric system (e.g. "He has 3 km to go" but "It was hundreds

of metres long"). In general books, use per cent not %; in academic books % may be used. Always use % in tables.

- When printing inclusive numbers, use the fewest possible figures, unless the numbers or dates are spoken otherwise (68–9, 126–7, 1616–83; but 1688–1744, 216–18, 10–11). Use an unspaced en rule to separate them.

Footnotes and endnotes

- Notes are most easily found if printed at the foot of the page, but footnotes are expensive, and minor corrections may entail considerable rearrangement. For these reasons footnotes are to be avoided.
- If footnotes are essential, these should not be consecutively numbered: footnotes are numbered afresh on each page if there are more than one per page. If there is no more than one footnote per page, use an asterisk, not a number. It is acceptable to use a double asterisk for the second footnote on a page.
- Do not combine source references and explanatory notes in footnotes. The explanatory notes can be kept as footnotes but the source reference should be included as endnotes. Renumber as necessary.
- Preferable to the above (in academic works only) is the Harvard system for source references: the reference (author, date, page) is placed in brackets immediately after the appropriate text (e.g. Rankin 1983:109). If this system is used, check that all works referred to in the text appear in the bibliography and that dates and the spelling of names coincide.
- If a manuscript has numerous explanatory notes, they are less obtrusive and much cheaper if printed at the end of the book immediately before the index. They should not be put at the end of chapters, where they are hard to find. Use superior figures (without parentheses) in the text, the sequence beginning afresh with each chapter.

Hyphen

- A hyphen may be used to connect the parts of an adjectival phrase; it should not be inserted unless the text would be ambiguous without it (e.g. "a well-known man", but "the man was well known").

- Hyphens should be used in compound words when one syllable ends and the next begins with the same letter, e.g. co-operate (but uncooperative), in spelt-out fractions and measurements and compound nouns not normally spelt as one word.
- Note *tonight, tomorrow,* and *anyone, everyone, someone,* when used as nouns, but *no one*—two words without hyphen—*in so far, for ever, dare say.*
- Hyphens should not be used with adverbs qualifying adjectives if the sense is already clear (e.g. a highly competent person).

Italic

- Italic type should be used for the following:
  - — for emphasis (sparingly);
  - — for foreign words and phrases (but not proper names or phrases of foreign origin that have become an everyday part of English, e.g. per cent, entrée—consult *Hart's Rules* pp. 25–8 if you are not sure);
  - — for titles of books, plays, journals and ships (excluding H.M.S., s.s., etc.);
  - — for Latin scientific names (genus, species and varieties only—orders, families, cultivars to be roman);
  - — for enumerative letters;
  - — for mathematical variables such as *x* and *a*.
- Roman double-quoted, not italic, should be used for titles of articles, chapters, poems, or any part of a book, works of art and songs.
- Words or letters referred to as such ("the word *good*", "the term *expense*", "the letter *e*") should be set consistently either in italic or in roman double-quoted. Care should be taken to avoid confusion either with titles or with quoted matter.
- Conventional Latin abbreviations and phrases (lb., ibid., e.g., i.e., etc.) should not be italicised except when a single letter, e.g. *c.* (circa), *v.* (versus), or when the roman abbreviation has another meaning.

Metric units

- Put space between figures and metric units (e.g. 10 mm, 5 kg).
- Mathematical variables (*x, A*) are italic, while metric units and abbreviations are roman without full stops (kg, cm).

- Metric units, when spelt out, take lower case (e.g. millimetre, kilojoule).
- All metrication must be in line with specifications laid down by the SABS.
- Ensure that all measurements in a manuscript are in metric, not imperial (except in direct quotations).

Punctuation

- The apostrophe is used to mark an elision and the possessive case. The possessive *s* is omitted after plural words ending in s, but ONLY when it is not spoken after singular words ending in s, so in "Charles's friend" the possessive *s* is retained. Letters in the plural need 's, but figures and abbreviations consisting of initials take plain *s* (e.g. f's but 90s). No apostrophe should be put before teens, twenties, thirties, etc., or before phone, plane, cello, flu or bus, or in 1980s, 1870s, etc.
- If in doubt whether to insert a comma or not, omit it.
- Enclose parenthetic expressions between commas: "It was, she felt, too cold". If the interruption to the flow of the sentence is slight, BOTH commas may be omitted: "She was however not well". Never omit only one comma in such cases: "Her friend, Joan was late" is wrong.
- Place a comma before a conjunction introducing an independent clause: "The situation is perilous, but escape is still possible."
- Do not join independent clauses by a comma; use a colon or semi-colon instead, or break the text into separate sentences.
- Do not break sentences into two where there should be a comma; in other words, do not use full stops for commas.
- Omit full stops after all headings and after names and addresses printed below prefaces, after quotations, letters, etc. Figure captions do not need a full stop, unless they form a complete sentence or sentences. Even then the final full stop is optional.
- Parentheses (round brackets) should be used for simple interpolations; square brackets should be reserved for editorial notes or interpolations in quoted matter.
- Use double quotes for quoted words or passages and single for quotations inside quoted matter; revert to double for inside

quotes. Punctuation that is part of the quoted matter should be inside quotes. All punctuation, including terminal commas and full stops, that is not part of the quoted matter should be outside quotes.

Quotations

- Extended quotations (of more than about six lines) should be indented 1 em on the left, with 1 line space above and below. They should be typed with double-spaced lines like the main text; do NOT single-space the lines. They should not be enclosed within quotation marks.
- Interpolated unquoted matter (e.g. [he said], etc.)—should be placed within square brackets.
- Never edit direct quotations or change them to conform to house style. They should appear exactly as in the original.

References

- References to sources should run as follows. For books: author's surname, initials, title in italic (i.e. underlined in typewritten text or in italic in work done on a word processor), number of edition other than first, publisher, place and date of publication, volume and page number, all separated by commas, thus:
  Van Zyl, A.E., *Introduction to Marketing,* 2nd ed., Southern Book Publishers, Cape Town, 1994, Vol. 2, p.73.
  However, any sequence the author uses is acceptable, provided the order and the use of punctuation are consistent.
- After the first citation per chapter, references may be abbreviated to the shortest form that will still avoid confusion with the other references—normally surname, title and chapter and page reference:
  Hare, *Introduction,* 2 73.
  If the same reference occurs in a subsequent chapter, it must again be given in full the first time.
- For contributions to books: surname, initials, title of contribution in quotes, and for the rest as in the previous reference above:
  Peabody, R.W., "The Marketing Concept", in Van Zyl, A.E., *Introduction to Marketing,* etc.

This may be abbreviated to: name, book title, chapter and page reference:

Peabody, in *Introduction to Marketing,* 2 168.

- For articles in periodicals: name, title of article in quotes, name of journal in italics, volume and part number, place of publication, month or season and year, page number:

  Jones, A.B., "The Tribal Factor", in *Journal of Anthropology,* XII, London, 1991, p.20.
- Use capitals for all nouns, adjectives and other important words in book titles, e.g. *The First Principles of Physics* and not *The first principles of physics*. In scientific works, titles of papers are printed without quotation marks and with capital initials for proper nouns only.
- After the first citation of a reference in a chapter, subsequent references may also be given as "ibid." (not italic, no capitals) or "ibid. p.XXX" when the source is the same as the one directly above/preceding it. Omit author's name with "ibid." references. Repeat references to other sources already listed in full in that chapter should consist of the author's name and "op. cit. p.XXX". Avoid "idem" and "loc. cit.". Abbreviating the reference (see Peabody above) is however preferable in all cases.

Spelling

- The *-ise* spelling should be used in all words where *s* and *z* are alternatives (e.g. legalise, realisation).
- Spell: abridgement, acknowledgement, judgement and lodgement, artifacts, hyena, Mozambique (not Mocambique), Zaire, Malawi, per cent (not percent).
- Do not hesitate to use a good dictionary to check spelling, or use the spell-checking facility on your word-processing program (but beware Americanisms).

24

How to read proofs

In Chapter 16 we explained what proofs are and where they fit into the production process. We will now look at exactly what you are supposed to do with the proofs once you receive them.

An ordinary reader will tend to ignore spelling mistakes, and will even tend to read one sentence at a go. He or she concentrates on the author's meaning, and often barely takes in individual words. A good proofreader does exactly the opposite. He or she reads slowly, syllable for syllable, taking in every detail of punctuation, spacing and so on.

One of the main purposes of reading proofs is to make sure that the typesetter has not made any mistakes in keyboarding your material. If you handed in a disk and the typesetter worked straight from it, there should be little risk of wrong keyboarding, but you will still be required to read the proofs word for word against your original manuscript. This task can be greatly eased if you get another person to read the original out loud while you are checking the proof.

It is useful to read in two operations: first to check for details like spelling, capitalisation and other more mechanical points, and a second time to read for sense. You might also ask colleagues to read the proofs for you—one can never have enough proofreaders. It is one of the peculiarities of proofreading that everyone reading a set of proofs will pick up slightly different errors. In psychology there is even a term for such a condition: "proofreader's error".

Place a ruler under the sentence you are reading to isolate it from the other type and to make it easier to concentrate on that one line. If you find an error in the line, re-read that line a second time for you are inclined to miss a second error once you have focused on the first one.

On galley proofs you should check word breaks at the end of sentences very carefully. On page proofs you have far more things to check than merely the text itself. You should also look out for errors in the size and consistency of headings, page numbering, notes and references to notes in the text, the placing and size of illustrations and tables, etc. A major part of the job at page-proof stage is to fill in references to specific page numbers, chapters, illustrations, and so on.

A number of printing errors may need to be marked up: wrong type or size of letter, broken letters, unequal spacing, inconsistent indentations, and so on.

Marking corrections

There is normally room on the manuscript itself to write in alterations between lines, and that is accepted practice. In proofreading, however, the typesetter just runs his eye down the margin to see which lines contain corrections. A correction that is made in the text only will therefore not be picked up. The correction should be written in the margin (left or right, whichever is nearer) and level with the error. Two marks are needed: a textual mark in the line itself and an instruction in the margin. See Figure 24.1 for a list of commonly used proofreaders' marks, and Figure 24.2 for an example of how these marks are applied.

If the line of text contains a number of errors, the corrections in the margin should be marked in the order they are to be made in the line, reading from left to right. An oblique stroke separates one instruction from another. Where a number of errors occur in one sentence, it might be best to cross out the whole passage containing the errors and write it all correctly in the margin—it will take the typesetter less time to read the rewritten sentence than to do a number of small corrections.

Ask your editor what colour pen to use when making corrections. It is common for a publisher to have a colour-coding system when marking proofs so that the author's corrections can be separated from those of the editor or the printer's proofreader.

Always be aware that the person setting and correcting the text is unlikely to know anything about your subject, or even to have the slightest interest in it. Your marks should be absolutely clear and consistent. Suppress the temptation to make rude remarks in the margin where the typesetter has made a mess of things.

Corrections to proofs

The correction of proofs is a labour-intensive job and therefore expensive. The addition of one or two words in a sentence may lead to that sentence having to be reset, which may bump out the paragraph by one line, which may force the typesetter to take over that line to the next page, which might upset the balance on that page, and so on. You as author should look very carefully at the effect that any addition, deletion or change will have, especially at the page-proof stage. Unnecessary changes have four major drawbacks:

- The cost of author's corrections is often recouped by the publisher from the author.
- Unnecessary corrections can cause endless production delays.
- In correcting errors, the typesetter often makes further mistakes.
- Changes on page proofs might require the index to be redone.

All in all, the reading of proofs is a tedious but at the same time important job. Do it properly and thoroughly if you want to end up with a decent book.

Instruction	Mark in text	Mark in margin
Leave text unchanged	This is a hot potato	stet
Delete	This is not a hot potato	
Close up	This is a hot po tato	
Delete and close up	This is a hot pottato	
Insert in text	This is a potato	hot
Insert full stop, comma, semi-colon, colon, bracket	This is a hot potato	
Insert quotation marks	This is a hot potato	
Insert superior number	This is a hot potato	3
Insert hyphen	This is a hotpotato	-/
Insert dash	This is a hot potato	|—|
Change to italic type	This is a hot potato	ital
Change to roman type	This is a *hot potato*	rom
Change to bold type	This is a hot potato	bold
Change to capital letters	This is a hot potato	caps
Change to lower case	This is a HOT POTATO	l.c.
Insert space	Thisis a hot potato	#
Transpose letters	This si a hot potota	trs / trs
Insert new paragraph	This is a hot potato	
Run on (no new paragraph)	This is a hot potato	run on
Indent	This is a hot potato	
Align text with margin	This is a hot potato This is a hot potato This is a hot potato	||

Figure 24.1: A selection of the most commonly used proofreader's marks. Note that for each instruction there is a mark in the text and one in the margin.

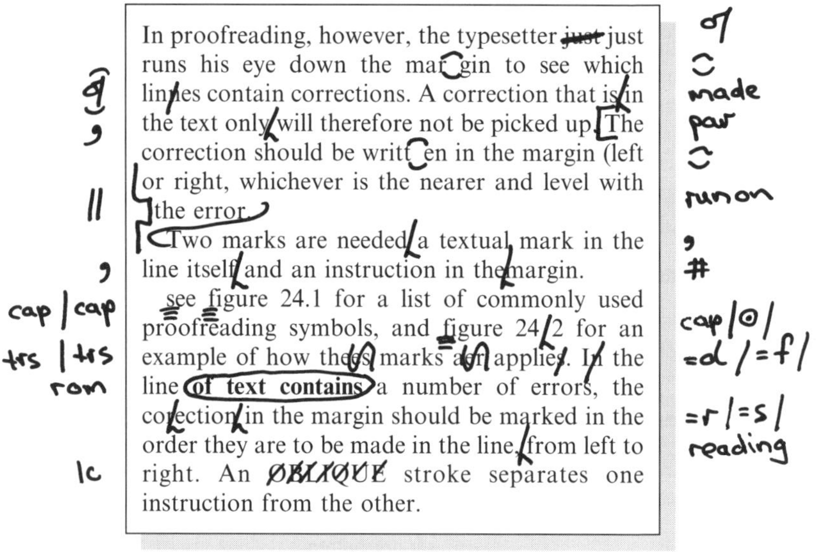
In proofreading, however, the typesetter just just runs his eye down the mar gin to see which linnes contain corrections. A correction that is in the text only will therefore not be picked up. The correction should be writt en in the margin (left or right, whichever is the nearer and level with the error.
Two marks are needed a textual mark in the line itself and an instruction in themargin.
see figure 24.1 for a list of commonly used proofreading symbols, and figure 24/2 for an example of how thees marks aer applies. In the line **of text contains** a number of errors, the corection in the margin should be marked in the order they are to be made in the line from left to right. An OBLIQUE stroke separates one instruction from the other.

Figure 24.2(a): Running text showing proofreading symbols as they are used in practice

In proofreading, however, the typesetter just runs his eye down the margin to see which lines contain corrections. A correction that is made in the text only, will therefore not be picked up.

The correction should be written in the margin (left or right, whichever is the nearer) and level with the error. Two marks are needed, a textual mark in the line itself, and an instruction in the margin.

See Figure 24.1 for a list of commonly used proofreading symbols, and Figure 24.2 for an example of how these marks are applied.

If the line of text contains a number of errors, the corrections in the margin should be marked in the order they are to be made in the line, reading from left to right. An oblique stroke separates one instruction from the other.

Figure 24.2(b): Running text after the corrections marked in Figure 24.2(a) were executed by the typesetter

25

How to prepare an index

The index usually begins on a right-hand page, and is set in two or three columns per page, in a type size smaller than that of the text itself. Like references, indices call for a great deal of close attention to tedious detail. Before starting to compile one, ask yourself a few questions.

The first question is: does the book really need an index? Many books do not. Examples are children's books, fiction, poetry, school textbooks (especially for lower standards) and numerous others where it is not particularly important to be able to find key concepts in an alphabetical manner. So the first rule of indexing is: don't unless you need to.

Even if an index is called for, consider whether the book needs a comprehensive one. Often it does not and you simply confuse the reader if you try to list every possible reference. For example: in a travel book you may well need nothing more than a place-name index; in a botanical field guide, you may need no more than an index to Latin names and an index to common names; in a who's who, you may need not more than an index of personal names. The most detailed index is not necessarily the most useful one.

However, many serious non-fiction books and certainly all books intended for serious reference and study should have a proper index to maximise their usefulness. To produce a good index, the indexer must be able to put him or herself in the position of the prospective reader of the book, decide which words, terms or phrases the reader is most likely to want to look up in the body of the text, and then set out the index in the simplest way possible so that the reader can gain easy access to the text. Whether a statement is pertinent or not is determined by the subject and purpose of the book, bearing in mind the kind of audience the book is aimed at. There is therefore no such thing as the perfect index, only the index most suitable for that particular book.

Apart from understanding the book's readership, the indexer should understand the content and context of the book and be able to work in an analytical, systematic and orderly way.

There are basically two ways of preparing an index: on cards or on a computer data base. Some word-processing packages also have indexing capabilities, but these will depend on the type of package you are working with and how much you know about that package. Most authors do not have an in-depth knowledge of the capacity of their word-processing packages and find it difficult to use the automatic indexing facilities.

In either event, it is usually only possible to prepare a proper index once you have received page proofs. The publisher should provide you with two sets of page proofs, one for reading and one for indexing purposes.

To prepare an index from cards, do the following:

- Underline each word in the text that you want to index. It is wise to do this first in pencil, because you will no doubt change your mind as you go on, after discovering either that you are underlining too many words or too few.
- Transfer the marked words on to index cards. Enter each word or phrase you underlined onto a separate card, together with the number of the page on which it occurs.
- The next step is to alphabetise all the cards, first according to the initial letter, and then alphabetically within each category of letter.
- You must now edit the cards to make the index meaningful. This involves grouping the headings, working out various classes of sub-headings, cross-references, and so on. You should try to supply at least one sub-entry if there are more than six references to any single heading. Don't overdo the sub-entries, though.
- The final step is to type the index in final form in double-spacing on A4 paper as you would the manuscript. The typing should be double-checked against the card entries at least twice, for mistakes are easily made.

Consult with your editor about the size the index should be. The index should be in proportion to the length of the book.

The best guide I know to card indexing and the principles of indexing in general is provided in Chapter 18 of *The Chicago Manual of Style*. It sets out in a logical and detailed fashion the mechanics and general principles of indexing, and the principles of alphabetising.

A shortcut to indexing is commonly used these days in the form of computerised data bases. Almost any computer data base can be used, including well-known ones like Lotus 1-2-3, and many word-processing programs have now also got the capacity to alphabetise words.

If you are using a data base, the procedure is initially the same: underline the words, names, phrases, and so on in the text that you would like to have taken up in the index; but then instead of transferring them manually to a card, you type them on to a data base. Once you have typed in all the words and phrases, you simply sort alphabetically. You will still need to edit extensively at this stage to create headings and sub-headings, cross-references, eliminate repeating entries, and so on, but it certainly speeds up the process and makes it more manageable.

In my experience authors make the best indexers for the simple reason that they know their subject and text better than anybody else. However, they often need to be guided by the editor on how to construct an index, and their first efforts might require a great deal of editing. If the author finds the task too daunting, the publisher can call in the services of a professional indexer. This can, however, be expensive, and the publisher is likely to deduct the cost of the indexer's services from the author's royalties.

The biggest problem with indices is that they have to be done in a late stage of production, after the author has received page proofs. Almost invariably there will be great pressure to meet publication deadlines, and most indices are done in a headlong rush that does not necessarily make for clear thinking and meticulous scrutiny of details. That is part of the reason why so many books appear with bad indices. If a good index is really necessary for your book, avoid the temptation to rush at this point.

Typographically indices can be arranged in one of two ways: set out or run on. The differences between the two is that in the set-out style, subentries are indicated by indentation, whereas in the run-on style, subentries are indicated by punctuation. See

Figure 25.1 for an example of each (taken from the index to *The Scramble for Africa* by Thomas Packenham). Agree with your editor at an early stage on the style to be used. Indices that are set out are easier to use but take up more space.

Jameson, Leander Starr: on Rhodes' expedition to Mashonaland, 374; accompanies Johnston to Lobengula, 388–90; invades Transvaal ('Jameson Raid'), 489–90, 498–503, 557–8; attack on Lobengula, 491–5; inaugurates Bulawayo, 497; prison sentence, 503; in South African union, 666.

Jameson, Leander Starr
on Rhodes' expedition to Mashonaland, 374
accompanies Johnston to Lobengula, 388–90
invades Transvaal ('Jameson Raid'), 489–90, 498–503
attack on Lobengula, 491–5
inaugurates Bulawayo, 497
prison sentence, 503
in South African union, 666.

Figure 25.1: Example of set-out (bottom) and run-on (top) styles of indexing. Note that the colon after "Starr" in the top example indicates that there are no page numbers relating to Jameson in general. Also note that the subentries follow the sequence of the book; they could also be arranged alphabetically by key word.

Part 5

A directory of South African publishers

Introduction

The following directory was compiled primarily by sending out questionnaires to members of PASA (The Publishing Association of South Africa). It is incomplete in several ways that the user should be aware of:

- It lists only South African publishers and not book importers.
- The reader should be aware that some overseas publishers with branches or agents in South Africa may also conceivably be interested in manuscripts from South African authors. I have, however, avoided listing overseas companies that do not actually publish in South Africa.
- Not all publishers returned the questionnaires, despite follow-up actions, so the list is not complete.
- I do believe, however, that all major publishers are included. Any publisher who is not included in this list, but would like to be included in a reprint, should write to me at P.O. Box 3103, Halfway House, 1685.
- It was not in all cases possible to get absolutely complete information from each publisher, so there are some slight variances in the information presented.
- Users of this directory should be aware that address and even name changes of publishers are not uncommon, as are changes in telephone and fax numbers.
- Inclusion in this list does not mean that I recommend these publishers to anyone or that they are somehow "better" than publishers not listed. This is merely a directory with no attempt made to indicate preference.

Note: Where the name of a company consists of the name of an individual, the company falls under the surname of the individual in the alphabetical listing, e.g. look for David Philip under *P* for Philip and not under *D* for David.

1. ACORN BOOKS

Address: P.O. Box 4845
Randburg
2125
Tel. no.: (011) 880-5768
Fax. no.: (011) 880-5768
Key contact names: Eleanor-Mary Cadell, Publisher
New titles published 1994: 2
1995: —
Number of titles in print: 8
Imprints: Acorn Books
Areas of publishing:

English:	Non-fiction, Africana, Natural history

2. BOOKCHAT

Address: P.O. Box 541
Grabouw
7160
Tel. no.: (021) 859-3081
Fax. no.: (021) 859-4000
Key contact names: Jay Heale, Editor
New titles published 1994: 3
1995: 2
Number of titles in print: 6
Imprints: Bookchat, Bookchat Booklets
Areas of publishing:

English:	Literature, Primary school, Juvenile, Children's, Reference

3. JONATHAN BALL PUBLISHERS

(incorporating AD Donker Publisher, Delta Books, Harper Collins SA and Who's Who of Southern Africa)
Address: P.O. Box 33977
Jeppestown
2043
Tel. no.: (011) 622-2900
Fax. no.: (011) 622-7610

Key contact names: Francine Blum
Maggie Fletcher
Parent company: Nasionale Boekhandel
New titles published 1994: 22
1995: 22
Number of titles in print: 196
Imprints: Jonathan Ball Publishers, AD Donker Publisher, Delta Books, Church of the Province of South Africa
Areas of publishing:

English:	Non-fiction, Literature, Academic and scholarly works, Reference, Religious, Africana, Business, Politics
Afrikaans:	Non-fiction, Reference, Religious
African Languages:	Religious

4. BUTTERWORTH PUBLISHERS

Address: P.O. Box 4
Mayville
4058
Tel. no.: (031) 268-3111
Fax. no.: (031) 268-3100
Key contact names: W.J. Last, Managing Director
J.E. Martens, Operations Director
M.B. Booth, Training and Seminars Director
C.A. Uniacke, Technical Director
V.A. Griffiths, Marketing Manager
T. Viljoen, Legal Publishing Manager
M. van Zyl, Financial Manager
New titles published 1994: 171
1995: 285
Number of titles in print: 450
Imprints: Butterworths, Digma, Blackstone Press (agents)
Areas of publishing:

English:	Tertiary textbooks, Professional, Reference, Legal and Taxation, Electronic publishing, Lexis-Nexis
Afrikaans:	Tertiary textbooks, Professional, Reference, Legal and Taxation

5. CAMBRIDGE UNIVERSITY PRESS

Address: 1 The Moorings
Portswood Ridge
Victoria and Alfred Waterfront
Cape Town
8001
Tel. no.: (021) 419-8414
Fax. no.: (021) 419-8418
Key contact names: S.A. Seddon, Director
Susan Joubert, Commissioning Editor
Fiona Thomson, Commissioning Editor
New titles published 1994: 0
1995: 0
Number of titles in print: 22
Imprints: Cambridge University Press
Areas of publishing:

English:	Non-fiction, Primary school, Secondary school, Tertiary textbooks, Academic and scholarly works, Professional, Children's, Reference, Religious

6. THE CARREFOUR PRESS

Address: P.O. Box 2629
Cape Town
8000
Tel. no.: (021) 64-4136
Key contact names: Dee Murch, Director
New titles published 1994: —
1995: —
Number of titles in print: 30
Areas of publishing:

English:	Non-fiction, Literature, Religious

7. CHAMELEON PRESS

Address: P.O. Box 117
Plumstead
7801
Tel. no.: (021) 75-3195
Fax. no.: (021) 75-8011

Key contact names: G. Waletzki, Office Manager
New titles published 1994: 1
1995: —
Number of titles in print: 25
Areas of publishing:

English:	Non-fiction, Reference, History, Cookery, Art, Gift books, Science (Physics)
Afrikaans:	Non-fiction, Reference, History, Gift books

8. CLEVER BOOKS

Address: P.O. Box 20113
Alkantrant
0005
Tel. no.: (012) 342-3263
Fax. no.: (012) 43-2376
Key contact names: Henda Steenhuisen
New titles published 1994: 12
1995: 7
Number of titles in print: 1 000
Areas of publishing:

English:	Primary school, Secondary school, Pre-primary
Afrikaans:	Primary school, Secondary school, Pre-primary
African Languages:	Pre-primary

9. DRAGON

Address: P.O. Box 116
St. James
7946
Tel. no.: (021) 788-6834
Fax. no.: (021) 788-6834
Key contact names: Erika van Greunen
New titles published 1994: 1
1995: —
Number of titles in print: 1
Imprints: Dragon

Areas of publishing:

English:	Religious, Philosophy
African Languages:	Religious, Philosophy

10. EDUCUM

Address: P.O. Box 3068
Halfway House
1685
Tel. no.: (011) 315-3647
Fax. no.: (011) 315-2757
Key contact names: Dr Wim de Wet, General Manager
Dr Ernest North, Publishing Manager
Mr Cyprian Mahlaba, Marketing Manager
New titles published 1994: 36
1995: 43
Number of titles in print: 900
Imprints: Educum, Varia, Bona Books, Umfolozi Books, Ukhozi Press, Lubombo Books, Capricorn Books
Areas of publishing:

English:	Primary school, Secondary school
Afrikaans:	Primary school, Secondary school, Reference
African Languages:	Literature, Popular fiction, Primary school, Secondary school, Reference

11. ENVIRONMENTAL DEVELOPMENT AGENCY TRUST

Address: P.O. Box 15840
Doornfontein, Johannesburg
2028
Tel. no.: (011) 402-5161
Fax. no.: (011) 402-0298
Key contact names: Lorraine Mutewera
Victor Munnick
New titles published 1994: —
1995: 1
Number of titles in print: 1
Areas of publishing:

English:	Non-fiction

12. FERNWOOD PRESS

Address: P.O. Box 15344
Vlaeberg
8018
Tel. no.: (021) 683-3784
Fax. no.: (021) 61-8574
Key contact names: Pieter Struik, Managing Director
New titles published 1994: 4
1995: 4
Number of titles in print: 14
Imprints: Fernwood Press
Areas of publishing:

English:	Non-fiction, Reference, Africana

13. FIRESIDE PUBLICATIONS

Address: 4th Floor
31 Adderley Street
Cape Town
8001
Tel. no.: (021) 45-5558/461-8498
Fax. no.: (021) 461-8470
Key contact names: Richard Gaskell, Marketing
Richard Grenville, Finance
Safia Abdullah, Administration
New titles published 1994: —
1995: 12
Number of titles in print: 18
Imprints: Hammond, United Memorial Bible Services, Ferguson, Academy for Mathematics and Science, Home Study Programmes, Comptons
Areas of publishing:

English:	Literature, Popular fiction, Primary school, Secondary school, Academic and scholarly works, Children's, Reference, Religious, Audiovisual, Mathematics and Science
Afrikaans:	Primary school, Secondary school, Academic and scholarly works, Audiovisual, Mathematics and Science
African Languages:	Reference

14. W.J. FLESCH & PARTNERS

Address: P.O. Box 3473
Cape Town
8000
Tel. no.: (021) 461-7472
Fax. no.: (021) 461-3758
E-mail: sflesch@aztec.co.za
Key contact names: Stephen Flesch, Managing Director
New titles published 1994: 1
1995: 3
Number of titles in print: 8
Areas of publishing:

English:	Non-fiction, Reference, Cookery, Aviation

15. FORESIGHT PUBLICATIONS

Address: P.O. Box 1079
Somerset West
7129
Tel. no.: (021) 855-2197
Fax. no.: (021) 855-2198
Key contact names: Ken Ramsden, Publisher
Cathy Ramsden, Marketing Manager
New titles published 1994: —
1995: —
Number of titles in print: 3
Areas of publishing:

English:	Non-fiction, Road transport management and legislation, Dangerous goods

16. FRANCOLIN PUBLISHERS

Address: P.O. Box 18726
Wynberg
7824
Tel. no.: (021) 72-0373
Fax. no.: (021) 75-5001
Key contact names: Douglas van der Horst, Publishing Director
New titles published 1994: —
1995: 6
Number of titles in print: 11

Imprints: Francolin Publishers, Peninsula Books
Areas of publishing:

English:	Primary school, Secondary school, Tertiary textbooks, Professional, Reference, Teacher education

17. GARAMOND PUBLISHERS

Address: P.O. Box 924
Durbanville
7551
Tel. no.: (021) 975-4046
Fax. no.: (021) 975-1318
Key contact names: Kees Hage, Owner
New titles published 1994: 68
1995: 74
Number of titles in print: 247
Areas of publishing:

English:	Children's
Afrikaans:	Children's
African Languages:	Children's

18. GECKO BOOKS

Address: P.O. Box 127
Pavilion
3611
Tel. no.: (031) 86-5178/25-3657
Fax. no.: (031) 25-3771
Key contact names: Gertrud Strauss
Veronica Klipp
New titles published 1994: 10
1995: 10
Number of titles in print: 26
Areas of publishing:

English:	Non-fiction, Literature, Primary school, Juvenile, Children's
Afrikaans:	Children's
African Languages:	Children's

19. HEINEMANN PUBLISHERS

Address: P.O. Box 371
Isando
1600
Tel. no.: (011) 974-1181
Fax. no.: (011) 974-4311
Key contact names: Kevin Kroeger, Managing Director
Laura Czerniewicz, Director: Strategy and Staff Development
Mike Smuts, Financial Director
Jannie Wilken, Sales and Marketing Director
Nick Evans, Publishing Director
Sabelo Zulu, Publishing Director
Margarethe Mostert, Director: Higher and Further Education
New titles published 1994: 80
1995: 100
Number of titles in print: 2 000
Imprints: Heinemann, Heinemann-Centaur, Centaur, Isando Books, Lexicon, Ginn, Butterworth-Heinemann
Areas of publishing:

English:	Literature, Primary school, Secondary school, Tertiary textbooks, Academic and scholarly works, Professional
Afrikaans:	Literature, Primary school, Secondary school, Tertiary textbooks, Academic and scholarly works, Professional
African Languages:	Literature, Primary school, Secondary school

20. HIBBARD PUBLISHERS

Address: P.O. Box 40251
Arcadia
0007
Tel. no.: (012) 804-3990/1
Fax. no.: (012) 804-1240
Key contact names: Tersia Hibbard, Manager
Lynette Casey, Editor
New titles published 1994: 8
1995: 5
Number of titles in print: 66

Imprints: Bard, Galactic, Thandi Art Press, Manx
Areas of publishing:

English:	Non-fiction, Literature, Popular fiction, Primary school, Secondary school, Juvenile, Children's, Reference, Young adult, Study guides, Games, Posters
Afrikaans:	Non-fiction, Literature, Popular fiction, Primary school, Secondary school, Juvenile, Children's, Reference, Study guides
African Languages:	Non-fiction, Literature, Popular fiction, Tertiary textbooks, Secondary school, Academic and scholarly works, Juvenile, Children's, Reference, Young adult, Study guides

21. HIPPOGRIFF PRESS

Address: P.O. Box 191
Parklands
2121
Tel. no.: (011) 646-4229
Fax. no.: (011) 646-4229
Key contact names: E.M. MacPhail
New titles published 1994: —
1995: —
Number of titles in print: 6
Areas of publishing:

English:	Literature, Fiction

22. HODDER & STOUGHTON EDUCATIONAL

Address: P.O. Box 3948
Randburg
2125
Tel. no.: (011) 886-4920
Fax. no.: (011) 886-5326
Key contact names: G.E. de Villiers, Executive Chairman
D. Lea, Deputy Managing Director
New titles published 1994: 24
1995: 24
Number of titles in print: 235
Imprints: Hodder & Stoughton, Baobab Books (SA), The Fountain Press

Areas of publishing:

English:	Primary school, Secondary school, Tertiary text-books, Juvenile, Children's, Reference
African Languages:	Literature, Primary school, Secondary school

23. HOUSTON PUBLISHING

Address: P.O. Box 35
Greenpoint
8051
Tel. no.: (021) 439-9772
Fax. no.: (021) 439-9772
Key contact names: Desmond J. Thompson
New titles published 1994: 1
1995: 2
Number of titles in print: 3
Areas of publishing:

English:	Non-fiction, Literature, Primary school, Secondary school, Children's, Health cookery

24. HUMAN & ROUSSEAU

Address: P.O. Box 5050
Cape Town
8000
Tel. no.: (021) 25-1280
Fax. no.: (021) 419-2619
Key contact names: Kerneels Breytenbach, General Manager
New titles published 1994: 159
1995: 145
Number of titles in print: 1 242
Imprints: Human & Rousseau
Areas of publishing:

English:	Non-fiction, Juvenile, Children's (trade and mass market), Religious, Arts and crafts, Cookery, Leisure books
Afrikaans:	Fiction, Non-fiction, Juvenile, Children's (trade and mass market), Religious, Arts and crafts, Cookery, Leisure books
African Languages:	Children's trade publications

25. HUMAN SCIENCES RESEARCH COUNCIL (HSRC)

Address: 134 Pretorius Street
Pretoria
0002
Tel. no.: (012) 202-2330
Fax. no.: (012) 202-2891
Key contact names: R. Keet, Assistant Publisher
New titles published 1994: 60
1995: 64
Number of titles in print: 250
Areas of publishing:

English:	Non-fiction, Academic and scholarly works, Professional, Reference
Afrikaans:	Non-fiction, Academic and scholarly works, Professional, Reference

26. INDICATOR SA

Address: University of Natal
Private Bag X10
Dalbridge
4014
Tel. no.: (031) 260-2526
Fax. no.: (031) 260-2813
Key contact names: Karen MacGregor, Editor and Head
Rob Evans, Production and Design
Pat Fismer, Administration and Marketing
New titles published 1994: 1
1995: 5
Number of titles in print: 12
Imprints: Indicator Press, Indicator SA
Areas of publishing:

English:	Non-fiction, Academic and scholarly works, Reference, Journals, Booklets

27. INSTITUTE FOR DEMOCRACY IN SOUTH AFRICA (IDASA)

Address: P.O. Box 575
Rondebosch
7700

Tel. no.: (021) 689-8389
Fax. no.: (021) 689-3261
Key contact names: Sue Valentine, Media Director
Lindiwe Kulu, Administrator
Moira Levy, Media co-ordinator, IDASA Information Centre
New titles published 1994: 1
1995: 7
Number of titles in print: 22
Imprints: IDASA
Areas of publishing:

English:	Non-fiction, Secondary school, Tertiary textbooks, Academic and scholarly works, Democracy education, Good governance, Public information on parliament, the budget, public opinion surveys, migrancy
Afrikaans:	Non-fiction
African Languages:	Non-fiction

28. INTERNATIONAL THOMSON PUBLISHING

Address: P.O. Box 2459
Halfway House
1685
Tel. no.: (011) 805-4819
Fax. no.: (011) 805-3648
E-mail: lmartini@thrasher.co.za
Key contact names: Fergus Hall, Managing Director
Leanne Martini, Academic Publishing Manager
Eloise Wessels, Commissioning Editor
New titles published 1994: 12
1995: 15
Number of titles in print: 110
Areas of publishing:

English:	Tertiary textbooks, Academic and scholarly works, Professional
Afrikaans:	Tertiary textbooks, Academic and scholarly works, Professional

29. ISIMU YELWAZI PUBLISHERS

Address: 90 Harris Street
Colbyn
Pretoria
0083
Tel. no.: (012) 342-1236
Fax. no.: (012) 342-1236
Key contact names: Barend Joubert, Manager
New titles published 1994: —
1995: 21
Number of titles in print: 39
Imprints: Isimu Yelwazi Publishers, Eulitz Productions
Areas of publishing:

Afrikaans:	Children's, Religious
African Languages:	Literature, Secondary school

30. IVY PUBLISHING

Address: 18 Cardiff Road
Parkwood
2193
Tel. no.: (011) 880-4117
Fax. no.: (011) 880-2483
Key contact names: F. Suzor, Secretary
New titles published 1994: —
1995: —
Number of titles in print: —
Areas of publishing:

English:	Non-fiction, Literature, Primary school, Secondary school, Academic and scholarly works, Fiction

31. JUTA & COMPANY

Address: P.O. Box 14373
Kenwyn
7790
Tel. no.: (021) 797-5101
Fax. no.: (021) 762-7424

Key contact names: J.E. Duncan, Managing Director
R.J.H. Cooke, Deputy Managing Director
C.W. Wallander, Director: Retail
J.C. Potgieter, Director: Education
P.M. Nel, Director: Finance
New titles published 1994: 364
1995: 344
Number of titles in print: 3 108
Imprints: Juta, Prima Books/Boeke
Areas of publishing:

English:	Literature, Primary school, Secondary school, Tertiary textbooks, Academic and scholarly works, Professional, Adult basic education, Non-formal education
Afrikaans:	Literature, Primary school, Secondary school, Tertiary textbooks, Academic and scholarly works, Professional, Adult basic education, Non-formal education
African Languages:	Literature, Primary school, Secondary school, Adult basic education, Non-formal education

32. JUTASTAT

Address: P.O. Box 14373
Kenwyn
7790
Tel. no.: (021) 797-9261
Fax. no.: (021) 761-0771
Key contact names: Anton van Dorsten, Managing Director
Welna Kruger, Branch Manager, Johannesburg: (011) 803-8770
New titles published 1994: 6
1995: 4
Number of titles in print: 14
Imprints: Jutastat (Pty) Ltd (a subsidiary of Juta & Co Ltd)
Areas of publishing:

English:	Electronic publishing
Afrikaans:	Electronic publishing

33. KAGISO PUBLISHERS

Address: P.O. Box 629
Pretoria
0001
Tel. no.: (012) 328-4620
Fax. no.: (012) 328-4706
Key contact names: Lindelwe Mabandla, Managing Director
Colin Bower, Publishing (021) 47-1368
Bruce Ferreira, Operations
Jan Wilken, Central Warehouse (012) 666-9033
New titles published 1994: 245
1995: 179
Number of titles in print: 2 393
Imprints: Kagiso Publishers, Kagiso Tertiary, Kagiso Literary, HAUM, Juventus, Femina, Rostrum, Out of Africa, Engedi
Areas of publishing:

English:	Non-fiction, Literature, Popular fiction, Primary school, Secondary school, Tertiary textbooks, Academic and scholarly works, Professional, Juvenile, Children's, Religious, Audio-visual materials, ABET, ECE, Distance education
Afrikaans:	Non-fiction, Literature, Popular fiction, Primary school, Secondary school, Tertiary textbooks, Academic and scholarly works, Professional, Juvenile, Children's, Religious, Audio-visual materials, ABET, ECE, Distance education
African Languages:	Non-fiction, Literature, Popular fiction, Primary school, Secondary school, Tertiary textbooks, Academic and scholarly works, Juvenile, Children's

34. HANS KIRSTEN PUBLISHERS

Address: P.O. Box 35890
Menlo Park
0102
Tel. no.: (012) 348-5426
Fax. no.: (012) 348-5429
Key contact names: Mr Hans Kirsten
Mr Adolph Kirsten
Mrs Gisela Johannes
New titles published 1994: 30
1995: 30

Number of titles in print: 137
Imprints: Ace Publishers, Colibri Publishers
Areas of publishing:

English:	Primary school, Secondary school, Tertiary textbooks, Academic and scholarly works, Children's
Afrikaans:	Literature, Primary school, Secondary school, Tertiary textbooks, Academic and scholarly works, Children's, Religious, Africana
African Languages:	Primary school, Secondary school, Tertiary textbooks, Academic and scholarly works

35. KNOWLEDGE UNLIMITED

Address: Private Bag 16
Centurion
0046
Tel. no.: (011) 652-1800
Fax. no.: (011) 314-2984
Key contact names: M.A.C. Jacklin, Managing Director
B.H. Mason, Production Manager
H.J.M. Retief, Rights and Permissions
Ansie Fouché, Sales Manager
New titles published 1994: 100
1995: 150
Number of titles in print: 100
Imprints: Daan Retief, Knowledge Unlimited, Kennis Onbeperk, Mike Jacklin
Areas of publishing:

English:	Children's
Afrikaans:	Popular fiction, Children's
African Languages:	Children's

36. KWELA BOOKS

Address: P.O. Box 6525
Roggebaai
8012
Tel. no.: (021) 406-3191
Fax. no.: (021) 406-3196

Key contact names: Dr Annari van der Merwe, Manager
Erika Gouws, Editor
New titles published 1994: —
1995: 12
Number of titles in print: 23
Imprints: Kwela Books, Kwela Boeke
Areas of publishing:

English:	Non-fiction, Literature, Popular fiction, Reading matter for newly literate adults
Afrikaans:	Non-fiction, Literature, Popular fiction, Reading matter for newly literate adults
African Languages:	Literature, Popular fiction, Reading matter for newly literate adults

37. KZN BOOKS

Address: P.O. Box 2413
Pinetown
3600
Tel. no.: (031) 701-4591
Fax. no.: (031) 701-7564
Key contact names: S.C. Scholtz, Manager
New titles published 1994: —
1995: —
Number of titles in print: 20
Areas of publishing:

English:	Literature, Primary school, Secondary school, Tertiary textbooks, Academic and scholarly works, Juvenile, Children's
Afrikaans:	Primary school, Secondary school
African Languages:	Literature, Primary school, Secondary school, Tertiary textbooks, Academic and scholarly works, Juvenile, Children's

38. LEXIS

(A division of Nasionale Boekhandel)
Address: P.O. Box 5496
Cape Town
8000

Tel. no.: (021) 406-3752
Fax. no.: (021) 406-2926
Key contact names: H.D. Büttner, Manager
Peter Martin, Marketing Manager
New titles published 1994: 3
1995: 4
Number of titles in print: 61
Imprints: Lexis
Areas of publishing:

English:	Dictionaries
Afrikaans:	Dictionaries
African Languages:	Dictionaries

A new imprint of the Nasionale Boekhandel Group under which all dictionaries in Afrikaans, English and African languages previously published by Tafelberg, J.L. van Schaik, Nasou and Via Afrika have been consolidated since 1996.

39. LEX PATRIA

Address: P.O. Box 17040
Doornfontein
2028
Tel. no.: (011) 776-9111
Fax. no.: (011) 402-7226
Key contact names: Koos van Niekerk, General Manager
New titles published 1994: 6
1995: 8
Number of titles in print: 35
Imprints: Lex Patria
Areas of publishing:

English:	Tertiary textbooks, Academic and scholarly works, Professional
Afrikaans:	Tertiary textbooks, Academic and scholarly works, Professional

40. LOVEDALE PRESS

Address: Private Bag 1346
Alice
5700

Tel. no.: (0404) 3-1135
Fax. no.: (0404) 3-1871
New titles published 1994: 3
1995: 7
Number of titles in print: 105
Areas of publishing:

English:	Popular fiction, Primary school, Tertiary textbooks, Academic and scholarly works, Professional, Juvenile, Children's, Africana
Afrikaans:	Popular fiction
African Languages:	Literature, Popular fiction, Primary school, Secondary school, Reference, Religious

41. LUX VERBI

Address: P.O. Box 1822
Cape Town
8000
Tel. no.: (021) 21-5540
Fax. no.: (021) 419-1865
Key contact names: H. Stephan Spies, CEO
M. Volschenk, Marketing Manager
New titles published 1994: 35
1995: 65
Number of titles in print: 405
Imprints: Lux Verbi, NG Kerk-Uitgewers, Waterkant-Uitgewers
Areas of publishing:

English:	Juvenile, Children's, Religious
Afrikaans:	Juvenile, Children's, Reference, Religious, Social

42. MACMILLAN S.A.

Address: P.O. Box 32484
Braamfontein
2017
Tel. no.: (011) 339-2935
Fax. no.: (011) 403-1627
Key contact names: T. Ball, Sales and Marketing Director
P. Murby, Publishing Director
New titles published 1994: 120
1995: 140

Number of titles in print: 650
Imprints: Macmillan Boleswa, Macmillan South Africa, Macmillan Botswana, Nolwazi Educational Publishers
Areas of publishing:

English:	Non-fiction, Literature, Popular fiction, Primary school, Secondary school, Tertiary textbooks, Academic and scholarly works, Professional, Reference
Afrikaans:	Literature, Primary school, Secondary school
African Languages:	Literature, Primary school, Secondary school

43. MACMILLAN ACADEMIC, SOUTHERN AFRICA

Address: P.O. Box 31487
Braamfontein
2017
Tel. no.: (011) 403-8435
Fax. no.: (011) 403-8315
E-mail: coryv@iafrica.con
Key contact names: Cory Voigt, General Manager
New titles published 1994: —
1995: —
Number of titles in print: —
Imprints: Macmillan Press, W.H. Freeman, Worth Publishers, Sinauer Associates
Areas of publishing:

English:	Tertiary textbooks, Academic and scholarly works, Reference

44. MAKRO BOOKS

Address: P.O. Box 913-042
Voortrekkerhoogte
0143
Tel. no.: (012) 666-8710
Fax. no.: (012) 666-8710 ask for 23
Key contact names: Johan Nel
Jannie Malan
New titles published 1994: 15
1995: 23
Number of titles in print: 200
Imprints: Makro, Benedic, Trumpet, Connoisseur

Areas of publishing:

English:	Non-fiction, Primary school, Secondary school, Tertiary textbooks, Academic and scholarly works, Professional, Children's
Afrikaans:	Non-fiction, Literature, Popular fiction, Primary school, Secondary school, Tertiary textbooks, Academic and scholarly works, Professional, Juvenile, Children's, Religious, Large print fiction
African Languages:	Literature, Popular fiction, Juvenile, Children's, Religious

45. MASKEW MILLER LONGMAN

Address: P.O. Box 396
Cape Town
8000
Tel. no.: (021) 531-7750
Fax. no.: (021) 531-4049
Key contact names: M.A. Peacock, Chief Executive
F. Dada, Managing Director: Education Division
S. Connolly, Managing Director: Development Division
New titles published 1994: 150
1995: 200
Number of titles in print: 3 000
Imprints: Maskew Miller Longman, MML
Areas of publishing:

English:	Literature, Primary school, Secondary school, Tertiary textbooks, Academic and scholarly works, Professional, Juvenile, Children's
Afrikaans:	Literature, Primary school, Secondary school, Tertiary textbooks, Children's
African Languages:	Literature, Primary school, Secondary school, Tertiary textbooks, Juvenile, Children's

46. NASOU

Address: P.O. Box 5197
Cape Town
8000

Tel. no.: (021) 406-3313
Fax. no.: (021) 406-2922
Key contact names: L. Naudé, General Manager
E. van der Lingen, Senior Manager Publishing
New titles published 1994: 27
1995: 38
Number of titles in print: 500
Imprints: Nasou
Areas of publishing:

English:	Primary school, Secondary school, Tertiary textbooks
Afrikaans:	Primary school, Secondary school, Tertiary textbooks
African Languages:	Literature, Primary school, Secondary school

47. NEW GUILD SA

Address: P.O. Box 11476
Bloubergrant
7443
Tel. no.: (021) 557-0704
Fax. no.: (021) 557-0704
Key contact names: Terry Stobart, Director
Anthea Bartie, Promotions
Rachel Toping, Editor
New titles published 1994: —
1995: —
Number of titles in print: 11
Areas of publishing:

English:	Non-fiction, Popular fiction

48. NOLWAZI EDUCATIONAL PUBLISHERS

Address: P.O. Box 32484
Braamfontein
2017
Tel. no.: (011) 339-2935
Fax. no.: (011) 403-2505
Key contact names: Peter Murby, Director
New titles published 1994: —
1995: 6
Number of titles in print: 19

Areas of publishing:

English:	Non-fiction, Primary school, Secondary school
African Languages:	Literature, Primary school

49. OPTIONS PUBLISHING

Address: P.O. Box 1588
Somerset West
7129
Tel. no.: (021) 852-4728 / 852-7134
Fax. no.: (021) 851-2592 / 852-4728
Key contact names: Mick Cromhout, Publisher
Monica Cromhout, Editor
New titles published 1994: 6
1995: 8
Number of titles in print: 13
Imprints: Escreet Books, Writers World
Areas of publishing:

English:	Non-fiction, Literature, Popular fiction, Reference, Religious/Spiritual, Africana, Books for writers, Small business, 'How to' books, Specialist small run books, Autobiographies

50. OXFORD UNIVERSITY PRESS SOUTHERN AFRICA

Address: P.O. Box 1141
Cape Town
8000
Tel. no.: (021) 45-7266
Fax. no.: (021) 45-7265
Key contact names: Kate McCallum, Managing Director
Hanri Pieterse, Publishing Director
Colleen McCallum, Sales and Marketing Director
New titles published 1994: 120
1995: 70
Number of titles in print: 800
Areas of publishing:

English:	Non-fiction, Literature, Primary school, Secondary school, Tertiary textbooks, Academic and scholarly works, Professional, Juvenile, Children's, Reference, Africana

Afrikaans:	Non-fiction, Literature, Primary school, Secondary school, Tertiary textbooks, Academic and scholarly works, Professional, Juvenile, Children's, Reference
African Languages:	Non-fiction, Literature, Primary school, Secondary school, Tertiary textbooks, Academic and scholarly works, Professional, Juvenile, Children's, Reference, Africana

51. PENGUIN BOOKS (SA)

Address: Private Bag X14
Parkview
2122
Tel. no.: (011) 482-1520
Fax. no.: (011) 482-6669
Key contact names: John Allen, Managing Director
Alison Lowry, Publishing Manager
New titles published 1994: 12
1995: 35
Number of titles in print: 70
Imprints: Penguin SA, Puffin, Pelham, Viking
Areas of publishing:

English:	Non-fiction, Literature, Popular fiction, Academic and scholarly works, Professional, Juvenile, Children's, Reference, Religious, Africana, Sport

52. PERSKOR

Address: P.O. Box 3068
Halfway House
1685
Tel. no.: (011) 315-3647
Fax. no.: (011) 315-2757
Key contact names: Connie Nel, General Manager
Cecilia Britz, Chief Publisher: Fiction
Neels du Plooy, Chief Publisher: Religious
New titles published 1994: 64
1995: 52
Number of titles in print: 240
Imprints: Perskor, Orion, Vlaeberg

Areas of publishing:

English:	Religious
Afrikaans:	Literature, Popular fiction, Juvenile, Religious

53. DAVID PHILIP PUBLISHERS

Address: P.O. Box 23408
Claremont
7735
Tel. no.: (021) 64-4136
Fax. no.: (021) 64-3358
Key contact names: David Philip, Managing Director and Chair
Marie Philip, Rights Director and Chair
Russel Martin, Executive Director (Publishing)
Bridget Impey, Executive Director (Marketing)
Graham Elliott, Accounts
New titles published 1994: 35
1995: 25
Number of titles in print: 300
Imprints: Africasouth Paperbacks, Africasouth New Writing, Songololo Books
Areas of publishing:

English:	Non-fiction, Literature, Secondary school, Tertiary textbooks, Academic and scholarly works, Juvenile, Children's, Reference, Religious, Biography, Natural History
Afrikaans:	Juvenile, Children's
African Languages:	Literature, Juvenile, Children's

54. RAVAN PRESS

Address: P.O. Box 145
Randburg
2125
Tel. no.: (011) 789-7636
Fax. no.: (011) 789-7653
Key contact names: Monica Seeber, General Manager
Ipuseng Kotokoane, Marketing and Sales Manager
Matthew Seal, Production Manager

New titles published 1994: 7
1995: 7
Number of titles in print: 162
Imprints: Ravan
Areas of publishing:

Afrikaans:	Non-fiction, Literature, Secondary school, Tertiary textbooks, Academic and scholarly works, Professional, Juvenile, Africana

55. READER'S DIGEST ASSOCIATION

Address: P.O. Box 2677
Cape Town
8000
Tel. no.: (021) 440-5111
Fax. no.: (021) 440-5411
Key contact names: Nick McRae, Managing Director
Fay Bentley, Marketing Director
Christopher Walton, Editor-in-Chief
Jackie Dyble, Product Manager: General Books
Fay Davids, Public Affairs Manager
New titles published 1994: 8
1995: 8
Number of titles in print: 30
Imprints: The Reader's Digest Association of SA,
AA Motorist Publications
Areas of publishing:

English:	Non-fiction, Literature, Juvenile, Children's, Reference, Religious, Africana, Cooking, Do-it-Yourself, Gardening, Health Guide books

56. READ WELL

Address: P.O. Box 4573
Pietersburg
0700
Tel. no.: (0152) 295-2193
Fax. no.: (0152) 295-2194

Key contact names: Piet van Heerden, Managing Director
M.J. Matemane, Publisher
Ivy Raselomane, Secretary
New titles published 1994: —
1995: —
Number of titles in print: 3
Areas of publishing:

English:	Non-fiction, Literature, Popular fiction, Primary school, Secondary school, Tertiary textbooks, Children's, Geography, History, Mathematics
Afrikaans:	Non-fiction, Literature, Popular fiction, Primary school, Secondary school, Tertiary textbooks, Children's, Geography, History, Mathematics
African Languages:	Non-fiction, Literature, Popular fiction, Primary school, Secondary school, Tertiary textbooks, Children's

57. RHODES UNIVERSITY

Address: P.O. Box 184
Grahamstown
6140
Tel. no.: (0461) 31-8438
Fax. no.: (0461) 2-3487
E-mail: lbsr@giraffe.ru.ac.za
Key contact names: Sandra Rowoldt
New titles published 1994: 20
1995: 20
Number of titles in print: 250
Imprints: Rhodes University and Departments and Institutes of the University
Areas of publishing:

English:	Non-fiction, Literature, Tertiary textbooks, Academic and scholarly works, Professional, Reference, Religious, Africana
Afrikaans:	Academic and scholarly works
African Languages:	Non-fiction, Literature, Tertiary textbooks, Academic and scholarly works, Africana

58. ROEDURICO TRUST

Address: P.O. Box 810
Somerset West
7129
Tel. no.: (021) 852-3104
Fax. no.: (021) 851-6874
Key contact names: Philip van Rensburg, Managing Director
Nico van Rensburg, Director: Sales and Marketing
New titles published 1994: —
1995: —
Number of titles in print: 24
Areas of publishing:

English:	Secondary school
Afrikaans:	Secondary school

59. SACHED BOOKS

Address: Private Bag X08
Bertsham
2013
Tel. no.: (011) 496-1730
Fax. no.: (011) 496-1117
Key contact names: Mel Holland, Publishing Manager
Paul Miemi, Marketing Executive
New titles published 1994: —
1995: 15
Number of titles in print: 45
Imprints: Sached Books
Areas of publishing:

English:	Adult education: Readers and courses, and numeracy courses
Afrikaans:	Adult education: Readers and courses
African Languages:	Adult education: Readers and courses

60. SEYFFERDT PUBLISHERS

Address: P.O. Box 44
Bapsfontein
1510
Tel. no.: (011) 964-2778/1551

Fax. no.: (011) 964-2778
Key contact names: A.E. Seyfferdt, Director
New titles published 1994: 15
1995: 15
Number of titles in print: 35
Areas of publishing:

English:	Secondary school, Tertiary textbooks, Academic and scholarly works
Afrikaans:	Secondary school, Tertiary textbooks, Academic and scholarly works

61. SHUTER & SHOOTER

Address: P.O. Box 109
Pietermaritzburg
3200
Tel. no.: (0331) 94-6830/8881
Fax. no.: (0331) 42-7419
Key contact names: Dave Ryder, Managing and Publishing Director
Piet van Heerden, Regional Director
Terry Hepworth, Regional Director
New titles published 1994: 72
1995: 80
Number of titles in print: 1 015
Imprints: Edubooks
Areas of publishing:

English:	Non-fiction, Literature, Primary school, Secondary school, Tertiary textbooks, Juvenile, Children's, Reference, Religious
Afrikaans:	Non-fiction, Literature, Primary school, Secondary school, Children's, Reference
African Languages:	Non-fiction, Literature, Popular fiction, Primary school, Secondary school, Tertiary textbooks, Juvenile, Children's, Reference

62. SOUTHERN BOOK PUBLISHERS

Address: P.O. Box 3103
Halfway House
1685

Tel. no.: (011) 315-3633
Fax. no.: (011) 315-3810
Key contact names: Basil van Rooyen, Managing Director
Louise Grantham, Publishing Director
Debby de Groot, Local Sales Manager
Paul Steedman, Agency Sales Manager
New titles published 1994: 55
1995: 32
Number of titles in print: 221
Imprints: Southern Book Publishers
Areas of publishing:

English:	Non-fiction (including natural history, travel and leisure, gardening), Technical textbooks, Reference
Afrikaans:	Non-fiction, Reference

63. THE STORYTELLER GROUP

Address: P.O. Box 617
Melville
2109
Tel. no.: (011) 482-3008
Fax. no.: (011) 726-1632
Key contact names: Neil Napper, Managing Director
New titles published 1994: —
1995: —
Number of titles in print: 20
Areas of publishing:

English:	Comic books
Afrikaans:	Comic books
African Languages:	Comic books

64. STRUIK BOOK DISTRIBUTORS

Address: P.O. Box 624
Bergvlei
2012
Tel. no.: (011) 444-9473
Fax. no.: (011) 444-9472
Key contact names: Nick Pryke, Managing Director
Marga Collings, Publishing Manager: Zebra Press

New titles published 1994: 10
1995: 24
Number of titles in print: 43
Imprints: Struik Book Distributors, Zebra Press
Areas of publishing:

English:	Non-fiction, Professional, Computer/Internet
Afrikaans:	Professional

65. STRUIK CHRISTIAN BOOKS

Address: P.O. Box 193
Maitland
7405
Tel. no.: (021) 551-5900
Fax. no.: (021) 551-1124
Key contact names: A. Verschoyle, Managing Director
R. Crouse, Publishing Manager
New titles published 1994: —
1995: 25
Number of titles in print: 179
Imprints: SCB
Areas of publishing:

English:	Religious
Afrikaans:	Religious

66. STRUIK PUBLISHERS

Address: P.O. Box 1144
Cape Town
8000
Tel. no.: (021) 462-4360
Fax. no.: (021) 462-4379
Key contact names: Lois O'Brien, Director: Publishers
Linda de Villiers, Publishing Director
Janice Evans, Design Director
New titles published 1994: 90
1995: 120
Number of titles in print: 961
Imprints: Struik, Timmins, Struik Timmins, New Holland Publishers

Areas of publishing:

English:	Non-fiction, Children's, Reference, Home interest, Medical and sex, Natural history, Travel and leisure
Afrikaans:	Non-fiction, Children's, Reference, Home interest, Medical and sex, Natural history, Travel and leisure
African Languages:	General, Reference
German:	Natural history, Travel and leisure
French:	Travel and leisure

67. TAFELBERG PUBLISHERS

Address: P.O. Box 879
Cape Town
8000
Tel. no.: (021) 24-1320
Fax. no.: (021) 24-2510
Key contact names: Riana Scheepers, Public Relations Officer
New titles published 1994: 98
1995: 91
Number of titles in print: 1 617
Imprints: Tafelberg Publishers, Delos
Areas of publishing:

English:	Juvenile, Children's
Afrikaans:	Non-fiction, Literature, Popular fiction, Professional, Juvenile, Children's, Reference, Religious, Africana
African Languages:	Juvenile, Children's

68. UNIVERSITY OF CAPE TOWN PRESS (UCT PRESS)

Address: University of Cape Town
Private Bag
Rondebosch
7700
Tel. no.: (021) 24-4519
Fax. no.: (021) 23-2453
Key contact names: Ms R. Meny-Gibert, Publisher
Ms T. Petersen, Publishing Assistant
Parent company: Juta & Co Ltd and University of Cape Town

New titles published 1994: 8
1995: 15
Number of titles in print: 32
Imprints: UCT Press
Areas of publishing:

English:	Literature, Academic and scholarly works

69. UNIVERSITY OF NATAL PRESS

Address: Private Bag X01
Scottsville
Pietermaritzburg
3209
Tel. no.: (0331) 260-5225
Fax. no.: (0331) 260-5599
Key contact names: Ms M.P. Moberly, Managing Director
Dr J.J. Edley, Rights and Permissions
New titles published 1994: 9
1995: 6
Number of titles in print: 90
Imprints: Killie Campbell African Library, Hadeda Books
Areas of publishing:

English:	Non-fiction, Literature, Academic and scholarly works, Books on KwaZulu-Natal, Women's issues

70. UNISA PRESS

Address: P.O. Box 392
Pretoria
0001
Tel. no.: (012) 429-3051
Fax. no.: (012) 429-3221
Key contact names: Phoebe van der Walt, Director
Sarie Moolman, Head: Publishing Section
New titles published 1994: 46
1995: 29
Number of titles in print: 150
Imprints: Unisa Press
Areas of publishing:

English:	Non-fiction, Tertiary textbooks, Academic and scholarly works, Professional, Reference, Religious

Afrikaans:	Non-fiction, Tertiary textbooks, Academic and scholarly works, Professional, Reference, Religious
African Languages:	Tertiary textbooks, Academic and scholarly works

71. J.P. VAN DER WALT AND SON

Address: P.O. Box 123
Pretoria
0001
Tel. no.: (012) 325-2100
Fax. no.: (012) 325-5498
Key contact names: C.J. Steenkamp, Managing Director
R.J.J. van Rensburg, Manager
Imprints: JP van der Walt, Keurbiblioteek, Treffer-Boekklub, Eike-Boekklub, President-Boekklub, Romankeur, Symbol Books
Areas of publishing:

English:	Non-fiction, Literature, Popular fiction, Primary school, Juvenile, Children's
Afrikaans:	Non-fiction, Literature, Popular fiction, Primary school, Tertiary textbooks, Academic and scholarly works, Juvenile, Children's, Reference, Religious

72. J.L. VAN SCHAIK PUBLISHERS

Address: P.O. Box 12681
Hatfield
0028
Tel. no.: (012) 342-2765
Fax. no.: (012) 43-3563
Key contact name: George Louw, General Manager
New titles published 1994: 70
1995: 66
Number of titles in print: 86
Imprints: J.L. van Schaik, J.L. van Schaik Academic, Academica, Joan Lötter Publications
Areas of publishing:

English:	Non-fiction, Literature, Primary school, Secondary school, Tertiary textbooks, Academic and scholarly works, Professional, Juvenile, Children's, Reference, Religious

Afrikaans:	Non-fiction, Literature, Popular fiction, Primary school, Secondary school, Tertiary textbooks, Academic and scholarly works, Professional, Juvenile, Children's, Reference, Religious
African Languages:	Non-fiction, Literature, Popular fiction, Primary school, Secondary school, Tertiary textbooks, Academic and scholarly works, Juvenile, Children's, Reference, Religious

73. VIA AFRIKA

Address: P.O. Box 151
Pretoria
0001
Tel. no.: (012) 342-1964
Fax. no.: (012) 342-1846
Key contact names: D.H. Schroeder, General Manager
E.R. Arnold, Senior Manager: Publications
A. Gouws, Senior Manager: Marketing and Associated Companies
C. van Jaarsveld, Manager: Administration and Systems
New titles published 1994: 73
1995: 45
Number of titles in print: 1 400
Imprints: Acacia, Afro, Afritech, Via Afrika, Atlas, Bateleur, KZN
Areas of publishing:

English:	Primary school, Secondary school, Juvenile, Religious, Adult basic education
Afrikaans:	Primary school, Reference, Religious
African Languages:	Primary school, Secondary school, Tertiary textbooks, Juvenile, Children's, Religious, Adult basic education

74. VIVA BOOKS

Address: P.O. Box 28510
Kensington
2101
Tel. no.: (011) 616-2980/615-5250
Fax. no.: (011) 622-7169

Key contact names: Kevin French, Publisher
Linde Woolley, Publisher
Karin Griessel, Commissioning Editor
New titles published 1994: 4
1995: 10
Number of titles in print: 25
Areas of publishing:

English:	Non-fiction readers, Primary school readers, Secondary school readers, Adult basic education and training readers
Afrikaans:	Non-fiction readers, Primary school readers, Secondary school readers, Adult basic education and training readers
African Languages:	Non-fiction readers, Primary school readers, Secondary school readers, Adult basic education and training readers

Publishers of supplementary readers for ABET and schools.
South African literature in an adapted form and autobiographies and biographies.

75. VIVLIA PUBLISHERS

Address: P.O. Box 1014
Florida Hills
1716
Tel. no.: (011) 472-3912
Fax. no.: (011) 472-4904
Key contact names: A.N. Nemukula, Managing Director
Grace Monate, Secretary
S. Mota, Sales and Marketing Director
H. Sekhote, Field Editor Manager
New titles published 1994: 17
1995: 25
Number of titles in print: 20
Imprints: Vivlia
Areas of publishing:

English:	Non-fiction, Literature, Popular fiction, Primary school, Secondary school, Tertiary textbooks, Academic and scholarly works, Children's

Afrikaans:	Non-fiction, Literature
African Languages:	Literature, Tertiary textbooks, Children's, Religious

76. WITWATERSRAND UNIVERSITY PRESS

Address: P.O. Wits
2050
Tel. no.: (011) 484-5907
Fax. no.: (011) 484-5971
Key contact names: Franscois McHardy, Acting Director
Pat Tucker, Managing Editor
Cheryl Brant, Commissioning Editor
New titles published 1994: 20
1995: 25
Number of titles in print: 110
Imprints: WUP; Witwatersrand University Press
Areas of publishing:

English:	Non-fiction, Literature, Secondary school, Tertiary textbooks, Academic and scholarly works, Professional, Reference, Religious, Africana, Drama
Afrikaans:	Tertiary textbooks
African Languages:	Literature, Secondary school

77. Y PRESS

Address: 801 Berea Centre
249 Berea Rd
Durban
4001
Tel. no.: (031) 21-6084
Fax. no.: (031) 21-6488
Key contact names: Belinda Yiangou, Publishing Director
New titles published 1994: 1
1995: 2
Number of titles in print: 12
Imprints: Publishing Works, LRA Charts
Areas of publishing:

English:	Non-fiction, Tertiary textbooks, Academic and scholarly works, Professional
African Languages:	Literature

78. ZACHEN UITGEWERS/PUBLISHERS

Address: P.O. Box 38190
Garsfontein
0042
Tel. no.: (012) 98-4636
Fax. no.: (012) 998-6621
Key contact names: Adri van Rooyen
Dirk Benadé
New titles published 1994: —
1995: —
Number of titles in print: 24
Areas of publishing:

English:	Technical and engineering drawing
Afrikaans:	Technical and engineering drawing

Miscellaneous information

There are several trade associations that cater for various parts of the book trade:

PASA (Publishers' Association of South Africa)

PASA was formed in 1992 when the then existing trade associations catering for publishers (SAPA – the South African Publishers' Association, which represented mainstream local publishers; IBDA – the International Book Distributors' Association, which represented overseas publishers and distribution agents; and IPASA – the Independent Publishers' Association, which represented on the whole smaller and "alternative" publishers) decided to amalgamate into one major trade association for the publishing industry.

PASA is made up of three major interest groups: one for educational (read school) books; one for academic books (read tertiary textbooks); and one for general or consumer books. A fourth interest group looks after publishing training and development.

PASA has a permanent office in the Western Cape. You can contact the PASA administrator at the following address:

Address: PASA Office
P.O. Box 116
St James
7946
Tel. no.: (021) 788-6470
Fax. no.: (021) 788-6469

Please note that it is not the PASA office's function to provide authors with advice on where to publish – it is devoted to internal cooperation and communication among publishers, and to liaising between PASA and other stakeholders in the book trade.

ABSA (Associated Booksellers of South Africa)

ABSA is the equivalent of PASA for the bookselling community. It has a trade magazine called *Bookmark* which is published every three months. ABSA does not have a permanent administrator but can be contacted through the office of the President.

Address: P.O. Box 870
Bellville
7535
Tel. no.: (021) 951-6611
Fax. no.: (021) 951-4903

PIFSA (Printing Industries Federation of South Africa)

This is the trade association for printers – not only book printers, but all printers. PIFSA runs a very modern and impressive training facility for the whole printing industry at Honeydew, north of Johannesburg. You can contact PIFSA at:

Address: P.O. Box 1084
Honeydew
2040
Tel. no.: (011) 794-3810
Fax. no.: (011) 794-3964

Publishing training available in South Africa

Some authors may feel the need to get to know more about the business of publishing, and indeed, many authors are interested in a publishing career. Formal training in publishing skills is quite a recent event in South Africa. Up until a few years ago the only way one could learn was by doing. While experience will probably always be the best teacher, there are now a number of formal courses available in the country.

The Publishing Training Project (PTP)

Contact person: The coordinator
Address: PO Box 95379
Grant Park
2051
Tel. no.: (011) 728-2898
Fax. no.: (011) 728-3164

The PTP runs under the auspices of PASA and offers short courses from one day to five days long. While these are predominantly aimed at people already working within the industry, individuals who wish to attend courses are welcome to do so.

The PTP monitors industry needs and plans courses on a six-months basis.

Regular courses include:

- An overview of book publishing
- Commissioning
- Introduction to production processes
- Introduction to book marketing
- Editing for accessibility
- Copyright and contracts
- Copy-editing

Other courses which have been offered include:

- Senior publishing management (with The Book House, London)
- Senior management training for production managers (with The Book House, London)
- Developing distance education materials
- Editing for technical subjects
- Editing for maths and science
- Textbook design
- Textbooks and educational methodology

(The Book House is the training organisation affiliated to the British Publishers' Association.)

University of the Witwatersrand

Contact person: Professor Isabel Hofmeyer
Address: African Literature Department
Private Bag 3
Wits
2050
Tel. no.: (011) 716-4082
Fax. no.: (011) 716-8030 (marked African Literature)

The African Literature Department at Wits offers an Honours in Publishing Studies. The course comprises four modules, a research report and a placement. The four courses are:

- Publishing Studies A (covering key issues in SA publishing)
- Publishing Studies B (a series of workshops)

- Teaching African literature in the classroom
- Developing English teaching/learning materials for different educational contexts

University of Pretoria

Contact person: Christa North, lecturer in Publishing
Address: Department of Information Science
University of Pretoria
Pretoria
0002
Tel. no.: (012) 420-9111
Fax. no.: (012) 420-3686

The University of Pretoria offers an Honours in publishing in the Department of Information Studies. A Master's degree is also offered. From 1997 Pretoria University will be offering a BA degree in publishing studies. This course will include courses in Information Science, a language, Visual Communication, Library Science and Business Management.

The university also offers part-time introductory certificate publishing courses as well as occasional short courses.

University of Western Cape

Contact person: Professor Tony Parr
Address: Department of English
University of Western Cape
Private Bag X17
Bellville 7535
Tel. no.: (021) 959-2964
Fax. no.: (021) 959-2202

From 1997 the English Department at UWC plans to offer a special option in publishing studies at Honours and Master's level.

University of Cape Town

Contact person: Ian Glenn
Address: English Department
University of Cape Town
Private Bag
Rondebosch
7700

Tel. no.: (021) 650-2836
Fax. no.: (021) 650-3726 (marked English Department)

Third-year students in the English Department at UCT are able to select a double module in publishing as one of their chosen options. Obviously you have to be majoring in English already to be able to choose this option.

Plans to start a post-graduate diploma in publishing at UCT have not taken off.

INTEC College

Contact person: Moira Edmunds, Publishing Executive
Address: P.O. Box 19
Cape Town
8000
Tel. no.: (021) 448-3405
Fax. no.: (021) 47-9004

INTEC is a private commercial college offering courses by distance education. INTEC plans to offer courses in publishing studies from 1997.

Further reading

In this section I look at each part of this book and suggest works that may be of use for particular aspects of writing. In many cases editions are not listed, since these works tend to be of a type that are constantly updated. It obviously makes sense to acquire the latest edition wherever possible.

Part 1: The book publishing industry in South Africa

The list below, compiled by Laura Czerniewicz of Heinemann, is a selection of readings focusing on publishing in South Africa. A comprehensive list can be found in Hans Zell's bibliography (listed below) – this list simply attempts to highlight those readings that are the most relevant and useful for people particularly interested in South African publishing.

Books

Altbach, P.G. and Hoshino, E.S. (eds.), *International Book Publishing: An Encyclopedia*, Garland Publishing, 1995. A comprehensive and valuable book comprising 34 articles on key publishing topics many of which are relevant to South Africa, and 30 essays on specific regions/countries.

Bethlehem, L., *An Industrial Strategy for the Pulp and Paper Sector*, UCT Press, 1994. A useful background document for those interested in publishing as part of the broader book chain.

Book Publishing in South Africa for the 1990s, South African Library, 1991. A collection of papers covering a number of issues in SA publishing.

Kromberg, S. (ed.), *Publishing for Democratic Education*, Sached Books, 1993. Articles adapted for publication from the presentations at the conference of the same name. Deals with a range of the key issues in South African publishing.

PASA Directory, PASA, 1996. The official directory of all publishers belonging to the Publishers' Association of South Africa (PASA). Available from the PASA Office (see address under Miscellaneous).

Priestley, C., *Development Directory of Indigenous Publishers*, APNET, 1995. Includes information about publishers and publishing in Southern Africa.

Taitz, L. (ed.), *Directory of Book Publishing in South Africa*, Publishing Training Project and British Council, 1995. Useful, as it describes what kinds of books each South African publisher produces. Also lists information about people and organisations working for and with South African publishers.

Zell, H., *Publishing and Development in the Third World*, London, Vistaar Publications, 1992. The standard reference work highlighting key publishing development issues. Papers by a good selection of important people in this field.

Zell, H. and Lomer, C., *Publishing and Book Development in Sub-Saharan Africa: An Annotated Bibliography*, Hans Zell Publishers, 1996.

Journals and newsletters

African Book Publishing Record. A long-established journal, including articles, news and a regular update of books being published in Africa. Available from P.O. Box 56, Oxford, OX1 2SJ, England.

African Publishing Review. The newsletter of the African Publishers Network (APNET), distributed free to publishers in Africa as well as those interested in publishing in Africa. Available from P.O. Box 4209, Harare, Zimbabwe.

Book Development Council Newsletter. An occasional newsletter from the South African Book Development Council, available from P.O. Box 30994, Braamfontein, 2017.

Bookchat. This publication focuses on what is happening in children's writing and publishing in South Africa. Available from P.O. Box 541, Grabouw, 7160.

Bookmark. Published by the Association of Booksellers of South Africa (ABSA). Available from P.O. Box 23660, Claremont, 7735.

Publish! A newsletter by subscription to keep South African publishers, editors, writers and booksellers informed; includes extracts from recent newspaper articles, information about competitions and so on. Available from P.O. Box 1588, Somerset West, 7129.

Pegboard. An occasional publication of the Professional Editors' Group (PEG), mostly freelancers working for South African publishers. Available from P.O. Box 85410, Emmarentia, 2029.

Papers, articles, etc.

British Publishers' Association: *Mission Report on the Book Trade in South Africa*, 1994.

Czerniewicz, L, 'Training for a Change,' Report for Independent Publishers' Association (IPASA) and African Literature Department of University of Witwatersrand, 1994.

Czerniewicz, L, 'South African Publishing: The Transition Edition,' *African Publishing Review*, 1994.

Czerniewicz, L. *et al.*, 'Report on Textbook Provision and Procurement,' for the Implementation Project of Education and Training (IPET) for the CEPD, 1994.

Davis, G. and Holger, G., 'Levelling the Playing Fields: An Interview with David and Marie Philip,' *Matatu*, 11, 1994.

De Villiers, I.F.A., 'Government Publishing in South Africa Today,' *Government Information Quarterly*, 3(4), 1986.

Denning, C., 'South African Textbook Study,' unpublished research report for Overseas Development Administration (British Government), 1992.

Donker, A.D., 'English Language Publishing in South Africa,' in Gardner, S. (ed.), *Sociology of Southern African Literature*, Wits, 1986.

Evans, N., 'Book Publishing in South Africa: Some Facts and Figures,' for UNESCO seminar on publishing in Africa, 1995.

Gunderson, H. and Rudolph, J. (eds.), *Together as One: Copyright Protection against Unauthorised Reproduction: The Seminar on Copyright and the Collective Administration of Rights within the Southern African Development Co-ordination Conference*, August 1991, published by Kopinor, 1992.

Holland, M., 'The State of Publishing in South Africa,' paper presented at ANC conference, April 1993.

Horwitz, E., Talk to Bibliophiles Conference on the state of South African publishing today – article to be published in *Cape Librarian*, 1996.

Joubert, S., 'Publishing in the New South Africa,' *African Book Publishing Record*, 1991.

Joubert, S., 'Publishing in Another South Africa: Problems and Projections,' dissertation in part requirement for the M.Phil., University of Stirling, 1990.

Kantey, M., 'The Provision of Textbooks in South Africa,' research report to the National Education Policy Investigation, 1992.

Kantey, M., 'Book Publishing in South Africa: A Provisional Sketch,' 1989.

PASA documents. The PASA office has a number of valuable documents, particularly about educational publishing in South Africa. These include information about the costs involved in textbook publishing and purchasing, selection procedures for school book buying and so on. As these documents are specifically for PASA members, you would need to become an associate member of PASA in order to have access to them.

Philip, D. and Kantey, M. 'Publishing in South Africa,' in Altbach, P.G. and Hoshino, E.S. (eds.), *International Book Publishing: An Encyclopedia*, Garland Publishing, 1995.

Randall, P., 'An Overview of Publishing in South Africa,' in Gardner, S. (ed.), *Sociology of Southern African Literature*, Wits, 1986.

Seeber, M., 'Woman to Woman Communication: A Report on Women and Development Material in South Africa,' prepared for Women Ink, New York, 1995.

'Special Focus on Southern Africa,' *Publishers Weekly*, August 1996.

'Textbook tremor,' *Finance Week*, 14 October 1993.

'Women in Publishing and Book Development in Africa: A Provisional Listing' prepared by the African Books Collective, Oxford, 1995.

It needs to be said that the above readings tend to concentrate on socio-political matters, political change, and textbook provision. More commercial snippets of news about South African publishing can be gleaned from occasional articles in *The Bookseller*, the organ of the British book trade.

One section for which an enormous range of books exists, is the one dealing with publishing overseas. Apart from the commonly used and available *The Writers' and Artists' Yearbook* from A.C. Black and *The Writer's Handbook* from Macmillan that were also mentioned in the main body of the text, there is a steady stream of books available on various aspects of breaking into print in the United Kingdom and the United States, useful only to the extent that you intend to get published there.

Major sources about the publishing industry world-wide are *International Literary Market Place* (dealing with countries outside the USA) and *Literary Market Place* (dealing with the USA itself), published annually by Bowker, which provide endless information on publishers, distributors, literary agents and the like. Also useful is the much less ambitious *Directory of Publishing: United Kingdom, Commonwealth and Overseas* published annually by Cassell in the UK. Both contain some (rather oddly selected) information about South African publishers as well.

Part 2: How to find the right publisher

The information in this section tends to be fairly generic. It is based on general knowledge and common sense, and further reading on the subject is unlikely to enlighten the prospective author greatly.

Part 3: How publishing works

There are several books available that discuss publishing agreements. They are, however, all written from British or American perspectives. They are also written with publishers and literary agents in mind, so they tend to be too technical for the purposes of the author. If you have problems with publishing and royalty agreements, it is probably better to consult your family lawyer or a lawyer specialising in copyright matters, since the South African law of contract applies to such agreements

The publishing process is admirably explained in *Basic Editing: A Practical Course* by Nicola Harris. This is one of the excellent texts developed by The Book House training centre, which is administered by the British Publishing Association. These courses, which also cover matters such as marketing and production, were developed for UNESCO, and are sufficiently generic to be used world-wide. I leaned more heavily on this text than any other in writing the book, also with regard to the sections on editing and manuscript preparation.

Book costing is not a matter on which an author needs a great deal more information than the few simple principles explained here. Cost accounting principles are the same in publishing as in any other industry.

There are any number of books available that discuss production. If you use such a book, make sure that the production techniques discussed are in fact ones that pertain to the book industry and are in fact used by the publisher or printer you work with. A commonly used work for production training purposes is *The Print Production Handbook* by Davis Bann, published by Little, Brown and Company. It contains all the information a technically inclined author is likely to want to know about book production.

Part 4: How to prepare a manuscript

In this area there is an embarrassment of riches: there are so many excellent books available that one does not know which to mention and which not.

Dictionaries and thesauri. No one should seriously contemplate writing a book without having a couple of dictionaries and a good thesaurus at hand. My own favourite dictionary is *Merriam-Webster's Third International Dictionary*. There is nothing to beat it as a working dictionary for an author or translator, especially of technical material, but it may be a bit overwhelming for most authors. For the rest, I am not sure that there is much to choose among the numerous ones on the market. The Oxford and Collins ranges are the most popular. There are a similar number of thesauri available. My favourite is the *Bloomsbury Thesaurus*, one of the latest.

The choice when working in Afrikaans is more restricted. I would put my money on the latest edition of the *HAT (Handwoordeboek van die Afrikaanse Taal)*, published by Perskor, as the most useful descriptive dictionary in Afrikaans. Southern recently published the first full-blown thesaurus in Afrikaans: *Groot Tesourus van Afrikaans* by Leon de Stadler, now also available in electronic form.

The standard translating dictionary is *Tweetalige Woordeboek/ Bilingual Dictionary* by Bosman, Van der Merwe and Hiemstra, published by Tafelberg, and the Reader's Digest's *Afrikaans-Engelse Woordeboek/English-Afrikaans Dictionary*, which is based on the former but has additional very useful notes.

Style. For a thorough if slightly old-fashioned approach there is nothing to beat Fowler: *Modern English Usage* and *The King's English*. There are numerous very good American books available, the bible for publishers being *The Chicago Manual of Style*, published by the University of Chicago Press. Britain's answer to this is the excellent work of Judith Butcher called *Copy-editing: The Cambridge Handbook*, published by Cambridge University Press.

As a general reference on matters of style, you cannot go wrong if you use *Hart's Rules for Compositors and Readers at the Oxford University Press,* published naturally enough by that press.

For DTP work, *Editing for Desktop Publishing* by John Taylor and Shirley Heale (Spa Books) is a useful text, but there are many others available. Make sure the book you use is a recent one, for DTP technology is changing rapidly.

Design. There are a great many books available on design – both book design and typographical and graphic design in general. This is an area where a little knowledge is a dangerous thing. A good designer will probably have a university degree in graphic design and a number of years' experience; it is not possible to become a designer by reading a couple of manuals. Do not be seduced into putting your own book together on a DTP system simply because you know how to operate the program. A DTP program is merely a design tool; you still need to understand the basics of design to use it effectively. It is a little like thinking you can be a good author simply because you can operate a typewriter. If you have an irrepressible urge to apply DTP to your work, first consult your publisher.

Index

Abbreviations 169, 174
Academic books 64–76
Academic publishers, focus areas of 66
Academic publishing, high-level 74
Academic textbooks 67–8
  American 64–5, 145–6, 172
  auctioning of 68
  author's questionnaire for 75
  availability of 67–8
  cooperation on 73
  decision criteria for 68
  high prices of 71
  language medium of 70
  local content in 66
  perception of prices 73–4
  print runs for 65–6, 73
  reading levels of 70
  revision of 68
  subjects for 65–6
Acknowledgement of source 152
Acronyms 174
Advance material 132
Advances on royalties 16
African languages 48–9
  and educational publishing 52–4
  political role of the language boards 51
  publishing in 47–54
Afrikaans fiction, categories of 39
Afrikaans fiction publishing 5–6
Afrikaans market 38–46
Afrikaans publishers, development of 3
Agreement, see Contract 113
Aiken, Joan 34
A Long Walk to Freedom 12
Alphabetising of words 189
Americanisms 181
Anansi 32
Annotations 156
Apartheid 38
Apostrophe 179
Appendix 161
Approaching publishers 95
Areas of concentration 100
Armstrongs 6
Articles in periodicals 181
Artists 157
  briefings for 157
  commissioning of 158
  references for 158
Artwork, creative 157
Assessing a manuscript 101–2, 126
Assessment questions 102
Audience 168, 188
Author-publisher 86, 87, 88, 92
Authors
  as indexers 189
  motivation of 125
  suggestions from 108
Author's
  copies 118
  copyright 116
  corrections 122
  corrections, penalties for 129
Average sentence length 170
A. & C. Black 81

Back flap 132
Balkema, A.A. 10
Bannister, Anthony 14
Belles-lettres 27–8
Berne Convention 69, 152
Bertelsman 17
Bibliography 162, 174–5
Bilingualism 38
Binding 130–1
Blurb copy 131–2
Bold type 149
Bond, Frances 34
Bonsai as topic 13

Book
  average 132
  structuring of 159–67
Book club publishing 77–9
  constraints of 77–8
  quality of 78
Books, categorisation of 55
Booksellers 6–8
  as unofficial censors 15
Bookselling, structure of 17
Bookshops 95
  campus 6
  school 7
Brackets, round 179
Brackets, square 179
Breytenbach, Breyten 38
Brink, André P. 27, 38, 42
British educational publishers in SA 3
Bunyan, Paul 47
Bureau for University Teaching 172
Buthelezi, J.C. 51
Butterworth 3, 5, 66

Camera-ready copy 130
Cameron, Trewhella 42
Cape Town 131
Capital outlay 141
Capitals 175–6
  in book titles 181
Captions 156
  for photographs 156
Cash payments to authors 79
Catalogues 95
  publisher's 60
Channels of distribution 16–17
Chapter 163
  new 150
Chicago Manual of Style, The 189
Children's book publishing in South Africa 29–37
  market constraints of 29–30
  language 30
  Afrikaans 30
  African languages 30
  awards and rewards 31
  non-fiction 32–3
  fiction 33–4
  assessing new manuscripts 35–6
  future developments in 36–7
Clear Cut 171
Clements, Alan 70
Clichés 169
CNA 6, 7, 11, 15, 17, 18, 39, 40, 108, 109
  Prize 39
  sales statistics 4
CNA-Gallo 6, 7, 29, 53
Colon 179
Colour reproduction 156
Colour-coding, in proofs 183
Columns 166
Comma 179
Commissioning 103–4
Commissioning editor 97, 105–6
  functions of 105
  tasks of 104
Computer illustration packages 158
Computer programs 171
Computerised data base 189
Conrad, Joseph 171
Consistency 156, 163, 173, 183
Contract
  early 113
  negotiable clauses in 113
  publishing 124–5
  sample 114–23
  termination of 123
  standard 114
Contributions to books 180
Conventional publishing process 134
Conventional typesetting 128, 129
Co-publishing, international 82–3
Copyright
  author's 116
  duration of 152
  material 121
  notice 116
  owner, reaching 154
  page 160
  permission, fees for 154
  permission, sample letter for 153
  permissions 152–4
Copyright Act, 1981 69, 152
Copy-editing 128

Copy-editing *(continued)*
need for 106
Copy-editor 106, 128, 173
functions of 106
Corel Draw 158
Correct Grammar 171, 174
Correction cost 129, 184
Corrections, in a manuscript 149
at final proof stage 130
marking of 183–4
Cost
of correction 184
of production 138–9
of books, how to reduce 146
Costing, sample 138–40
Costing or budgeting, initial 101
Counterproposal of publisher 96
Cover 130
design 131
Craven, Margaret 55
CRC 130
Creative artwork 157–8

Daan Retief Kinderklub 78
Daly, Niki 33
Data base, computerised 189
Dates 176
David Philip Publishers 3, 5, 21, 53, 66
De Villiers, Mrs S.J.A. 41
Deadline, in contract 120
Decision criteria
for educational books 101–3
for general books 101
Dedication page 161
Definite article 176
Deletion of page, in manuscript 150
Demographics, changes in 69–70
Design
of cover 131
of jacket 131
elements 164–7
improvement in 10
Designer 107, 128, 131
in non-fiction publishing 14–15
Desk Top Publishing 72, 136–7
Development period 99
Diagrams 155
Dickens, Charles 171
Direct address 169
Directory of South African Publishers 8
Disclaimer 154
Discount 124
bookseller 138
Disk 122, 136
editing on 136
hard copy of 150
illustrations on 151, 155
instructions for 151
preparation of 150–1
sample material on 151
Dispatch 131
Distribution channels for general books 6
Distribution overseas 82
Domestic hardbacks 145
Dorling Kindersley 83
Double spacing 149
Drama 27
Drawings, author's 155
Drawings, original 157
DTP 136–7
advantages of 136
capabilities of 136
compared to conventional typesetting 136
constraints of 136
program 136
publishing process 136
Dust-jacket 130

Economy of scale 114
Editing 134
comment on by author 128
on screen 136
queries arising from 127
Edition, subsequent 114, 122
Editor, managing 69
Editorial and production time 99
Education
language policy in 59
need for good materials in 60
departments, changes in 59
books, overseas distribution of 82
material, innovative 58

Education *(continued)*
publisher, criteria for choosing 61–3
publishing, changes in 59
publishing, corruption in 59–60
publishing, defining of 58
publishing, in Afrikaans 38–9
publishing, standard of 59
writer, qualifications for 58
writing, constraints on 58
Educum 5, 53
Eike-Boekklub 79
End matter 161–2
End notes 161, 177
Evaluate 171
Examples, concrete 169–70
Exclusive Books 7
Eybers, Elisabeth 39

Facts & Fiction 6
Fiction 22–5
Afrikaans 39–40
Figures 155–6, 176–7
cost of 156
numbering of 155
roughs for 155
Film 130
Financial
risk 99
viability 101
First refusal rights 116
Fixed costs 138
Flag heading 164
Flap
back 132
front 132
Flow charts 155
Focus 100
Fog Index 170–1
Footnotes 161, 177
Foreword 161
Format 165–6
control over 116
Fowler 168
Frankfurt Book Fair 82
French title 159
Friction, between author and publisher 108–9
Fromm, Jurgen 10
Front flap 132
Full stops 174, 179
Functional books 11

Galley proofs 129, 183
collation of 129
proofreading of 134
Garamond 32
Gardening as topic 12–13
General book publishing 5–6
General books
as luxury 16
decline in total sales 17
exports of 11
overseas printing of 16
General market, books needed for 13–14
General publishing, quality of 11
Geographic locations, capitals in 175
Glossary 162
Good writing 168–72
rules of 169–70
Gospel according to St John 171
Grammatic 5, 171, 174
Graphs 155
Greene, Graham 171
Griet Skryf 'n Sprokie 40
Gross margin 140
Guide to Creative Writing 34
Gunning Fog Index 170–1
Gut feel 100

Haggard, Rider 47
Half title 159
Handwriting, in a manuscript 149
Hard copy 151
copy-editing on 151
Hardback 144
versus paperback 143–6
HarperCollins 32, 81
Hart's Rules for Compositors and Readers 174
Harvard system 177
Heading, flag 164
Headings 163
capitals in 176
Heinemann 3, 5, 7, 53

Hertzog Prize 39
Historical data 99
Hodder and Stoughton Educational 5, 53
Hong Kong 16, 131
House style 173–81
 definition of 173
Hughes, Shirley 33
Huisgenoot Wenresepte 41
Human, Annette 41
Human & Rousseau 5, 7, 10, 21, 32, 38, 53
Hyphen 145

I Heard the Owl Call my Name 55
Illustration packages, on computer 158
Illustrations 121–2
 on disk 155
 preparation of 155–8
Illustrators 14
Image printing 72
imPrint 22
Imprint page 160
Income statement 138
Indentation 164
Index 122, 162
 comprehensive 187
 from cards 188
 need for 187
 preparation of 187–90
 size of 188
Indexer, professional 187
Indexing, by authors 187
Individual publishers 4
Informal learning, material for 56
Inspection copies 118
Institutional publishers 4
Instruction, in margin 183
Insurance of colour photographs and artwork 119
Intellectual property 69
Interest 140
International publishing houses in SA 3
International Standard Book Number 161
International student editions 145
International Thomson Publishing 65, 66
Introduction 161
ISBN 92, 161
ise- ending 174, 181
Italic, use of 178
Italic type 149
ize- ending 174

Jacket design 131
James, Henry 171
Jeppe, Barbara 14
Johannesburg 131
Jonathan Ball Publishers 5, 7, 53
Journals, academic 74
Joyce, James 171
Justified type 167
Juta 3, 5, 6, 66
Juvenile literature 26–7
J.L. van Schaik 5, 7, 53
J.P. van der Walt 6, 38, 79

Kagiso 5, 9, 53
Katrina Harries Award 78
Keurbiblioteek 79
Khoi languages 49
King's English, The 168
Kirsten, Keith 41
Knowledge Unlimited 78
Kook en Geniet 41
Kwela 7

Labels 156
Late additions, in manuscript 150
Launch party 108
Layout of page 129–30
Legal Deposit of Publications Act, 1982 8
Leipoldt, Louis 19
Leisure Books, Afrikaans 41
Leserskring 6, 7, 17, 29, 39, 40, 53, 77
Liability for loss and damage 119
Libel 119
Liberation publishers 3
Libraries 40, 95
 local 96
 provincial 39
Life skills, as non-fiction topic 42–3

Limpbacks 145
Lists 164
  construction of 164
  examples of 164
  numbering of 164
Literary agents, approaching 80, 81–2
Literary prizes, Afrikaans 39
Literary publishing 19–28
Literary work, overseas distribution of 82
Literature for the classroom 63
Living standards, decline in 17
Logic, in sentence 169
Longman 3
Lovedale Missionary Press 47
Lux Verbi 39

Maake, Nhlanhla 51
Macmillan 3, 11, 53, 81
Main text 162–4
Mandela, Nelson 12
Manuscript 126, 128
  assessment and revision of 126
  assessment of 97
  part 126
  queries on 106
  unsolicited 103
Marais, Eugène 19
Margin, corrections in 183
Margins 166
Marianhill Missionary Press 47
Mark, textual 183
Market
  information, lack of 100
  research, lack of 99
Marketing 108–9
  manager 108
  plan 108
Marking corrections 183–4
Maskew Miller 3
Maskew Miller Longman 5, 53
Mass-market children's books, Afrikaans 39
Mast 7
Master set, of page proofs 130
Mathematical variables 178
Matric students 171
Matthee, Dalene 38, 39
Maximums, in contract 120
Maxiread 171
McGraw-Hill 65
Metric
  abbreviations 178
  system 176
  units 178
Mokae, Gomolemo 51
Molteno Project 58
Molver, Eileen 34
Monopolistic tendencies in book trade 7
Morija Press 47
Multi-author panels 68
My Land van Hoop 42
M-Net Prize 39

Nasionale Pers 3, 6, 7, 10, 17, 53
Nasou 5, 6, 7, 9
Natural history 11, 41
  use of capitals in 175
Net price 138
Net receipts, royalties on 117
Netherlands 39
New chapter 150
New Contrast 22
New paragraph, in a manuscript 149
Newman, Ken 14
Niehaus, Carl 42
Niehaus, Carmen 41
Non-fiction
  booksellers' perception of 15
  commissioning of 14
  consumer's perception of 15
  general 10–18
  illustrated children's 41
  overseas distribution of 82
  photographic dimension of 16
  subjects for 11–12
Non-formal learning, material for 56
Non-institutional learning, material for 56
Non-profit-making publishers 100
Notes
  at end of book 161
  at end of chapter 161
  explanatory 177

Notice, copyright 116
Novellas 22–3
Novels 23–6
Numbering
  inclusive 177
  of typescript 150
  roman 159
Nuwe Geskiedenis van Afrikaans 42

Obscenity 119
Om te Veg vir Hoop 42
Origination cost 138, 141
Overhead cost 140
Oxford Dictionary for Writers and Editors 174
Oxford University Press 5, 53, 66, 74, 174
Ozrovec, Solly 42

Packager 83
Page
  numbers, even 159
  numbers, odd 159
  plan or diagram 129
  proofs 130, 136, 183, 184, 188
  proofs, revised 130
Pages, specimen 128
Pan South African Language Board 51
Paper, cheaper 72
Paperbacks
  history of 143
  mass-market 143–4
  versus hardbacks 143–6
Paragraphs 167
Parentheses 179
Part title 162
PASA 8, 9, 90
Pass 171
Passive voice 169
Paste-up, rough 129
PC Style 171
Peires, Jeff 19
Penguin 5, 53, 143
Percentage of hard words 170
Permissions 152–4
  cost of 154
  guideline for 152
Perskor 3, 5, 9
Philip, David 53, 66
Photocopy 150
Photocopying 69, 116
Photographer 14, 156
Photographs 156–7
  black-and-white 156, 157
  captions for 156
  choice of 157
  colour 156
  handling of 157
  numbering of 156
  relative sizes of 156
  screened 156
Photo-typesetting 151
Pioneers of publishing 3
Plagiarism 119
Plays 6
PNA 6
Poetry 6, 20–2, 95
  Afrikaans 21, 40
Politics, books on 12
Politics and local history 42
Polysyllables 170
  number of 171
Popular fiction, English 6, 80
Popular novels, Afrikaans 79
Potgieter, Herman 14
Preface 161
Preliminary pages 159–61
  sequence of 160
Prentice-Hall 65
Preparing illustrations 155–8
Preparing index 187–90
Pre-press costs 138
Presentation copies 118
President-Boekklub 79
Press costs 138
Price perceptions 143, 146
Print and bind cost 138, 139, 141
Print period 141
Print run 140, 141, 144
  as determinant of book price 140
Printing 130–1
  errors 183
  in multiples of 16 159
  machine 130
  plates 130

Procedure, explanation of 170
Production
  stages of 134
  undue delays in 135
  cost 137, 138
  lead times 132–3
  manager 107
  period 126
    reasonable 114
  schedule, average 133–4
  reducing 134–5
Profit before interest and tax 140
Promotion copies 118
Proofreader 129
Proofreader's error 182
Proofreader's marks 183, 185–6
Proofreading 182–6
  purpose of 182
Proofs
  galley 129, 183
  page 130, 183, 184, 188
  reading of 122, 182–6
Proper names 175, 176
Proposal package 96–7
Provision for write-off 140
Public relations officer 107
Publication dates 135
Publicist 107–8
Publicity plan 108
Publishers of non-fiction 5
Publishers' Association of South Africa 9
Publishing
  as business 100–1
  central dilemma of 141
  changes in 104
  contract 113–25
  creative role of 104
  decision 97, 99–104
  educational 55–63
  effectiveness 100
  expertise 99
  in African languages 47–54
  industry, annual turnover of 4
  overseas 80–3
  process 126–36
  process, conventional 126
  proposal 96–7
  reasons for 100
  risk 99
Punctuation 179–80
P.C. Hooft Prize 39

Qualifiers 169
Quality assessment 97
Quotations 180
  direct 180
  extended 180
Quotes
  double 180
  single 180

Rand, weakening of 71
Ravan Press 3, 53
Readability 170–1
  formulae 170–1
Reader's Digest 14, 171
Reading levels 170–2
Reading of proofs 182–6
Recession 17
Red-lined printout 151
References 180–1
  abbreviated 180, 181
  repeat 181
  sequence of 180
  subsequent 181
Remaindering 118–19
Response
  negative 98
  of editor 97
Retief, Daan 78
Review copies 118
Revision of manuscript 126
Rights
  American 80–1
  first refusal 116
  subsidiary 115
  UK and Commonwealth 80–1
RightWriter 171
Risk, financial 114
Romankeur 79
Roman numbering 159
Rough paste-up 130
Rough visual 131
Roughs, for artists 158
Royalties 117, 139

Royalties *(continued)*
  advantages of 124
  as source of income 125
  comparison of net and list 124, 125
  on list 124, 125
  on net receipts 117, 124, 125
  on published price 124
Royalty
  book club 117
  export 117
  sliding scale of 117
  payments, date of 118
  percentages 124

SACHED 3
Sales and marketing infrastructure 108
Sample costing 138–40
Schoeman, Karel 38
School
  books, distribution channels for 56
  publishing 5
  textbooks 172
    submission system for 59
    time needed for 58
Schools, range of materials published for 55
Screen editing 136
Second-language users 171
Section divider 162
Self-publishing 84–92, 98
  advantages and disadvantages of 85–6
  pre-requisites 86–7
  important considerations when 88–9
  costing 89
  preparing the manuscript 90
  marketing and 90
  responsibilities of 91
Selling price 138, 139
  reduction of 141
  retail 124
Semi-colon 179
Sendak, Maurice 33
Sentence length 171
Sentences 167
  short 169
Short stories 6, 22, 95
Shuter & Shooter 3, 5, 53
Singapore 16, 131
Small publishers 4
Snailpress 21, 29, 31
Softcovers 145
Songololo Books 30
South African National Biography 8
Southern Book Publishers 5, 11, 53, 114, 124, 173
Spacing 164, 166
  double 149
  between paragraphs 149
Specialisation 100
Specimen pages 128, 167
Spelling 181
  British versus American 174
Spell-checking facility 174, 181
Springbok Biblioteek 79
Square brackets 179
St John 171
State Library 8
State Library of Pretoria 92
Structuring, of a book 159–67
Struik 5, 7, 10, 32, 38, 53
Struik, Gerry 10
Struik family 10
Style 173
Styled 171
Subbing 132
Subjective judgement 101
Subscriptions 132
Substantial part, of work 152
Sub-headings 163–4
  level of 163
  metrically numbered 163

Table of contents 161
Tafelberg 5, 7, 10, 32, 53
Tax 140
Technical drawings 155
Technology, cheaper and better 72
Tertiary publishers 5
Tertiary-level books 64–76
Text
  main 162–7

Text *(continued)*
  preparation of 149–54
Textbooks
  American 71
  school 172
The Way to Write for Children 34
Third World editions 145
Time Magazine 171
Times Mirror 65
Title page 160
Title verso 160
Towards Understanding 34
Towards More Understanding 34
Trade paperback 144
Trade risks 104
Translations 38, 114
Transparencies 156, 157
Travel books 11
Travel guides 11
Treffer-Boekklub 79
Triomf 40
Type
  bold 149
  italic 149
  size 166
  face 166
Typescript
  extent and form of 120
  preparation of 149–50
Typesetter 107
Typesetter's errors 129
Typesetting 128–9
  time needed for 128

Uitgewery Bezuidenhout 79
Unisa Fog Index 172
Unit cost 140
University books 64–76
University of Cape Town Press 53, 74
University of Natal Press 53, 74
University of Pretoria 53, 67
University of South Africa 53, 67, 171–2
University of the Witwatersrand 53, 67
Unjustified type 167

Van der Vyver, Marita 38, 40
Van Niekerk, Marlene 40
Van Onselen, Charles 19
Van Schaik 3, 6, 7, 53
Variable cost 138
VAT 138
Via Afrika 5, 7
Viking-Penguin 81
Visual, rough 131
Vlaeberg 5
Vocabulary 168–9
  level 168

Warehouse 131
Wassenaar, Dr A.D. 42
Weights and measures, specific 177
Wildlife books 11
Winkel oor die Pos 79
Witwatersrand University Press 53, 74
Wood, Marilyn 53
Wordperfect 136, 150
Word-processing program 151, 174, 188
Works, competing 115
Writers
  teams of 57
Writers' and Artists' Yearbook 81
Writers' Handbook 81
Write-off, provision for 140

Xhosa literature 19